THE ANTHROPOLOGY OF PEACE AND RECONCILIATION

This book offers a uniquely comparative, case-study perspective on the anthropology of peace and reconciliation.

In the contemporary world, the end of violent conflict often gives way to one, or a combination, of five interventions designed to strengthen "peace" and facilitate "reconciliation". These interventions are: the reinvigoration of "traditional" conflict management mechanisms; the collection and preservation of testimony; truth commissions; international criminal trials; and memorialisation. Social anthropologists have challenged the received wisdom on which these interventions are based, arguing that they fail to adequately take into account and sensitively manage the needs and expectations of those who have lived through conflict. Exploring the five interventions through detailed ethnographic accounts from around the world, this book demonstrates that although social anthropologists adopt a critical stance, they do not dismiss "received wisdom" out of hand; rather, they advocate that interventions should be subject to continuous evaluation according to the evolving, often contradictory, needs and wishes of those who strive to survive among the ruins of their former lives.

This is essential reading for scholars of peace studies, conflict resolution studies and those taking an anthropological approach to conflict, violence, human rights and law.

Nigel Eltringham is Reader in Anthropology at the University of Sussex, UK.

CRITICAL TOPICS IN CONTEMPORARY ANTHROPOLOGY
Series editor: Alan Barnard

Anthropology and the Economy of Sharing
Thomas Widlok

The Anthropology of Peace and Reconciliation
Pax Humana
Nigel Eltringham

https://www.routledge.com/Critical-Topics-in-Contemporary-Anthropology/book-series/CTCA

THE ANTHROPOLOGY OF PEACE AND RECONCILIATION

Pax Humana

Nigel Eltringham

LONDON AND NEW YORK

First published 2021
by Routledge
2 Park Square, Milton Park, Abingdon, Oxon OX14 4RN

and by Routledge
52 Vanderbilt Avenue, New York, NY 10017

Routledge is an imprint of the Taylor & Francis Group, an informa business

© 2021 Nigel Eltringham

The right of Nigel Eltringham to be identified as author of this work has been asserted by him in accordance with sections 77 and 78 of the Copyright, Designs and Patents Act 1988.

All rights reserved. No part of this book may be reprinted or reproduced or utilised in any form or by any electronic, mechanical, or other means, now known or hereafter invented, including photocopying and recording, or in any information storage or retrieval system, without permission in writing from the publishers.

Trademark notice: Product or corporate names may be trademarks or registered trademarks, and are used only for identification and explanation without intent to infringe.

British Library Cataloguing-in-Publication Data
A catalogue record for this book is available from the British Library

Library of Congress Cataloging-in-Publication Data
Names: Eltringham, Nigel, author.
Title: The anthropology of peace and reconciliation : Pax Humana /
Nigel Eltringham.
Description: New York : Routledge, 2021. | Series: Critical topics in contemporary anthropology | Includes bibliographical references and index.
Identifiers: LCCN 2020048371 | ISBN 9780815349730 (Hardback) | ISBN 9780815349747 (Paperback) | ISBN 9781351164122 (eBook)
Subjects: LCSH: Peaceful societies. | Peace–Cross-cultural studies. | Reconciliation–Cross-cultural studies. | International cooperation.
Classification: LCC GN396 .E58 2021 | DDC 303.6/6–dc23
LC record available at https://lccn.loc.gov/2020048371

ISBN: 978-0-8153-4973-0 (hbk)
ISBN: 978-0-8153-4974-7 (pbk)
ISBN: 978-1-351-16412-2 (ebk)

Typeset in Bembo
by Taylor & Francis Books

CONTENTS

List of figures	*vi*
Acknowledgements	*viii*
Abbreviations	*ix*

Introduction: "Peace" and "reconciliation": Challenging "received wisdom"	1
1 "Traditional" conflict management mechanisms	25
2 *Re*-traditionalising conflict management	45
3 Memory and testimony in the aftermath of violent conflict	68
4 Seeking "truth" in the aftermath of violent conflict	90
5 International criminal justice	108
6 Memorial sites	131
Conclusion	151

Index	*160*

FIGURES

1.1	Dou Donggo elders engaged in dispute–resolution. (Photo courtesy of Peter Just)	31
2.1	An *Inkiko-Gacaca* hearing in 2006. (Photo courtesy of Karen Brounéus)	52
2.2	*Mato oput* in Gulu, northern Uganda, January 1998. (Photo courtesy of Sverker Finnström)	57
2.3 and 2.4	A *gamba* healing session at night. (Photos courtesy of Victor Igreja)	62
3.1	A neighbour walking home past a *wang-o* ("telling stories around the fire pit") set up for the evening in Pabo, northern Uganda. (Photo courtesy of Erin Baines)	77
4.1	At a 2011 Truth and Reconciliation Commission of Canada event in Inuvik, Alan and Rosie Kagak weep as they recall their experience as Inuit in Canada's residential school system. (Photo courtesy of Michael Swan)	95
5.1	Pronouncement of the judgement in Case 002/02 (Khieu Samphan and Nuon Chea) on 16 November 2018. (Photo courtesy of the Extraordinary Chambers in the Courts of Cambodia)	112
5.2	Residents of the former Khmer Rouge stronghold of Pailin visit Tuol Sleng Genocide Museum as part of an ECCC outreach visit in November 2010. (Photo courtesy of the Extraordinary Chambers in the Courts of Cambodia)	117

5.3	The ICTR courtroom from the prosecution end. (Photo courtesy of the International Residual Mechanism for Criminal Tribunals)	121
6.1	The entrance to Tuol Sleng Museum. (Photo courtesy of Alexander Laban Hinton)	137
6.2	The portrait room at Tuol Sleng. (Photo courtesy of Elena Lesley)	138
6.3	The half-completed Murambi Technical School in southern Rwanda. (Photo: Nigel Eltringham)	142
6.4	Sign in English, French and Kinyarwanda at Murambi. (Photo: Nigel Eltringham)	143

ACKNOWLEDGEMENTS

Many thanks to the Routledge team of Katherine Ong, Marc Stratton, Louisa Vahtrick, Louise Peterken and Amy Doffegnies for their patience and support in bringing this book to completion and to Roger Browning, the copy editor. Special thanks to Alan Barnard for the invitation to contribute to the series. As always, my profound thanks to my wife, Anna, and our daughters for their unswerving support.

Chapter 5 draws upon Eltringham, Nigel (2019) *Genocide Never Sleeps: Living Law at the International Criminal Tribunal for Rwanda*. Cambridge: Cambridge University Press. I am grateful to Cambridge University Press for granting permission to use those extracts.

Chapter 6 draws upon Eltringham, Nigel (2014) *Bodies of Evidence: Remembering the Rwandan Genocide at Murambi*. In Eltringham, Nigel and Maclean, Pam (eds.) *Remembering genocide. Remembering the Modern World*. London: Routledge pp. 200–219. I am grateful to Routledge for granting permission to use those extracts.

ABBREVIATIONS

AAR	Agreement on Accountability and Reconciliation
ACP	Ardoyne Commemoration Project
ADR	Alternative Dispute Resolution
BLWM	Bangladesh Liberation War Museum
CAVR	Commission for Reception, Truth and Reconciliation (Comissão de Acolhimento, Verdade e Reconciliação de Timor Leste)
CPK	Communist Party of Kampuchea
CVR	Peruvian Truth and Reconciliation Commission (Comisión de la Verdad y Reconciliación del Perú)
DK	Democratic Kampuchea
ECCC	Extraordinary Chambers in the Courts of Cambodia
FRELIMO	The Front for the Liberation of Mozambique (Frente de Libertação de Moçambique)
HSA	Holy Spirit Army
HRVC	Human Rights Violations Committee
ICC	International Criminal Court
ICTR	International Criminal Tribunal for Rwanda
ICTY	International Criminal Tribunal for the Former Yugoslavia
IMS	Information Management System
JHMRC	Jewish Holocaust Museum and Research Centre
KR	Khmer Rouge
LRA	Lord's Resistance Army
NRA	National Resistance Army
PAR	Participatory Action Research
PRK	People's Republic of Kampuchea
RENAMO	Mozambican National Resistance (Resistência Nacional Moçambicana)

x Abbreviations

RPA/F	Rwandan Patriotic Army/Front
RUF	Revolutionary United Front
SATRC	South African Truth and Reconciliation Commission
SCSL	Special Court for Sierra Leone
SITRC	Solomon Islands Truth and Reconciliation Commission
SLTRC	Sierra Leone Truth and Reconciliation Commission
SPSC	Special Panels for Serious Crimes in East Timor
TRCC	Truth and Reconciliation Commission of Canada
UNHCR	United Nations High Commissioner for Human Rights
USHMM	United States Holocaust Memorial Museum
UTP	Unofficial Truth Project
VRS	Army of Republika Srpska (Vojska Republike Srpske)

INTRODUCTION: "PEACE" AND "RECONCILIATION"

Challenging "received wisdom"

Given that the title of this book is "The Anthropology of Peace and Reconciliation", it would be reasonable for the reader to assume I would begin by defining "peace" and "reconciliation". To take such an approach, however, would be to ignore the first part of the title, "The Anthropology of ...". Jeffrey Sluka, in his discussion of the "Anthropology of Conflict", states that the strength of anthropology lies in its "cross-cultural and comparative perspective ... and a commitment to getting as close as possible to the participant's ... point of view" (Sluka 1992, 20). Rather than pre-empt the meaning of "peace" and "reconciliation", the search for meaning must begin with "insider" points of view and remain open to alternative and possibly contradictory definitions (see Falk Moore 1989, 300). Accessing such points of view is achieved through ethnography, the principal method employed by anthropologists, which:

> involves the researcher participating, overtly or covertly, in people's daily lives for an extended period of time, watching what happens, listening to what is said, and/or asking questions through informal and formal interviews, collecting documents and artefacts – in fact gathering whatever data are available to throw light on the issues that are the emerging focus of inquiry.
>
> *(Hammersley & Atkinson 2007, 3)*

Ethnography is not, however, just a set of activities. Rather, as Kevin Avruch (2009, 12), a prominent figure in the anthropology of conflict resolution, notes:

> What sets ethnography apart as a methodology is not so much a set of techniques as its underlying *rationale*: the commitment first to listening, and then valuing (if not always privileging) what your respondents tell you about their world and their experience of it. This is the hallmark of ethnographic inquiry.

2 Introduction

The value of taking such an approach is that we are forced to "challenge our assumptions [and] received wisdom" because we "understand particular processes, events, ideas and practices in an informant's own terms rather than ours" (Shaw 2007b, 188).

In order to consider an "insider view" and challenge received wisdom, I have chosen not to define "peace" or "reconciliation" at the outset of this book. Rather, I will consider in this Introduction four (counter-intuitive) propositions made by anthropologists regarding "peace": that conflict is constructive; division maintains "peace"; "harmony" is coercive; and "peace" is not the absence of violence. I will draw on ethnographic examples from Rwanda, South Sudan, Malawi, Zambia, Mexico, South Africa and Sierra Leone to illustrate these propositions. I will then consider how "insiders" who have survived violent conflict have sought to reconstruct viable relationships in Mozambique, Sierra Leone, Cambodia, Indonesia, Rwanda, Bosnia-Herzegovina and East Timor.

Conflict is constructive

Conflict, whether or not it involves physical violence, may be assumed to be innately destructive; the opposite of "peace", which is assumed to be constructive. Defining "peace" in such a way is not, however, convincing if we consider conflict also to be constructive. Anthropologists have tended to adopt the position taken by the sociologist Georg Simmel (1955) and the commentary on his work by the sociologist Lewis A. Coser (1956). Simmel argued that conflict was socially constructive in two ways: that it is (1) a binding element between groups that are in conflict; and (2) that it is a binding element within a group (Coser 1956, 121–128). Regarding the first proposition, Simmel argued that conflict requires a "common acceptance of rules governing the conduct of hostilities" and that such rules contribute to viable relations between "contending parties by imposing restraints on both of them" (Coser 1956, 123). Simmel goes further, arguing that "by bringing about new situations, which are partly or totally undefined by rules and norms, conflict acts as a stimulus for the establishment of new rules and norms" (Coser 1956, 124). In other words, rather than entirely alienating opposing groups from one another, conflict requires the continuous (re)construction of new understandings of appropriate behaviour between conflicting parties. The same constructive quality of conflict applies to the effect of conflict within a "group". For Simmel, conflict within a social group serves to revitalise the norms by which members are supposed to live. By making members of a group aware of norms that they are supposed to share, conflict is a means by which a group's values are reaffirmed and dormant norms made explicit (Coser 1956, 128) (see Chapter 1). Coser (1956, 125) illustrates this with a quote from the classic account of the law of the Cheyenne (the indigenous people of Montana) co-written by the anthropologist E. Adamson Hoebel and the legal scholar Karl Llewellyn:

[Conflict] dramatizes a "norm" or a conflict of "norms" which may have been latent. ... it forces the defining of issues ... It forces solution, which may be creation. It forces solution in a fashion to be remembered, perhaps in clear, ringing words. It is one more experiment toward new and clearer or more rigorous patterning both of behavior and of [a] recognized and recognizable "norm".

(Llewellyn & Hoebel 1941, 21)

Conflict, in other words, brings clarity, reaffirming existing rules that a group should live by or creating rules that reflect changing circumstances. Coser (1956, 127) concludes that "conflict, rather than being disruptive and dissociating, may indeed be a means of balancing and hence maintaining a society as a going concern". If we accept the argument that conflict is constructive for the maintenance of social groups, this can imply there is no "peace" without conflict, as intermittent conflict is needed to re-educate members of a group on how to live "in peace" with one another.

Coser's proposition that conflict is a means by which a group's values are reaffirmed is supported by the work of anthropologist Neil Whitehead (2004b, 68), who argues that violent acts "are creative and constitutive of social relations and identities". While violence tends to be seen as "the absence of order and meaning, a total [absence] of culture", in reality violence "is both rule governed and meaningful" and, therefore, "culturally authentic and significant" because individuals who commit violent acts draw on and manipulate "cultural forms, symbols, and icons" (Whitehead 2004a, 8–9). This is illustrated by the 1994 Rwandan genocide of the Tutsi. Anthropologist Christopher Taylor (1999, 101–102) observes that "Beneath the aspect of disorder there lay an eerie order to the violence. ... Many of the actions followed a cultural patterning, a structured and structuring logic." While Taylor (1999, 99–102) makes it clear that the 1994 genocide was not "caused" by Rwandan "culture", he does argue that perpetrators drew on Rwandan cultural symbols (see Mironko 2006). Taylor (1999, 110–126) notes, for example, that Rwandans conceive of the body through a "flow/blockage symbolism" (especially the orderly flow of fluids – milk, semen, blood) and that, within this symbolism, "unobstructed connection and unimpeded movement" are valued. Taylor (1999, 128) suggests that this "flow/blockage" metaphor was reflected in the methods employed by the perpetrators of the genocide, who displayed "a preoccupation with the movement of persons and substances and with the canals, arteries, and conduits along which persons and substances flow: rivers, roadways, pathways, and even the conduits of the human body such as the reproductive and digestive systems". In terms of the disposal of bodies, for example, Taylor sees an expression of the flow metaphor in the dumping of bodies in the Nyabarongo/Akagera River, with at least 40,000 bodies being recovered from Lake Victoria in Uganda, into which the Akagera River flows (see Dallaire & Beardsley 2004, 336; Eltringham 2014). Violence can, therefore, be understood not simply as disorderly destruction but as an expression of cultural norms that existed before and may very well continue to exist after the violence has subsided.

4 Introduction

Division maintains peace

While Simmel and Coser proposed that intermittent conflict was socially constructive, the anthropologist Max Gluckman (1963) suggested it was an individual's "conflicting loyalties" to different groups that kept the "peace". Gluckman drew on the anthropologist E.E. Evans-Pritchard's (1940) ethnographic account of the Nuer, a pastoral people in what is now South Sudan. The most important tie among the Nuer is that of kinship by blood through male ancestors. Evans-Pritchard reported that if a member of a group sharing a male ancestor was killed, the whole group would be obliged to exact vengeance on the killer's group. However, given that Nuer men were required to marry women from outside their kin group, a Nuer man could simultaneously be a member of the kin group seeking vengeance and a member of his wife's kin group against whom revenge was sought. Such divided loyalty, Gluckman (1963, 19) argues, inhibited the spread of disputes and fighting and meant there was "only pressure towards the establishing of peaceful relations". As Gluckman (1963, 4) argues, "these societies are so organized into a series of groups and relationships, that people who are friends on one basis are enemies on another. Herein lies social cohesion, rooted in conflicts between men's different allegiances."

Gluckman (1963, 23) suggests that a reliance for "peace" on division is universal, quoting from T.S. Eliot's (1948) observation regarding the United Kingdom that "everyone should be an ally of everyone else in some respects, and an opponent in several others, and no one conflict, envy or fear will predominate". For Gluckman (1963, 25), therefore, it was division and conflicting loyalties that kept the "peace" (see Koch et al. 1977, 271; Robarchek 1979, 107). It is important to note that contemporary anthropologists are wary of accounts, such as Gluckman's, which assume consensus regarding a group's norms and which downplay that norms inevitably change over time (see Chapter 1). Sally Falk Moore (1992, 33), for example, warns that what appears to be consensus may only be a "temporary moment of agreement in which a dominant segment of the group has prevailed". Anthropologists have, therefore, "abandoned theories of social structure that assume social integration" in favour of approaching "social life as a creative process rather than a steady state or equilibrium in which all elements work together for good" (Colson 1995, 70). Despite these reservations, Gluckman's key observation that "peace" relies on cross-cutting conflicts that cancel each other out remains persuasive.

"Harmony" is coercive

For Simmel, Coser and Gluckman, "peace" was not the absence of conflict but was, to some extent, dependent on it. One reason why this proposition seems counter-intuitive is a consequence of what anthropologist Laura Nader (1991b, 53) describes as "harmony ideology", which sees "conflict as dysfunctional and threatening to the social order, a phenomenon to be diffused" (see Gulliver 1979, 168–169). Nader argues that "harmony ideology" can be used to suppress legitimate grievances. This coercive nature can be seen, for example, in the shift from the demand for civil rights in the United States of

America in the 1960s to the emergence of the Alternative Dispute Resolution (ADR) movement in the 1970s. Nader (1997, 713–714) suggests that ADR is a means of further disempowering the working class by delegitimising legitimate grievances and personalising conflict, rather than challenging the actual causes of social and economic inequality (see discussion of "structural violence" below).

In Chapter 1 I will consider "local" conflict resolution mechanisms that are designed to restore "harmony" in small-scale communities, and in Chapter 2 I will discuss the contemporary promotion of such mechanisms by national governments and international aid organisations. While such harmony-restoring mechanisms are considered "authentic" because they are "local" and appear to be of long-standing, Nader (1991a, 44) argues that colonial rule was the likely source of such harmony models. Nader (1991b, 46–47) draws on research by Martin Chanock (1987) in Malawi and Zambia to demonstrate that while in the colonial period the institutions of groups such as the Chewa (in contemporary Malawi) were characterised as expressing the "harmony model" of patient examination and persuasion, the pre-colonial period was, in reality, a time of harsh punishment for sorcery, theft and adultery. Chanock demonstrates how from the early 1860s missionaries became heavily involved in the settlement of disputes and imposed the principles of "Christian harmony ideology". In this way, "harmony ideology" was a form of pacification because it was a "coercive harmony" used to repress conflict and extend colonial authority (Nader 1997, 715).

Nader's (1997, 712–713) own research among the Zapotec people in Mexico suggested a similar process to that in Zambia and Malawi, in which the harmony model was introduced by Spanish colonial authorities and missionaries. Nader (1997, 713) suggests, however, that, having been exposed to the harmony model, the colonised "began using it as a tool for restricting the encroachment of external [power] by encouraging harmonious rather than contentious behavior". In other words, the Zapotec transformed an ideology that had been imposed upon them into a technique of social control to reduce interference in their affairs by the colonial state. Nader (1991a, 307) argues that if colonial authorities were the likely "source of the harmony ideology that anthropologists often attribute to 'the natives'", then what is claimed as "traditional" may, in reality, be the result of colonial imposition. This suggests a degree of caution is needed when reading accounts of "traditional" conflict management based on the restoration of "harmony" (see Chapter 1) and raises concerns about contemporary efforts to harness "traditional" mechanisms in the aftermath of violent conflict (see Chapter 2).

Despite questions regarding the origins of "harmony ideology", "harmony" remains a common aspiration. Anthropologist Richard Ashby Wilson (2000, 80) notes how the dominant view on "reconciliation" in the South African Truth and Reconciliation Commission (SATRC, created in 1995, see Chapter 4) was "an amalgam of transnational human rights values and a Christian ethic of forgiveness and redemption". Wilson (2000, 80–81) notes how at the hearings of the Human Rights Violations Committee (HRVC) commissioners would urge those testifying to "forgive perpetrators and abandon any desire for retaliation against them". This

6 Introduction

was a form of "coercive harmony", Nader (2000) suggests in a comment on Wilson's article. The SATRC's emphasis on "harmony" diverged from popular notions of retributive justice as expressed in a daily court (*kgotla*) in a township (a very poor, racially segregated community) observed by Wilson to which local people turned to mediate and adjudicate disputes. Claiming to be an expression of "traditional authority and customary law" (although the township court was actually a product of recent assertions of autonomy in relation to the state, see Chapter 2), the court achieved justice through physical punishment, frequently involving severe public beating with *sjamboks* (whips) and golf clubs. Wilson (2000, 79) notes the irony that it was the threat of physical punishment from the *kgotla* that had allowed "colla-borators" who formerly worked for the apartheid state to return to their homes and "coexist" with their neighbours, thereby achieving the "reconciliation" the SATRC was designed to achieve. Wilson's account suggests that the use of "coercive harmony" at the hearings of the SATRC was not only at odds with what was working on the ground in the townships but that it possibly reflected a "sen-timental version" of African societies originating in the colonial period, which is "a mixture of African self-idealization [an exaggerated positive image of oneself] and colonial/anthropological political theory" (Falk Moore 1992, 32).

"Peace" is not the absence of violence

So far I have illustrated Shaw's (2007b, 188) claim that ethnography can "challenge our assumptions" by suggesting that conflict can be constructive, that "peace" relies on division and that seeking "harmony" can be coercive. A final counter-intuitive posi-tion is that "peace" does not necessarily refer to the absence of violent conflict. Whereas the anthropologist David Riches (1986, 8) defines "violence" as "an act of physical hurt", other anthropologists have been influenced by sociologist Johan Gal-tung's notion of "structural violence" (see Farmer 1996). In a far-reaching article, Galtung (1969, 168) defined "violence" as: "the cause of the difference between the potential and the actual, between what could have been and what is." Galtung illus-trates this with reference to someone dying from tuberculosis. In the 18th century this would have been unavoidable, but if someone dies from tuberculosis today, despite all the medical resources, this is an example of "indirect violence" as it is technically avoidable. Likewise, if people are starving when food is available (as is often the case in contexts of famine; see Sen 1990), "indirect violence" is also committed. Galtung (1969, 170) therefore makes a distinction between "personal or direct" violence and "structural or indirect" violence. Understood in this way, violence is not just a matter of physical hurt but "is embedded in everyday life and touches on spheres like poverty, hunger, nudity, displacement, loss of dignity and the like" (Honwana 2005, 87).

A preoccupation with "personal or direct" violence can mask "structural" violence, as can be seen in the case of the SATRC. The Commission was established "To pro-vide for the investigation and the establishment of as complete a picture as possible of the nature, causes and extent of gross violations of human rights committed during the period from 1 March 1960" (Government of South Africa 1995). The term "gross violations of human rights" was defined as "the killing, abduction, torture or severe ill-treatment of any person" by "any person acting with a political motive" (Government of South Africa 1995) and resulted in 21,298 statements, of which 2,400 were heard by the HRVC (Ross 2003b, 328). The political scientist Mahmood Mamdani (2000, 179) criticises the emphasis on direct violence against individuals within the definition of "gross violations of human rights", given that apartheid was "aimed less at individuals than entire communities" and the violence was not just "political" but designed to "dispossess people of means of livelihood". Mamdani (2000, 179) notes that the 3.5 million people who were forcibly removed between 1960 and 1982 did not count as victims under the SATRC's definition of "gross violations of human rights". From this perspective, because the SATRC was concerned with "personal or direct" violence rather than "structural or indirect" violence, the vast majority of the victims of apartheid were excluded from consideration by the HRVC and the SATRC "wrote the vast majority of apartheid's victims out of its version of history" (Mamdani 2000, 183). Anthropologist Paul Farmer (2004, 308) suggests that an "erasure of history" of this kind is integral to how "structural violence" operates.

The way in which the SATRC privileged "personal or direct" violence over "structural or indirect" violence is further illustrated by anthropologist Fiona Ross's account of women giving testimony to the HRVC. Ross (2001, 253) notes that the definition of human rights violation considered by the SATRC was "largely to do with what can be done to the body – it can be abducted, tortured, killed, 'disappeared'". As a consequence, women appearing before the HRVC told stories about direct violence experienced by others, primarily their sons, husbands and brothers. Many of the testimonies, however, were framed in relation to the domestic sphere. Eunice Miya, for example, when testifying about the shooting of her son Jabulani by security forces in 1986, used her domestic world as a framework for her account of the events leading up to his death, describing how she had last seen her son when she was about to leave the house to go to her job as a cleaner, how she fed him water and bread in the kitchen, gave him money to help in his search for work and locked the kitchen behind her (Ross 2001, 263). Ross (2001, 270) argues that it was stories such as these, rather than those concerned with direct violence, that revealed the true "depths of apartheid". Even when restricted by the SATRC's mandate to speak only about direct violence, women gave accounts of how they struggled to "maintain families in the face of great odds" (Ross 2001, 272), thereby forcing a recognition of the structural/indirect violence of apartheid (see Laplante 2007, 438; Theidon 2007, 458–459).

The example of the SATRC suggests that Galtung's definition of "violence" and his distinction between "personal or direct" violence and "structural or indirect" violence has consequences for how "peace" is envisaged, whether as "negative peace" (the absence of "direct, personal violence") or "positive peace" (the absence of "indirect, structural violence") (Galtung 1969, 183). In other words, peace is not simply the absence of violent conflict but requires action to end poverty and discrimination, which continue to obstruct achieving what could be. The hollow

8 Introduction

quality of "negative peace" is summed up by Adama, whose hand had been amputated and husband killed in the civil war in Sierra Leone: "I cannot be struggling and say that I am living in peace. ... If our problem is left behind, the war will not end" (Shaw 2007b, 201).

In this section I have suggested that the perspectives of anthropologists challenge assumptions by suggesting that conflict can be constructive; that "peace" relies on division; that seeking "harmony" can be coercive; and that peace is not the absence of violent conflict. In the next section I will consider how anthropologists have defined "reconciliation" in abstract terms and how such definitions relate to the response of those who have survived violent conflict.

What might "reconciliation" refer to?

Definitions of "reconciliation" abound outside anthropology, including "a process through which a society moves from a divided past to a shared future" (Bloomfield 2003, 12); "the process of healing traumas of both victims and perpetrators of violence, producing a closure of the bad relation" (Galtung 2001, 3); and "a process of change and redefinition of relationships" (Lederach 2001, 847). The variety of definitions has led human rights scholar Harvey Weinstein (2011) to conclude that "the amount of writing on reconciliation reinforces the view that we are searching for a concept that defies clarity". Not only may a universal, scholarly definition be elusive, the term may also defy easy translation in contexts in which anthropologists and other ethnographers conduct research. For example, in Chapter 2 I will consider the conflict between the Lord's Resistance Army (LRA) and the Ugandan government in northern Uganda, an area inhabited primarily by the Acholi people. Anthropologist Tim Allen (2010, 250–251) notes the ambiguity of the term "forgiveness" in that context, given that in the Acholi language the term *timokeca* is used for the English word "forgiveness" but is also used for "amnesty" and "reconciliation", meaning that discussions about Acholi "forgiveness" might refer to a range of things. This suggests that finding equivalent terms in a language is not the same as finding equivalent meanings.

A prominent definition of "reconciliation" within anthropology is that proposed by John Borneman (2002, 282) who, writing in the context of ethnic conflict, notes that "to reconcile" means "to render no longer opposed" and defines "reconciliation" as a "project of departure from violence" in the present (without needing to share a vision of the past or future). A benefit of this definition is that it defines a flexible, context-specific process (see Finnström 2010, 136). Borneman argues there are two processes that enable a departure from (i.e., non-repetition) of violence. The first is "witnessing" as a form of "cultivated listening" for "truth" by a third party which will enable "truth telling" (Borneman 2002, 289). This "third party listening", according to Borneman, gives victims a voice which gives "a sense of ending, rupture, and break with the past" (Borneman 2002, 296; see Chapter 3). Second, Borneman (2002, 297–300) argues that "retributive justice" (i.e., criminal trials, see Chapter 5) will contribute to "reconciliation" by supporting the "sense of an ending" through punishing perpetrators and vindicating victims.

While Borneman's suggestions are reflected in two contemporary responses to violent conflict, truth commissions (see Chapter 4) and international criminal courts (see Chapter 5), fellow anthropologist Steven Sampson (2003, 182–182) suggests that Borneman's concept of "reconciliation" relies on a naive trust in the power of dialogue when, in reality, leaving things "unsaid" may be preferential. Rather than "reconciliation", Sampson recommends the notion of "coexistence" in which violence is absent and conflicting parties "simply ignore each other". Likewise, Wilson (2003, 188), commenting on Borneman's definition of reconciliation, argues that "truth telling may in fact exacerbate conflict as much as remedy it" and that calls for "reconciliation" (rather than just "coexistence") may serve the interests of both outgoing and incoming political elites, who sacrifice the needs of those who have suffered in the pursuit of avoiding punishment and gaining power. Wilson (2003, 189) suggests that "reconciliation", as such a project that serves the interests of political elites, has the potential to "coerce individuals into compliant positions they would not adopt of their own volition" (see discussion of *Inkiko-Gacaca* in Rwanda in Chapter 2). Wilson (2003, 189) concludes by asking if individuals are required to "coexist" (i.e., not commit violent acts), do they still not "have the right to think and feel what they like, including hatred for their former enemy"?

Clearly, Borneman's definition of "reconciliation" as a "project of departure from violence" does not meet with unanimous approval among anthropologists. One possible reason for this is that Borneman (2002, 281) makes a virtue of the fact that his definition "neither elaborates a specific case nor makes detailed historical-cultural comparisons". This is contrary to Sluka's (1992, 20) position with which I began this Introduction, that the strength of anthropology lies in its "cross-cultural and comparative perspective". This suggests that, rather than posit a universal definition of "reconciliation" as Borneman chooses to do, it may be preferable to consult accounts of how those living in areas affected by violent conflict respond to the situations in which they find themselves. Such an approach allows us to be sensitive to that fact that "reconciliation", like the violence that precedes it, is "not a finished and self-contained behaviour" that can be pre-defined, but something that is "always a matter of degree, intensity, and culturally competent judgment" (Whitehead 2004b, 63). It also allows us to distinguish between "reconciliation" as a pre-defined objective and "reconciliation" as a context-specific process that unfolds in unanticipated ways (see Bar-Tal & Bennink 2004). For these reasons I will now consider two responses by those in areas affected by violent conflict: (i) the choice to remain silent about the past; (ii) placing an emphasis on (re)establishing mundane, day-to-day relations while avoiding the term "reconciliation".

i. Remaining silent about the past

As indicated above, Sampson (2003, 182) suggests that Borneman's concept of "reconciliation" relies on a naive trust in the power of dialogue, when leaving things "unsaid" may be better. A common assertion following violent conflict is that the truth about what happened must be salvaged and shared and that members

10 Introduction

of opposing groups must "freely discuss the past conflict and take responsibility for past injustice and wrongdoing" (Bar-Tal & Cehajic-Clancy 2013, 131). It has been argued, however, that the assumption that there is a need for such "inter-group dialogue, establishing a common truth about the past", originates from Europe/North America (Stefansson 2010, 70). Shaw (2007b, 189) suggests that a global paradigm of "redemptive remembering through truth-telling", which argues that personal recovery cannot proceed without "psychological ventilation" (Summerfield 1999, 1455; see Chapter 3), originated in Europe/North America. If such an approach is not, in reality, universal, then it may be the case that "truth telling may in fact exacerbate conflict as much as remedy it" (Wilson 2003, 188) and that avoiding discussion of the past may be a pragmatic choice (see Millar 2011a). This is borne out by the ethnographic studies I will consider below which suggest that discussion of the past is avoided because of "cultural" beliefs, socio-economic survival or, simply, because people want to move on. I will consider each of these in turn.

However, before I consider these three reasons why discussion of the violent past is avoided in order to form and sustain "relations important to viable local life" (Eastmond & Mannergren Selimovic 2012, 507), it is important to acknowledge that silence can also be imposed on survivors of violent conflict who lack adequate language to express their experience (see Caruth 1996, 5–9; Scarry 1985, 4) or because they fear they will not be believed (see Langer 1991, xiv). As an aside, I am aware that the term "survivor" is problematic. Werner Weinberg (1985, 152), a survivor of the Nazi concentration camp Bergen-Belsen, suggests that "survivor" becomes "a constricting designation that can easily make its bearer appear – to others and himself – as a museum piece, a fossil, a freak, a ghost". Survivors, it can be argued, are "produced through the occupation of the signs of injury" that suppresses their identity and who they were before the catastrophe (Ross 2003a, 12). While acknowledging these concerns with the term "survivor", I choose it to refer to those who have experienced violent conflict. Given the abnormality of violent conflict, survivors may find "the difficulty of narrating, from the context of normality now, the nature of the normality then" (Langer 1991, 22). As a consequence, "the urge to tell meets resistance from the certainty that one's audience will not understand" (Langer 1991, xii; see Donnan & Simpson 2007, 14). This is illustrated by anthropologist Harry West's (2003) reflection on the life stories of FRELIMO (Front for the Liberation of Mozambique/Frente de Libertação de Moçambique) activists who had been tortured by the Portuguese authorities during the war for independence (1965–1975). West (2003, 357) found that these men "felt the inadequacy of the language they knew to speak of what they had experienced". Speaking to them in the mid-1990s, West (2003, 357) found that although these men "felt a persistent need to tell of what had been done to them", the hostility of the post-independence FRELIMO government to public discussion of such things meant that fellow villagers were deeply suspicious of the former-FRELIMO activists and did nothing to help them "in crafting a language adequate to their needs" (West 2003, 357). As a consequence, the men "seemed resigned to the elusiveness of healing and redemption" (West 2003, 359).

Introduction 11

While West's example illustrates how survivors may be prevented from speaking about the violent past because of the inadequacy of language, Alcinda Manuel Honwana (1997), also writing in the context of Mozambique (following the 1977–1992 civil war), notes how people avoided taking about the violent past because they believed this would open the door to attack by the spirits of those who had been killed. Recalling experiences of the war was not considered part of coming to terms with that experience, and people would "rather not talk about the past, not look back, and prefer to start afresh following certain ritual procedures" (Honwana 1997, 296; see Chapter 2). Honwana (1997, 301) provides an example of a twelve-year-old boy, Nando, who had begun military training when he was eight years old. Having returned after the war, the boy underwent various reintegration rituals designed to enable him to forget about the past and start a new life (see Chapter 2). The rituals were designed to mark a break with the past traumatic experience. These rituals did not involve "verbal exteriorisation" (i.e., the past was not talked about); rather, relief for Nando was achieved through "nonverbal symbolic procedures" because recounting and remembering the traumatic experience would be like opening the way for the bad spirits to return (Honwana 1997, 303). Despite these rituals Nando continued to speak of the war, which was of concern to his father because "he believed that talking about bad things from the past could reopen the door to the evil spirits once more" (Honwana 1997, 301).

While Honwana describes how cultural reasons meant the violent past was not spoken about among her respondents in Mozambique, in other contexts the past is discussed, but in indirect ways. Discussing the aftermath of the conflict in Sierra Leone (1991–2002), Shaw (2007a, 68) found that people "chose not to 'encourage' the return of violence by giving it a public reality" (see Millar 2011b). People spoke of "forgetting", not in terms of the "erasure of personal memories" but "their containment in a form that would enable them to recover their lives" (Shaw 2007b, 194). Shaw (2007a) describes how members of the youth ministry of the Gospel Prayer Ministries Church in Freetown, Sierra Leone, who had been displaced in the war and lost family members, struggled "against insistent memories of death and violence, dreaming about it, anticipating its return". Shaw (2007a, 89) describes how the youths "forget" the war as a "direct realist account" and retold their memories through the metaphor of a Satanic "Underworld" which could be fought through prayer, Bible reading and exorcism (see Perera 2001; Warren 1993). While such avoidance could be interpreted as "repressing" a past that should have been openly discussed, Shaw (2007a, 89) argues that speaking about the past in metaphorical terms was, in reality, "enabling rather than constraining", creating "a moral life course". Whether it is a refusal to speak about the past at all, as in Mozambique, or speaking through metaphor, as in Sierra Leone, the examples provided by Honwana and Shaw suggest that, in attempting to reconstruct their lives, those affected by violent conflict avoid the kinds of direct truth-telling advocated by the global paradigm of "redemptive remembering through truth-telling" (Shaw 2007b, 189).

Related to cultural reasons for not speaking about the past, ethnographic research also suggests that individuals may choose to be silent about the past for reasons of socio-economic survival, what political scientist Lina Strupinskienė (2016, 3–5) describes as "economic or pragmatic" reconciliation. Craig Etcheson (2005, 212) notes, for example, that despite an ongoing desire for revenge and retribution, most people in rural areas of Cambodia managed to live alongside people suspected of involvement in killing by the Khmer Rouge regime (1975–1979) because the "imperatives of daily survival in a largely subsistence economy impel the population to focus on essentials like obtaining enough food to feed their families". Likewise, anthropologist Christopher Duncan (2016, 468) reports that in the aftermath of violence between Muslims and Christians in North Maluku, eastern Indonesia (1999–2000), many of those who took part in the "reconciliation ceremonies" imposed by political elites (see Chapter 2) did so because they needed to return home to "where they had access to gardens or other livelihoods", and if that meant living with those they did not fully trust "that was a risk they would take for economic security". Finally, anthropologist Bert Ingelaere (2007, 22–24) notes that following the 1994 Rwandan genocide of the Tutsi, "silence on the past was the order of the day" because "neighbours and villagers depend upon each other in their daily activities and their fight for survival in mutual impoverishment" (see also Waldorf 2010).

The contexts described by Etcheson, Duncan and Ingelaere imply a tolerance of former enemies in order to survive. Other ethnographers, however, report an even closer, economic interdependence between former enemies. Anthropologist Anders Stefansson (2010) illustrates this in the context of Bosnia-Herzegovina following ethnic cleansing (1992–1996). He notes that international agencies, such as the United Nations High Commissioner for Refugees (UNHCR), believed that "ethnic remixing" (where those driven away by ethnic cleansing return to their homes) would result in "reconciliation". Stefansson examines the results of this policy in Banja Luka, the capital of Republika Srpska (a breakaway entity established in 1992 in which Serbs were the majority). Bosniaks (non-Serbs) had returned to areas traditionally populated by Bosniaks into which displaced Serbs had moved. Between these two groups, Stefansson (2010, 66) found "co-existence and tolerance … based on economic interdependence" which entailed "silencing sensitive political and moral questions" regarding the conflict. Economic interdependence ranged from Bosniaks renting rooms to displaced Serbs; Bosniaks shopping in Serb-owned shops; and informal, non-paid work such as helping each other with agricultural activities. Stefansson (2010, 68) reports how such economic, practical interdependence resulted in "coffee visits", a central custom in pre-war Bosnia-Herzegovina, which "worked to maintain harmonious social relations" (see Chapter 1). As an elderly Bosniak returnee told Stefansson (2010, 69), "We have to live together. We don't have to love each other. We must respect each other and help each other." Whether or not such socio-economic interdependence paved the way for resolving the more fundamental disagreements of whether Republika Srpska was the outcome of ethnic cleansing (the Bosniak view) or the struggle for

Introduction   13

liberation (the Serb view), it led to a "nascent sense of trust and local sharedness" (Stefansson 2010, 72; see Strupinskienė 2016, 12–13).

While avoiding talking about the violent past could be interpreted as a "condition of subordination and repression" (Kent 2016, 31), the examples above suggest it can also be an empowering, pragmatic choice. Drawing on fieldwork in a multi-ethnic community in Bosnia-Herzegovina (Foča) in which crimes against humanity and war crimes were committed in the 1990s, Marita Eastmond and Johanna Mannergren Selimovic (2012, 507) suggest that avoiding discussion of the past is a strategy actively employed in everyday interactions with "ethnic others" in ways that "empower by communicating respect and even trust, thus forming and sustaining relations important to viable local life". Around a quarter of the Bosniaks who were ethnically cleansed from Foča in 1992 returned after the war. These Bosniaks believed that avoiding discussion of the past was "a way to build peace", given that because everyone knew what had happened "open acknowledgement would be counterproductive" to rebuilding a "normal life" in precarious socio-economic circumstances (Eastmond & Mannergren Selimovic 2012, 512 514). Not discussing the past openly, therefore, was necessary, given socio-economic need, but it was not the same as erasing or denying a past of which everyone was aware. As Milorad, a Bosnian Serb in his twenties stated, "Today we have our own problems. ... We don't have time to spend on thinking [about the past]. We try to earn money, to buy some things for the house, to make a better living. We don't look into the past" (Eastmond & Mannergren Selimovic 2012, 512). In Foča, therefore, avoiding discussion about the past was an act of social communication rather than just the absence of speech, as a pragmatic "strategy for coexistence" (Eastmond & Mannergren Selimovic 2012, 507). This is an example of what Shaw (2005, 1) describes as "social forgetting", which in Sierra Leone at least was a "cornerstone of established processes of reintegration and healing".

Lia Kent's (2016) research in East Timor further supports Eastmond and Mannergren Selimovic's argument that pragmatic avoidance of discussing the violent past is not the same as erasing or denying that past. In 2002 a UN-sponsored Commission for Reception, Truth and Reconciliation (CAVR: Comissão de Acolhimento, Verdade e Reconciliação de Timor Leste) was established in Timor-Leste (East Timor) in the aftermath of the 24-year occupation by Indonesia (see Chapter 4). The CAVR exemplified the global paradigm of "redemptive remembering through truth-telling" (Shaw 2007b, 189; see Chapter 3), given that it was tasked with "establishing the truth regarding human rights violations" between 1974 and 1999 and preparing a report "based on factual and objective information and evidence collected or received by it" (Commission for Reception, Truth and Reconciliation 2006, 2). Kent (2016, 42) found, however, that East Timorese people were rebuilding their lives in ways that "foregrounded relational and embodied forms of communication, rather than public, verbal disclosure". Kent (2016, 45) describes efforts by East Timorese to return from West Timor to their families and communities in East Timor. These returnees (around 100,000 in 2016) were relatives of East Timorese who had been members of the Indonesian security forces or pro-Indonesian militia. Having made

14 Introduction

visits to their communities over a period of years, their "embodied presence in their communities" communicated that they had not cut links with their homeland (Kent 2016, 46). On their permanent return, Kent (2016, 47) notes how the repair and rebuilding of homes by returnees further reasserted ties to kin, land and ancestors. Kent provides the example of Joao who, having returned from West Timor with his family, rebuilt and repaired, with his extended family who had remained in East Timor, the family's *uma lulik* (sacred house). Once complete, pigs, chickens and goats were slaughtered and the family shared a meal together, an important form of communication that "the family was united again and that it would no longer be divided" (Kent 2016, 47). In such a context, avoiding direct discussion about the violent past was not the same as denying or forgetting the past, because "individuals and communities are acknowledging [the conflict's] legacy in other ways" (Kent 2016, 33 36).

While the ethnographic research conducted in Bosnia-Herzegovina (discussed above) indicated that socio-economic survival was a reason for avoiding direct discussion of the past, it may also be a pragmatic choice by survivors of violent conflict who see no value in speaking about the past and simply want to move on. The anthropologist Carolyn Nordstrom (1998, 115), for example, describes how demobilised soldiers in Mozambique underwent communal reintegration ceremonies because "We have to take the war out of these soldiers". Although many people had suffered at the hands of soldiers, they explained to Nordstrom that "to harbor revenge and anger would simply fan the flames of war and violence". Likewise, Susan Thomson (2011, 374) provides an account of how, in the aftermath of the 1994 Rwandan genocide of Tutsi, the requirement that people give testimony to *Inkiko-Gacaca* (communal courts; see Chapter 2) could disrupt individuals' attempts to live in "peace". Thomson (2011, 385) quotes Jeanne, a forty-seven-year-old Tutsi widow, who was instructed by the local authorities to testify against the individual who was accused of killing her family:

> [I have tried] my best to stay silent so that I can live the rest of my days in peace. I just want peace. … So I was as happy as I could be after the genocide. Then I am told they found the man who did this to my people. I was horrified. Now I have to relive all that bad memory. … I would rather stay out of the way of *gacaca* if I could.

Likewise, Holly Guthrey (2016, 15) quotes Jacinta, who described how giving testimony to the CAVR in East Timor had "done nothing to make her life better or easier", that:

> Now my thoughts are normal, but when they [the CAVR] came, they were digging and asking me the same questions over and over again, and it made me remember all those things again, and made my life more complicated.

Perspectives like that of Jeanne and Jacinta support the idea that at "a common-sense level it would seem obvious that most people want to forget the pains of the past and get on with their lives" (Rigby 2001, 1–2). Choosing not to speak directly about the violent past can, therefore, be a pragmatic means of (re)establishing "relations important to viable local life" (Eastmond & Mannergren Selimovic 2012, 507); chosen for "cultural" reasons, for reasons of economic survival or simply because it is the only way in which people like Jeanne and Jacinta can live their days in relative "peace".

Shaw (2005, 1) refers to the choice of not talking about the past as "social forgetting", which in Sierra Leone at least was a "cornerstone of established processes of reintegration and healing". Despite using the term "forgetting", Shaw does not mean that personal memories were erased, but that they were contained "in a form that would enable them to recover their lives" (Shaw 2007b, 194). Likewise, while Eastmond and Mannergren Selimovic (2012) report that avoiding open discussion of the past was necessary, given socio-economic need, this was not the same as erasing or denying a past of which everyone was aware. The anthropologist Paul Connerton's (2008) discussion of different forms of "forgetting" are helpful in this discussion. At one extreme, Connerton (2008, 60) suggests there is "repressive erasure" in which political authorities prohibit mention of certain past events. Another version is "forgetting as humiliated silence", which refers to the way in which people "fall silent out of terror or panic or because they can find no appropriate words" (Connerton 2008, 68), as illustrated by West's account of FRELIMO activists in Mozambique discussed above. However, two of Connerton's other types of "forgetting" are particularly relevant in relation to the ethnographic accounts considered above: "prescriptive forgetting" and "forgetting that is constitutive in the formation of a new iden- tity". Connerton (2008, 61) describes "proscriptive forgetting" as forgetting that "is believed to be in the interests of all the parties to the previous dispute". Although Connerton associates "proscriptive forgetting" with an "act of state", it can also be envisaged as a voluntary choice made by those who have survived violent conflict and who must live in close proximity to their former opponents. Regarding the other type of "forgetting that is constitutive in the formation of a new identity", Connerton (2008, 63) describes this as involving the discarding of "memories that serve no practicable purpose in the management of one's current identity and ongoing purposes", so that what "is allowed to be forgotten provides living space for present projects". In this way, "the desire to forget may be an essential ingredient in the process of survival" (Connerton 2008, 68).

ii. Re-establishing a "normal life"

While the choice to not speak about the violent past may seem to be the opposite of pursuing "reconciliation", which tends to be associated with acknowledging the past, the discussion above suggests that choosing to avoid direct discussion of the past can, in reality, be "an instrument that fosters relationships and opens up common ground" (Eastmond & Mannergren Selimovic 2012, 515). Taken further, this suggests it is in everyday, mundane interactions that viable relationships are (re)

16 Introduction

established, rather than in processes that are explicitly proclaimed as enabling "reconciliation" (especially when there is lack of agreement on what the term means). Laura Martin (2016, 400), drawing on research in Sierra Leone, suggests that what is often desired by those who have survived violent conflict "is the ordinary … the establishment of a 'new normal'" (see Das & Kleinman 2001, 4). Sierra Leoneans interviewed by Martin (2016, 403) chose to employ pre-existing communal structures to achieve "normality" as a desired state of affairs. Martin (2016, 404) suggests that people first "imitate" what they perceive to be "normal" in order to reaffirm "social and economic practices that may have become less familiar or altogether absent" during the conflict. Martin (2016, 407–413) provides details of how "enacting ordinary activities" that had been detrimentally affected by the war, including social and economic relations and agricultural and religious associations, facilitated a transition to a "new normal". Martin argues that these mundane mechanisms are ignored as they are not amenable to the same kinds of instrumental replication, monitoring and evaluation by international organisations and national governments as is the case with "recognizable" mechanisms (such as "traditional reconciliation rituals" considered in Chapter 2).

Like Martin, anthropologist Stef Jansen (2013, 234) found that many people in Bosnia-Herzegovina considered "reconciliation" to be a "Western-imposed idea" and that, in contrast, "the object of hope for many ordinary people was a 'normal life'". Many of Strupinskienė's (2016, 13) respondents in Bosnia-Herzegovina also spoke of the importance of the mundane, such as "falling in love across ethnic lines, drinking coffee, going to school together" (see Helms 2010; Mannergren Selimovic 2010, 57). As with coffee visits in Bosnia-Herzegovina, when Ingelaere (2016, 148) asked Rwandans how they defined "living with" one another (*kubana*), they described "the sharing of food and drinks, ceremonies of conviviality, and the exchange of gifts as signs of good social cohesion" (see also Buckley-Zistel 2006, 140 142). As a survivor of the Rwandan genocide told Eugenia Zorbas (2009b, 135), "It's not exactly like before 1994. But when there is beer, we invite neighbours and they too invite us." Taken together, this suggests that "practices of redress and repair may … draw upon the performance of everyday life as a means of remaking relationships" (Shaw & Waldorf 2010, 20).

Although not concerned with the recreation of an existing community divided by violent conflict, the anthropologist Stephanie Hobbis Ketterer's (2014, 3) study of a Japanese–South Korean reconciliation initiative provides insight into the importance of mundane commensality (the practice of eating and drinking together). Japan's colonisation of the Korean peninsula (1910–1945) was marked by labour camps, forced prostitution and attacks on Korean cultural identity. From the perspective of South Koreans, Japanese politicians have been unwilling to atone for Japanese aggression, while the Japanese population is either ignorant of this history or refuses to engage with it (Ketterer 2014, 3–5). Ketterer (2014, 5) conducted fieldwork with Koinonia, a grassroots Japanese–Korean reconciliation initiative formed in 1999 as an exchange programme between a church in South Korea and a church in Japan to "encourage conscious reflections about the atrocities committed by Imperial Japan".

During the alternating exchanges there were "truth-telling events" at which Japanese participants would publicly admit guilt. Participants, however, highlighted the importance of social interaction, "especially of sharing food with each other" and the "seemingly mundane conversations during and about these very meals" (Ketterer 2014, 5). For Ketterer (2014, 5) it was clear that, in the context of Koinonia, "reconciliatory relationships have, to a notable extent, been forged in the seemingly mundane". Drawing on the work of David Sutton (2001), Ketterer (2014, 11) argues that, because we consume food on a daily basis and regularly with others, the seemingly mundane act of eating serves the purpose of reproducing our social relations. As a consequence, "food events", whether drinking coffee together in Bosnia-Herzegovina or sharing beer in Rwanda, allow for "a new inclusivity based on largely non-verbal interactions, and by so doing, can alter perceptions of the other in a more comprehensive manner than verbal-only exchanges ever could" (Ketterer 2014, 11). Eating and drinking together, therefore, is another form of Kent's (2016, 42) "relational and embodied forms of communication" in the aftermath of violent conflict.

If, as Martin (2016, 404) suggests, those who have survived violent conflict need to imitate what they perceive to be "normal", then they require an idealised image of that "normal". While Borneman (2002, 283) argues that "traumatic loss cannot be stopped or overcome by presenting the possibility of return to a prior state of innocence or fullness", Sampson (2003, 181) suggests that "reconciliation" relies on a return to a situation prior to conflict marked by "peace, friendship and understanding", although he also suggests that "these circumstances most likely existed only as someone's nostalgia". Nostalgia should not, however, be underestimated. When Zorbas (2009b, 173–175) asked her respondents in post-genocide Rwanda what a "reconciled community" would look like, they expressed a desire to "live like we lived before", in which "we had mixed marriages, we helped carry each other's sick, we shared beer". While Zorbas (2009a, 174) considered such descriptions to be a romantic, "highly partial, idyllic picture of life before the genocide", such nostalgic and idealised accounts allowed people to envisage a future, because "any narrative of the past is interwoven with a vision of the future" (Leydesdorff 2009, 36). Eastmond and Mannergren Selimovic (2012, 509) likewise found that Bosnians' notion of a "normal life" was idealised; that having a job, a home and children in school was described as "the way most people used to live" and that helping neighbours, irrespective of ethnicity, was considered to be part of the "normal life" they aspired to recreate (Eastmond & Mannergren Selimovic 2012, 513). This suggests that the remaking of mundane relationships relies on an idealised, nostalgic account of life before the violent conflict (Shaw & Waldorf 2010, 20).

The importance of an idealised, nostalgic account of the past implies that imagination is important for rebuilding mundane, everyday relationships. For Nordstrom (1998, 103), violent conflict becomes reproduced in the "minutia of daily living" and so it must also be in everyday life that violent conflict is "resisted and ultimately defeated". The primary means through which it is resisted and ultimately defeated, according to Nordstrom, is through the imagination. As a Mozambican told

18 Introduction

Nordstrom (1998, 111), "we have to make our lives again. We have to imagine a future, a future safe from war, and then try to make it." Nordstrom (1998, 117) suggests that by "juxtaposing the broken life of war with remembrance of life 'as it should be lived'", this man was able to keep "alive the ideas and ideals that guided the reforging of a viable society". An idealised, nostalgic account of how life was lived before the violent conflict would, therefore, provide the man with a template for life "as it should be lived" in the future.

It is important, however, to recognise that a shared, nostalgic image of the past may not always be available. The historian Selma Leydesdorff (2009), for example, indicates that female survivors of the Srebrenica genocide of July 1995 (in which the army of Republika Srpska, Vojska Republike Speke (VRS), killed an estimated 8,000 Bosnian men and boys) found it too difficult to recall the pre-war past of peaceful co-existence; the memory of the betrayal of friends and neighbours preventing them from "developing any vision of the future, for such a vision can only be based on feelings about what was perceived as 'good' in the past" (Leydesdorff 2009, 25). Likewise, Jansen (2002, 81) reports how in a group of villages in Croatia, first "cleansed" of Croats and then of Serbs, Serbs were keen to remember pre-war "good neighbourhood", but Croats emphasised the betrayal of Serbian neighbours. The two sides remembered the past selectively, Croats downplaying pre-war good relations (such as mixed marriages) to emphasise a post-war, monoethnic Croatia now "liberated" from Serbian domination, while Serbs downplayed pre-war patterns of discrimination against Croats in favour of a "nostalgically reconstructed Yugoslav paradise" (Jansen 2002, 83). Given that survivors of ethnic cleansing remembered the past in different ways relevant to their current self-image as either Croat victim or innocent Serb, there was no shared, idealised "remembrance of life as it should be lived" (Nordstrom 1998, 117).

While there can be no doubt that "mundane" activities play an important part in reconstructing relationships (often drawing on an idealised image of "good neighbourliness"), they may also be strengthened by a shared aversion to the formal promotion of "reconciliation" by national governments and international agencies. Jansen (2013, 238–239) found that in post-war Bosnia-Herzegovina "mutual recognition" between those from opposing sides "was often established on a shared aversion of *politika*" (politicians), which people considered to be "the source of all evil". As a consequence, "many of the efforts to promote reconciliation … rely on mutual recognition precisely through a shared aversion to *politika* … a common distancing from the filthy machinations of politicians" (Jansen 2013, 239). Likewise in Rwanda, Zorbas (2009b, 131–132) found that both survivors and those accused of participation in the 1994 genocide denounced *hauts responsables* (leaders) for having taken advantage of the "ignorance" of the *bas people* (ordinary people). This supported an imagined, nostalgic image of community relations in the past; that it was political elites who had to "'reconcile' with each other and stop exporting their conflicts to otherwise 'harmonious' local communities" (Zorbas 2009b, 141). In other words, a shared distrust of political elites who promote "reconciliation" may, ironically, lead people to reject "reconciliation" as a political ploy and strengthen the re-creation of mundane relations according to nostalgic, imagined views of the past (see Hinton 2018, 7).

Conclusion

I began the chapter with a refusal to define the key terms of "peace" and "reconciliation" in order to avoid preordaining what those terms may mean for those who have survived violent conflict. The value of such an approach is demonstrated by the way in which terms whose meaning may otherwise be taken for granted have been interpreted in counter-intuitive ways by anthropologists: conflict can be constructive; "peace" relies on division; seeking "harmony" can be coercive; and "peace" is not the absence of violent conflict. The same challenge to "received wisdom" can be seen in the way that a decision to not speak directly about the past may seem to be the opposite of "reconciliation" but can, in many circumstances, be "an instrument that fosters relationships and opens up common ground" (Eastmond & Mannergren Selimovic 2012, 515). The ethnographic examples discussed above suggest that survivors of violent conflict tend to avoid discussion of the past and, instead, foreground "relational and embodied forms of communication, rather than public, verbal disclosure" (Kent 2016, 42). Such communication draws upon the "seemingly mundane" (Ketterer 2014, 5) performance of everyday life, such as eating and drinking, as survivors seek to (re)construct "normal life" (Jansen 2013, 234). This requires acts of imagination (Nordstrom 1998) that may draw on a fabricated, nostalgic image of past relations prior to violent conflict (Zorbas 2009b).

Taken together, this suggests that it is in everyday, mundane interactions that viable relationships are (re)established, rather than in processes that are explicitly proclaimed as enabling "reconciliation" (especially when there is lack of agreement on what the term means). Such mundane interactions may be ignored because re-establishing "everyday life" is not amenable to the same kinds of instrumental replication, monitoring and evaluation needed by national governments and international agencies for interventions explicitly designed to achieve "reconciliation" (Martin 2016). While such formal interventions and their emphasis on speaking about the violent past may, in fact, undermine the (re)construction of mundane relations (see Kent 2016, 37), such interventions may also, paradoxically, draw together those from opposing sides who share a distrust of political elites and suspect "reconciliation" is a political ploy. All in all, this suggests a need to seek out the "small local stories in which … communities are experimenting with ways of inhabiting the world together" (Das & Kleinman 2001, 16).

Bibliography

Allen, Tim. 2010. "Bitter Roots: the 'invention' of Acholi traditional justice". In *The Lord's Resistance Army: Myth and Reality*, edited by Tim Allen and Koen Vlassenroot, 242–261. London: Zed Books.

Avruch, Kevin. 2009. "Transforming conflict resolution education: applying anthropology alongside your students", *Learning and Teaching* 2 (2): 8–22.

Bar-Tal, Daniel and Gemma H. Bennink. 2004. "The Nature of Reconciliation as an Outcome and as a Process". In *From Conflict Resolution to Reconciliation*, edited by Yaacov Bar-Siman-Tov, 11–38. Oxford: Oxford University Press.

Bar-Tal, Daniel and Sabina Cehajic-Clancy. 2013. "From Collective Victimhood to Social Reconciliation: Outlining a Conceptual Framework". In *War, Community, and Social Change: Collective Experiences in the Former Yugoslavia*, edited by Dario Spini, Guy Elcheroth and Dinka Corkalo Birusk, 125–136. New York: Springer.

Bloomfield, David. 2003. "Reconciliation: An introduction". In *Reconciliation after Violent Conflict: A Handbook*, edited by David Bloomfield, Teresa Barnes and Luc Huyse, 10–18. Stockholm: International Institute for Democracy and Electoral Assistance.

Borneman, John. 2002. "Reconciliation after ethnic cleansing: Listening, retribution, affiliation", *Public Culture* 14 (2): 281–304.

Buckley-Zistel, Susanne. 2006. "Remembering to forget: Chosen amnesia as a strategy for local coexistence in post-genocide Rwanda", *Africa* 76 (2): 131–150.

Caruth, Cathy. 1996. *Unclaimed Experience: Trauma, Narrative, and History*. Baltimore, MD: Johns Hopkins University Press.

Chanock, Martin. 1987. *Law, Custom and Social Order: The Colonial Experience in Malawi and Zambia*. Cambridge, UK: Cambridge University Press.

Colson, Elizabeth. 1995. "The Contentiousness of Disputes". In *Understanding Disputes: The Politics of Argument*, edited by Pat Caplan, 65–82. Oxford: Berg Publishers.

Commission for Reception, Truth and Reconciliation. 2006. *"Chega!" Final Report of the Commission for Reception, Truth and Reconciliation in East Timor*. Dili: CAVR.

Connerton, Paul. 2008. "Seven types of forgetting", *Memory Studies* 1 (1): 59–71.

Coser, Lewis A. 1956. *The Functions of Social Conflict*. London: Routledge and Kegan Paul.

Dallaire, Roméo and Brent Beardsley. 2004. *Shake Hands with the Devil: The Failure of Humanity in Rwanda*. New York: Carroll and Graf.

Das, Veena and Arthur Kleinman. 2001. "Introduction". In *Remaking a World: Violence, Social Suffering, and Recovery*, edited by Veena Das, Arthur Kleinman, Margaret Lock, Mamphela Ramphela and Pamela Reynolds, 1–30. Berkeley, CA: University of California Press.

Donnan, Hastings and Kirk Simpson. 2007. "Silence and Violence among Northern Ireland Border Protestants", *Ethnos: Journal of Anthropology* 72 (1): 5–28.

Duncan, Christopher R. 2016. "Coexistence not Reconciliation: From Communal Violence to Non-Violence in North Maluku, Eastern Indonesia", *The Asia Pacific Journal of Anthropology* 17 (5).

Eastmond, Marita and Johanna Mannergren Selimovic. 2012. "Silence as Possibility in Postwar Everyday Life", *The International Journal of Transitional Justice* 6 (3): 502–524.

Eliot, T.S. 1948. *Notes Towards the Definition of Culture*. London: Faber & Faber.

Eltringham, Nigel. 2014b. "Display, concealment and 'culture': the disposal of bodies in the 1994 Rwandan genocide". In *Human Remains and Mass Violence Methodological Approaches*, edited by Jean-Marc Dreyfus and Élisabeth Anstett, 161–180. Manchester: Manchester University Press.

Etcheson, Craig. 2005. "The Limits of Reconciliation in Cambodia's Communes". In *Roads to Reconciliation*, edited by Elin Skaar, Siri Gloppen and Astri Suhrke, 201–224. Lanham, MD: Lexington Books.

Evans-Pritchard, E.E. 1940. *The Nuer: A Description of the Modes of Livelihood and Political Institutions of a Nilotic People*. Oxford: Clarendon Press.

Falk Moore, Sally. 1989. "History and the Redefinition of Custom in Kilimanjaro". In *History and Power in the Study of Law: New Directions in Legal Anthropology*, edited by J. Starr and J.F. Collier, 277–301. Ithaca, NY: Cornell University Press.

Falk Moore, Sally. 1992. "Treating Law as Knowledge: Telling Colonial Officers What to Say to Africans about Running "Their Own" Native Courts", *Law and Society Review* 26: 11–46.

Farmer, Paul. 1996. "On Suffering and Structural Violence: A View from Below", *Daedalus* 25 (1): 261–283.

Farmer, Paul. 2004. "An Anthropology of Structural Violence", *Current Anthropology* 45 (3): 305–325.

Finnström, Sverker. 2010. "Reconciliation Grown Bitter?: War, Retribution, and Ritual Action in Northern Uganda". In *Localizing Transitional Justice: Interventions and Priorities after Mass Violence*, edited by Rosalind Shaw, Lars Waldorf and Pierre Hazan, 135–156. Stanford, CA: Stanford University Press.

Galtung, Johan. 1969. "Violence, Peace and Peace Research", *Journal of Peace Research* 6 (3): 167–190.

Galtung, Johan. 2001. "After violence, reconstruction, reconciliation, and resolution: Coping with visible and invisible effects of war and violence". In *Reconciliation, Justice, and Coexistence: Theory and Practice*, edited by Mohammed Abu-Nimer. Lanham, MD: Lexington Books.

Gluckman, Max. 1963. *Custom and Conflict in Africa*. Oxford: Basil Blackwell.

Government of South Africa. 1995. Promotion of National Unity and Reconciliation Act 34.

Gulliver, Philip H. 1979. *Disputes and Negotiations: A Cross-Cultural Perspective*. New York: Academic Press.

Guthrey, Holly L. 2016. "Local Norms and Truth Telling: Examining Experienced Incompatibilities within Truth Commissions of Solomon Islands and Timor-Leste", *The Contemporary Pacific* 28 (1): 1–29.

Hammersley, Martyn and Paul Atkinson. 2007. *Ethnography: Principles in Practice*. London: Routledge.

Helms, Elissa. 2010. "The gender of coffee: Women and reconciliation initiatives in post-war Bosnia and Herzegovina", *Focaal* 57: 17–32.

Hinton, Alexander Laban. 2018. *The Justice Facade: Trials of Transition in Cambodia*. Oxford: Oxford University Press.

Hoebel, E. Adamson. 1954. *The Law of Primitive Man: A Study in Comparative Legal Dynamics*. Cambridge, MA: Harvard University Press.

Honwana, Alcinda Manuel. 1997. "Healing for Peace: Traditional Healers and Post-War Reconstruction in Southern Mozambique", *Peace and Conflict: Journal of Peace Psychology* 3 (3): 293–305.

Honwana, Alcinda Manuel. 2005. "Healing and Social Reintegration in Mozambique and Angola". In *Roads to Reconciliation*, edited by Elin Skaar, Siri Gloppen and Astri Suhrke, 83–100. Lanham, MD: Lexington Books.

Ingelaere, Bert. 2007. *"Does the Truth Pass Across the Fire without Burning?" Transitional Justice and its Discontents in Rwanda's Gacaca Courts*. Antwerp: Institute of Development Policy and Management.

Ingelaere, Bert. 2016. *Inside Rwanda's Gacaca Courts: Seeking Justice after Genocide*. Madison, WI: University of Wisconsin Press.

Jansen, Stef. 2002. "The Violence of Memories: Local narratives of the past after ethnic cleansing in Croatia", *Rethinking History* 6 (1): 77–93.

Jansen, Stef. 2013. "If reconciliation is the answer, are we asking the right questions", *Studies in Social Justice* 7 (2): 229–243.

Kent, Lia. 2016. "Sounds of Silence: Everyday Strategies of Social Repair in Timor-Leste", *Australian Feminist Journal* 42 (1): 31–50.

Ketterer, Stephanie Hobbis. 2014. "'Love Goes through the Stomach': A Japanese–Korean Recipe for Post-conflict Reconciliation", *Anthropology in Action* 21 (2): 2–13.

Koch, Klaus-Friedrich, Soraya Altorki, Andrew Arno and Letitia Hickson. 1977. "Ritual Reconciliation and the Obviation of Grievances: A Comparative Study in the Ethnography of Law", *Ethnology* 16 (3): 269–283.

22 Introduction

Langer, Lawrence L. 1991. *Holocaust Testimonies: The Ruins of Memory*. New Haven, CT: Yale University Press.

Laplante, Lisa J. 2007. "The Peruvian Truth Commission's Historical Memory Project: Empowering Truth-Tellers to Confront Truth Deniers", *Journal of Human Rights* 6 (4): 433–452.

Lederach, John Paul. 2001. "Civil Society and Reconciliation". In *Turbulent Peace: The Challenges of Managing International Conflict*, edited by Chester A. Crocker, Fen Osler Hampson and Pamela Aall, 841–854. Washington, DC: United States Institute of Peace.

Leydesdorff, Selma. 2009. "When communities fell apart and neighbours became enemies: stories of bewilderment in Srebrenica". In *Memories of Mass Repression: Narrating Life Stories in the Aftermath of Atrocity*, edited by Nanci Adler, Selma Leydesdorff, Mary Chamberlain and Leyla Neyzi, 21–40. New Brunswick, NJ: Transaction.

Llewellyn, Karl N. and E. Adamson Hoebel. 1941. *The Cheyenne Way: Conflict and Case Law in Primitive Jurisprudence*. Norman, OK: University of Oklahoma Press.

Mamdani, Mahmood 2000. "The Truth According to the TRC". In *The Politics of Memory: Truth, Healing and Social Justice*, edited by Ifi Amadiume and Abdullahi An-Na'im, 176–183. London: Zed Books.

Mannergren Selimovic, Johanna. 2010. "Perpetrators and victims: Local responses to the International Criminal Tribunal for the former Yugoslavia", *Focaal* 57: 50–61.

Martin, Laura S. 2016. "Practicing Normality: An Examination of Unrecognizable Transitional Justice Mechanisms in Post-Conflict Sierra Leone", *Journal of Intervention and State-building* 10 (3): 400–418.

Millar, Gearoid. 2011a. "Between Western Theory and Local Practice: Cultural Impediments to Truth-Telling in Sierra Leone", *Conflict Resolution Quarterly* 29 (2): 177–199.

Millar, Gearoid. 2011b. "Local Evaluations of Justice through Truth Telling in Sierra Leone: Postwar Needs and Transitional Justice", *Human Rights Review* 12 (4): 515–535.

Mironko, Charles. 2006. "Ibitero: Means and Motive in the Rwandan Genocide". In *Genocide in Cambodia and Rwanda: New Perspectives*, edited by Susan E. Cook, 163–190. New Brunswick, NJ: Transaction Publishers.

Nader, Laura. 1991a. *Harmony Ideology: Justice and Control in a Zapotec Mountain Village*. Stanford, CA: Stanford University Press.

Nader, Laura 1991b. "Harmony Models and the Construction of Law". In *Conflict Resolution: Cross-Cultural Perspectives*, edited by Kevin Avruch, Peter W. Black and Joseph A. Scimecca, 41–59. New York: Greenwood Press.

Nader, Laura. 1997. "Controlling Processes: Tracing the Dynamic Components of Power", *Current Anthropology* 38 (5): 711–737.

Nader, Laura. 2000. "Comment on: Reconciliation and Revenge in Post-Apartheid South Africa Rethinking Legal Pluralism and Human Rights", *Current Anthropology* 41 (1): 75–98.

Nordstrom, Carolyn. 1998. "Terror Warfare and the Medicine of Peace", *Medical Anthropology Quarterly* 12 (1): 103–121.

Perera, Sasanka. 2001. "Spirit Possessions and Avenging Ghosts: Stories of Supernatural Activity as Narratives of Terror and Mechanisms of Coping and Remembering". In *Remaking a World: Violence, Social Suffering, and Recovery*, edited by Veena Das, Arthur Kleinman, Margaret Lock, Mamphela Ramphele and Pamela Reynolds, 157–200. Berkeley, CA: University of California Press.

Riches, David (ed.). 1986. "The Phenomenon of Violence". In *The Anthropology of Violence*, 1–27. Oxford: Wiley-Blackwell.

Rigby, Andrew. 2001. *Justice and Reconciliation: After the Violence*. Boulder, CO: Lynne Rienner.

Robarchek, Clayton A. 1979. "Conflict, emotion and abreaction: Resolution of conflict among the Semai Senoi", *Ethos* 7 (2): 104–123.

Ross, Fiona. 2001. "Speech and Silence: Women's Testimony in the First Five Weeks of Public Hearings of the South African Truth and Reconciliation Commission". In *Remaking a World: Violence, Social Suffering, and Recovery*, edited by Veena Das, Arthur Kleinman, Margaret Lock, Mamphela Ramphela and Pamela Reynolds, 250–279. Berkeley, CA: University of California Press.

Ross, Fiona. 2003a. *Bearing Witness: Women and the Truth and Reconciliation Commission in South Africa*. London: Pluto Press.

Ross, Fiona. 2003b. "On Having a Voice and Being Heard", *Anthropological Theory* 3 (3): 325–341.

Sampson, Steven. 2003. "From Reconciliation to Coexistence", *Public Culture* 15 (1): 181–186.

Scarry, Elaine. 1985. *The Body in Pain: The Making and Unmaking of the World*. Oxford: Oxford University Press.

Sen, Amartya. 1990. *Poverty and Famines: An Essay on Entitlement and Deprivation*. Oxford: Oxford University Press.

Shaw, Rosalind. 2005. *Rethinking Truth and Reconciliation Commissions: Lessons from Sierra Leone*. Washington, DC: United States Institute of Peace.

Shaw, Rosalind. 2007a. "Displacing Violence: Making Pentecostal Memory in Postwar Sierra Leone", *Cultural Anthropology* 22 (1): 66–93.

Shaw, Rosalind. 2007b. "Memory Frictions: Localizing the Truth and Reconciliation Commission in Sierra Leone", *The International Journal of Transitional Justice* 1 (2): 183–207.

Shaw, Rosalind and Lars Waldorf. 2010. "Introduction: Localizing Traditional Justice". In *Localizing Transitional Justice: Interventions and Priorities after Mass Violence*, edited by Rosalind Shaw, Lars Waldorf and Pierre Hazan, 3–26. Stanford, CA: Stanford University Press.

Simmel, Georg. 1955. *Conflict and the Web of Group Affiliations*. New York: Glencoe Free Press.

Sluka, Jeffrey A. 1992. "The Anthropology of Conflict". In *The Paths to Domination, Resistance, and Terror*, edited by Carolyn Nordstrom and JoAnn Martin, 18–35. Berkeley, CA: University of California Press.

Stefansson, Anders H. 2010. "Coffee after cleansing? Co-existence, co-operation, and communication in post-conflict Bosnia and Herzegovina", *Focaal* 57: 62–76.

Strupinskienė, Lina. 2016. "What is reconciliation and are we there yet? Different types and levels of reconciliation: A case study of Bosnia and Herzegovina", *Journal of Human Rights* 16 (4): 1–21.

Summerfield, Derek. 1999. "A critique of seven assumptions behind psychological trauma programmes in war-affected areas", *Social Science & Medicine* 48 (10): 1449–1462.

Sutton, David E. 2001. *Remembrance of Repasts: An Anthropology of Food and Memory*. Oxford: Berg Publishers.

Taylor, Christopher C. 1999. *Sacrifice as Terror: The Rwandan Genocide of 1994*. Oxford: Berg Publishers.

Theidon, Kimberly. 2007. "Gender in Transition: Common Sense, Women and War", *Journal of Human Rights* 6 (3): 653–678.

Thomson, Susan. 2011 "The Darker Side of Transitional Justice: The Power Dynamics Behind Rwanda's Gacaca Courts", *Africa* 81 (3): 373–390.

Waldorf, Lars. 2010. "'Like Jews Waiting for Jesus': Posthumous Justice in Post-Genocide Rwanda". In *Localizing Transitional Justice: Interventions and Priorities after Mass Violence*, edited by R. Shaw, L. Waldorf and Pierre Hazan, 183–204. Stanford, CA: Stanford University Press.

24 Introduction

Warren, Kay (ed.). 1993. "Interpreting La Violencia in Guatemala: Shapes of Mayan Silence and Resistance". In *The Violence Within: Cultural and Political Opposition in Divided Nations*. Boulder, CO: Westview Press.

Weinberg, Werner. 1985. *Self-portrait of a Holocaust Survivor*. Jefferson, NC: McFarland & Co.

Weinstein, Harvey M. 2011. "Editorial Note: The Myth of Closure, the Illusion of Reconciliation: Final Thoughts on Five Years as Co-Editor-in-Chief", *International Journal of Transitional Justice* 5 (1): 1–10.

West, Harry G. 2003. "Voices Twice Silenced: Betrayal and Mourning at Colonialism's End in Mozambique", *Anthropological Theory* 3 (3): 343–365.

Whitehead, Neil L. (ed.). 2004a. "Introduction: Cultures, Conflicts, and the Poetics of Violent Practice". In *Violence*, 3–24. Santa Fe, NM: School of American Research Press.

Whitehead, Neil L. (ed.). 2004b. "On the Poetics of Violence". In *Violence*, 55–77. Santa Fe, NM: School of American Research Press.

Wilson, Richard A. 2000. "Reconciliation and Revenge in Post-Apartheid South Africa: Rethinking Legal Pluralism and Human Rights", *Current Anthropology* 41 (1): 75–98.

Wilson, Richard A. 2003. "Justice and Retribution in Postconflict Settings", *Public Culture* 15 (1): 187–190.

Zorbas, Eugenia. 2009a. *Reconciliation in Post-genocide Rwanda: Discourse and Practice*. London: London School of Economics and Political Science.

Zorbas, Eugenia. 2009b. "What does reconciliation after genocide mean? Public transcripts and hidden transcripts in post-genocide Rwanda", *Journal of Genocide Research* 11 (1): 127–147.

1
"TRADITIONAL" CONFLICT MANAGEMENT MECHANISMS

The means by which societies maintain "social cohesion" by managing conflict has been a long-standing concern of anthropologists (see Avruch 2007). Two principal positions emerged in anthropology in the first half of the 20th century regarding conflict management understood as "law". The first position conceived of "law" in relatively restricted terms as "the legitimate use of physical coercion by a socially authorized agent" (Hoebel 1954, 26). The second position was much broader and defined "law" as any activity (including gossip and ostracism) that promoted social conformity (Malinowski 1926), thereby "raising uncodified social rules to the status of law" (Wilson 2000, 76). The first position was criticised for only recognising processes which resemble the manner in which law is practised in Europe and North America (see Comaroff & Roberts 1981, 6–7), while the latter, in defining all social rules as "law", made it difficult to analyse the specific impact of "state law" that is (re)written by bureaucratic specialists and enforced by a monopoly of physical coercion (imprisonment, execution, etc.) (Wilson 2000, 77). Contemporary anthropologists have moved beyond the debates on the definition of "law" and, instead, have considered the "processes by which conflicts are handled and resolutions achieved" (Merry 2001, 8489; see Nader & Todd 1978). Rules are still relevant in managing conflict, but there is a recognition that rules are "strategic improvisations" (McWilliam 2007, 89) and that the "body of rules [is] continually undergoing transformations in separate cases" (Rose 1992, 191; see Comaroff & Roberts 1981, 19).

On one hand, this chapter has a stand-alone purpose in demonstrating the benefits of adopting an ethnographic approach to understanding "processes by which conflicts are handled and resolutions achieved" (Merry 2001, 8489). The chapter also prepares the ground for Chapter 2, in which I will discuss how, in recent years, "indigenous" or "traditional" conflict management mechanisms have been promoted as an "authentic", and more effective, response to violent conflict than externally conceived

26 "Traditional" conflict management mechanisms

interventions such as "truth commissions" or criminal trials (see United Nations 2004, 7–12). Given that this "re-traditionalisation" movement has drawn inspiration from ethnographic accounts of "traditional" conflict management mechanisms in countries formerly under colonial rule, this chapter will consider seven such mechanisms. I have chosen to employ the phrase "conflict management" rather than "conflict resolution" or "conflict settlement" as these alternative terms downplay the fact that a residue of antagonism is likely to remain and that "conflicting interests and personal animosities" do not simply disappear (Colson 1995, 66; see Falk Moore 1977, 186; Gulliver 1979, 78–79).

Before considering the seven case studies, I will reflect on three issues that suggest a degree of caution is required when reading ethnographic accounts of conflict management mechanisms: the need to avoid essentialising "culture" (i.e., avoid assuming that there is consensus among all members of a group regarding the validity of the mechanism and that the mechanism has not changed over time); the need to recognise that what is presented as "tradition" may be the result of a more recent colonial invention of "customary law"; and, finally, the need to ensure that in comparing mechanisms we do not privilege features that resemble the form taken by conflict management in Europe and North America.

Essentialising "culture"

In the Introduction I noted that classic anthropological accounts of conflict resolution, such as that of Max Gluckman (1963), reflect the approach of "structural functionalism", which emphasised how an existing socio-political order was maintained by shared values that acted to maintain equilibrium (see Nader 1991). It has been argued that such an approach underplayed internal disagreements and failed to account for change over time. The anthropologist James Clifford (1988, 235), for example, argues that such an approach privileges the "coherent, balanced and 'authentic' aspects of shared life", which implies that "culture" is "enduring and structural" when, in reality, the form it takes is temporary and constantly incorporates new influences. Writing in the context of conflict resolution, anthropologists Kevin Avruch and Peter W. Black (1993, 132) warn that "culture" is "often spoken of as though it were a thing, as if it were evenly distributed across members of the group … as though it were impervious to change over time". Of particular concern is the assumption that "culture is homogeneous", that a culture is "free of dissensions, of internal contradictions or paradoxes" (Avruch 2000, 341; see Avruch & Black 1991; Avruch 1998; Finlay 2006). In contrast to such an approach, contemporary anthropologists, including Avruch and Black, consider "culture" as a "field of creative interchange and contestation … and continuous transformation" (Cowan et al. 2001, 5). This means that "culture" is not a noun or a list of characteristics but a verb, "an active process, not as something which, once achieved, is fixed" (Falk Moore 2000, 6). As a consequence, "cultures" are "marked by hybridity and creolization rather than uniformity or consistency" (Merry 2003, 67).

When "traditional" conflict management mechanisms are considered, therefore, they should not be seen as a "stable body of rules" but as a "body of rules continually undergoing transformations in separate cases" (Rose 1992, 191), and as a "living, negotiated tissue of practices which are continually being adapted to new ecological and social circumstances" (Scott 1998, 34). From such a perspective there is a need to be cautious about views of culture that propose "a group is defined by a distinctive culture and that cultures are discrete, clearly bounded and internally homogeneous" (Cowan et al. 2001, 3). On encountering claims that "culture" is homogenous, Elizabeth Zechenter (1997, 334) encourages us to ask a series of questions: "(1) whose interests are being served by the 'traditional' customs and whose are infringed by them, (2) why some customs are abandoned while others are maintained or resurrected and by whom, (3) who benefits from change in cultural practices versus who gains from maintaining the status quo?"

The colonial invention of "customary law"

Reflecting the focus of the "re-traditionalisation" movement (see Chapter 2), the seven case studies considered below are drawn from countries that were colonised by European powers. Anthropologist Sally Merry (1988, 875) notes that, in colonial settings, pre-colonial mechanisms were adopted by colonial rulers and labelled "customary law", implying that it was of long-standing and had been left unchanged by the colonial powers. Ethnographic and historical accounts have demonstrated, however, that "the notion of an unchanging custom ... was a myth of the colonial era" and that, in reality, "customary law itself was a product of the colonial encounter" (Merry 1988, 875; see Snyder 1981), including "harmony ideology" discussed in the Introduction (see Nader 1997, 715). For these reasons, human rights scholar Lars Waldorf (2006, 6) warns that "what passes for harmonious, indigenous customs are more often than not 'invented traditions' designed to promote social control and political ideologies".

This is illustrated by anthropologist Sally Falk Moore's (1989) ethnographic fieldwork among the Chagga of Mount Kilimanjaro (Tanzania) in the later 1960s. Falk Moore (1989, 277 289) notes that while there is a tendency to refer to "customary law" as if "parts of previous traditions actually existed intact", it is, in reality, a "product of the colonial encounter", a "residual category", being the part of an "earlier way of life" with which colonial administrations chose not to interfere. Falk Moore describes how the political and economic conditions of the Chagga changed entirely with colonisation, with the Chagga chiefdom as it had existed in the late 19th century disappearing and the introduction of coffee as a cash crop generating new rules about land ownership. Despite these radical changes, in the 1960s Falk Moore (1989, 295) witnessed better-off men (such as salaried teachers) evoking "customary law" to try to do their poorer relatives and neighbours out of their land. Falk Moore (1989, 299) argues that the actions of these better-off Chagga men demonstrate that claims to continuity of "custom" over time, even if not true, can be used strategically by individuals (and national governments) to promote their interests (Falk Moore 1989, 277; 2000).

28 "Traditional" conflict management mechanisms

Falk Moore's research indicates a state of "legal pluralism" among the Chagga in which more than one legal system was at play: "state law" and "customary law" (see Wilson 2000, 76). All societies are "legally plural" to some extent, with individuals not only having their behaviour enforced by "state law" but also by other mechanisms of "normative ordering" (e.g., workplace disciplinary mechanisms). Falk Moore's study of the Chagga indicates that "state law" and "customary law" are not separate but in a "mutually constitutive relation" (Merry 1988, 880). In other words, rather than "customary law" in colonised states remaining "static and isolated" (Wilson 2000, 76), it was "utterly transformed by, controlled, and integrated within the administrative apparatus of the colonial state" (Wilson 2000, 77; see Chanock 1987; Colson 1995) and continues to be defined in reference to "state law".

This is evident in the seven case studies that I consider below. In Liberia, for example, those in matrimonial disputes chose the *moot* (an assembly held for debate) over the state's court "because [the court's] harsh tone tends to drive spouses farther apart rather than reconcile them" (Gibbs 1963, 2). In Indonesia, people chose *paresa dou* ("to investigate an individual") over going to the police because involving outsiders "is to relinquish a share of control over the outcome of a dispute" (Just 1991, 109; see Al-Krenawi & Graham 1999, 169). Finally, in Nigeria, cases were brought before the *esop isöñ* ("elders council") rather than the formal courts because of the corruption of police officers who would demand a bribe (*kola*) before investigating or prosecuting a case, with the consequence that "the court [people] dread most is the formal court" (Offiong 1997, 430). The preference for these "customary" conflict resolution mechanisms rather than "state law" demonstrates that the two forms of "law" remain in a "mutually constitutive relation" (Merry 1988, 880).

Examples such as Falk Moore's study of the Chagga indicate that "customary law" is not simply "tradition", but is the residue of a system "utterly transformed by, controlled, and integrated within the administrative apparatus of the colonial state" (Wilson 2000, 77; see Chanock 1987). This transformation continues as "customary law" continues to exist in a mutually constitutive relationship with "state law". As a consequence, when "customary law" is evoked, including in the form of conflict management mechanisms, it must be recognised that it is a "construct with political implications" (Merry 1988, 880) that can be used strategically by individuals (and governments) to promote their interests (Falk Moore 1989, 277).

The pitfalls of comparison

A further issue that suggests a degree of caution is required when reading ethnographic accounts of conflict management mechanisms is the longstanding debate within the "anthropology of disputes" regarding comparison and its potentially distorting effects (see Bohannan 1969; Comaroff & Roberts 1977). While on one hand it is argued that ethnographic research "cannot be a matter of locating identical phenomena masquerading under different names" (Geertz 1983, 216), it is also argued that "the presentation solely, allegedly, of the ideas of a folk system [i.e., without comparison] restricts

"Traditional" conflict management mechanisms **29**

one's analysis severely" (Gluckman 1969, 365). Put another way, if we argue that each conflict resolution mechanism is unique, are we restricted to only describing each mechanism in isolation without any comparison?

The dangers associated with "locating identical phenomena masquerading under different names" (Geertz 1983, 216) can be seen in James Gibbs' (1963) account of the Kpelle moot in Liberia, which I discuss in detail below. Gibbs (1963, 1–6) argues that the moot "is based on a covert application of the principles of psychoanalytical theory which underlies psychotherapy" including: support (presence of kin and neighbours); permissiveness (a suspension of every-day restrictions on anti-social statements); the denial of reciprocity (the therapist will not respond in kind to hostility or affection); and manipulation of rewards (one is rewarded by group approval if one makes/accepts an apology) (see Al-Krenawi & Graham 1999, 170). While such comparisons (suggesting that the mechanism "is like" psychoanalysis) may be tempting as a means of achieving understanding, they need to be used with caution. In Chapter 3 I will consider how, from the 19th century onward, psychoanalytical ideas of "repressed memories" and "cathartic release" have "seeped into American and European consciousness through the development of 'therapy culture'" (Shaw 2007, 192). Rosalind Shaw (2007) argues that while therapeutic approaches originated in Europe and North America, they have become so naturalised as to appear universal. In reality, however, as the psychiatrist Derek Summerfield (1999, 1449–1451) notes, what "constitutes psychological knowledge is the product of a particular culture at a particular point in time". The implications for interpreting the Kpelle moot or other conflict management mechanisms as being "like" psychotherapy are clear, that we may be further promoting the universalisation of approaches that are considered "natural" only in particular parts of the world.

On the other hand, as Gluckman (1969, 365) noted, describing conflict management mechanisms in a vacuum without any comparison will severely restrict or even paralyse our analysis. Seeking to overcome the comparison conundrum, the anthropologist Douglas Fry (2000, 334) suggests that although, on one hand, "conflict management mechanisms can be viewed as highly specific to the particular cultural system within which they operate", on the other hand "cross-cultural comparisons reveal general mechanisms of conflict management". Fry (2000, 347) argues, therefore, that "understanding conflict management can best be advanced through both culturally comparative studies and culturally specific research". The purpose of such an approach is "not to construct a manual with conflict-resolution steps" but to "expand the number of options to consider in approaching conflict" (Fry & Bjorkqvist 1996, 5). While remaining cautious about "pulling conflict-resolution 'tidbits'" from a specific cultural context because they only "acquire meaning as part of the cultural whole", paying attention to "recurring cultural patterns and isolating underlying principles is essential" (Fry & Bjorkqvist 1996, 5). In an effort to fulfil Fry and Bjorkqvist's suggestion, I will consider seven case studies which, on the one hand, demonstrate that conflict management mechanisms "are intimately related to other aspects of personality, society and culture" (Robarchek 1979, 104), but which, on the other, allow a tentative identification of common themes.

30 "Traditional" conflict management mechanisms

In preparation for considering the seven case studies, I have suggested three issues that demand a degree of caution when reading ethnographic accounts of conflict management mechanisms: to be aware of the tendency to essentialise "culture"; to recognise that, while the perceived longevity of a mechanism (as "tradition") may lend it prestige, its contemporary form may be a relatively recent development and it continues to evolve over time; and to resist the assumption that all conflict management mechanisms follow a universal logic. It is, of course, important for me to acknowledge that I too "essentialise" culture as I selectively cherry pick ethnographic accounts of mechanisms from all over the world and use the present tense as I summarise observations made up to sixty years ago. Such an approach is unavoidable if I wish to explore mechanisms of conflict management in cross-cultural comparison, but acknowledging the artificial nature of such an approach is also necessary to moderate the claims I make.

Conflict management mechanisms: seven case studies

1. Kpelle (Liberia)

The anthropologist James Gibbs (1963) provides an account of a conflict management mechanism among the Kpelle, a Mande-speaking group of rice cultivators who live in central Liberia. The Kpelle moot, or "house palaver" (*bɛrɛi mu memi saa*), considers domestic cases such as alleged mistreatment or neglect by a spouse, unpaid money for jobs and quarrels over inheritance. The moot takes place at the home of the complainant before an *ad hoc* assembled group of his kin and neighbours and is overseen by a "mediator" chosen by the complainant from among his/her kin (Gibbs 1963, 3). The proceedings begin with a blessing from one of the oldest members of the group, who asks the "supreme creator deity" to "bless all those who come to discuss this matter" (Gibbs 1963, 4). The complainant speaks first and may be questioned by anyone present. The accused then speaks and may be questioned by anyone present. Finally, the complainant and accused may question one another (Gibbs 1963, 4). After everyone has been heard, the mediator and others present "will point out the various faults committed by both parties" before the mediator expresses the consensus of the group (Gibbs 1963, 4). The person felt to be mainly at fault will then formally apologise to the other person and give them token gifts, such as an item of clothing or a few coins (Gibbs 1963, 4). A fine of beer or rum is also imposed and this is consumed by all present. The moot finishes with the elder pronouncing another blessing and offering "thanks for the restoration of harmony within the group" (Gibbs 1963, 4).

2. Dou Donggo (Indonesia)

The anthropologist Peter Just (1991) provides an account of conflict management in a village of Dou Donggo, subsistence farmers on Sumbawa island, Indonesia. In complicated cases, where there has been the threat of, or actual, violence, an *ad hoc* panel of village elders (*doumatuatua*) oversees a *paresa* ("to conduct an evidentiary proceeding") in which evidence is publicly presented and weighed, a ruling made and sanctions applied. The primary purpose of a *paresa* is to restore damaged status relationships and enforce the key expectation of "deference and respect by juniors for seniors" (Just 1991, 110). In the public forum of the *paresa* the accuser, or a *doumatuatua,* presents charges against the accused, evidence is provided and testimony given. A consensus on "a version of the 'truth' emerges through a process of give and take in which accuser, accused and presiding judges all engage in rhetorical claims and counter claims" (Just 1991, 134). If the accused confesses, he or she will be let off lightly. If not, the *doumatuatua* may take on an aggressive, hectoring style. This can continue for an hour or more and become "something of a morality play" in which "proverbs and clichés celebrating social values are recited to enlighten the victim and to edify the onlooking audience" (Just 1991, 134). Judgements may call for restitution or a fine. Just (1986, 54) argues that such proceedings are concerned less with determining guilt or innocence than fulfilling the "social priorities" of the Dou Donggo, especially deference and respect by juniors for seniors. In other words, false evidence may be accepted (and exonerating evidence ignored) to ensure "the recreation and reaffirmation of proper relationships" and status relations (Just 1991, 116). This "sociological truth" (Just 1986, 58), rather than the actual forensic truth, may be accepted because what actually happened is already known in the tight-knit community of around 3,000 and because the re-creation and reaffirmation of proper relationships is the priority.

FIGURE 1.1 Dou Donggo elders engaged in dispute-resolution. (Photo courtesy of Peter Just)

32 "Traditional" conflict management mechanisms

3. Hawaii

Anthropologist Karen Ito (1985, 213), in her discussion of *Ho'oponopono* in Hawaii, notes that Hawaiians conceptualise social relationships as interconnected pathways which are conduits for gestures of hospitality, kindness and respect (*aloha*). Negative actions – such as self-gratification, exploitation or neglect of others – make these pathways "jam-up" so that the emotional exchanges that flow down the pathways "bunch up", or "all jam up", causing "entanglements" (*hihia*) in the protective netting of positive inter-personal relationships. Left unresolved, such entanglements leave members of the group vulnerable to trouble (*pilikia*), including illness, injury, misfortune or death. In order to "unravel", "loosen" (*kala*) and "cut" (*'oki*) the negative entanglements a *Ho'oponopono* is "made". Although led by a senior member of the family, a *Ho'oponopono* can be called by any member of the family and all household members, including children, must attend. Having begun with prayers (*pule wehe*) for a "proper spiritual environment" (Ito 1985, 208), a discussion phase (*mahiki*) begins. Ito (1985, 208) notes that *mahiki* means "to pry; peel off, as a scab", implying a metaphor of needing to drain a festering wound. This is achieved by the leader constantly questioning and restating what each person says to clarify interpretations and emotional responses. As Ito (1985, 209) states: "The point of the leader's questioning is to make everything, even the implicit and covert, explicit and understandable for both the speaker and the other family members." Having discovered through discussion how the transgression (*hala*) became an entanglement, the family moves on to apology and forgiveness (*mihi*). *Ho'oponopono* finishes with a closing prayer and a shared meal.

4. Semai Sanoi (Malaysia)

Anthropologist Clayton Robarchek (1979) describes the *bcaraa'*, a process of conflict management employed by the Semai Sanoi, subsistence farmers who live in villages of fewer than a hundred people in the valleys that dissect the mountainous spine of the central Malay peninsula. Given that the integrity of the group is the source of individual security, the Semai "avoid open confrontation and conflict whenever possible" (Robarchek 1979, 106). When disputes (*hal,* meaning a "negative affair") can no longer be tolerated, the wronged party informs the elders who request the headman to convene a *bcaraa'*. This can be applied to cases of slander, disputes over territory and in cases of adultery and divorce. The *bcaraa'* involves calling together the disputants, their male kin and "any interested spectators" at dusk at the headman's house for "a debate and discussion of the entire affair" (Robarchek 1979, 106–108). Those in dispute do not directly confront one another. Rather, each participant will dispassionately "state his [or her] own conception of the affair and of the actions of the other party" (Robarchek 1979, 109). This will then be augmented by arguments from each participant's kin, who may question him or her to bring out particular points. This can continue for a few hours or non-stop for several days and nights. When all possible permutations of the events have been considered, the headman (who does not

"Traditional" conflict management mechanisms **33**

participate in the discussions) "gives voice to the group's consensus" (Robarchek 1979, 110) and may fine one (or both) of the disputants. The disputants are then instructed not to repeat or raise the dispute again. This is followed by speeches emphasising the need to maintain the unity and interdependence of the group before the matter is "deemed closed forever" (Robarchek 1979, 111).

5. Meto (Indonesia)

Anthropologist Andrew McWilliam (2007) provides an account of conflict management practices among the Meto, the main ethnic group in West Timor. The term *lasi* indicates separation or antagonism and requires "ritualised meetings accompanied by formal speech and commensality [eating and drinking together]" (McWilliam 2007, 76). The formal speech used at such meetings (*natoni*) is "metaphoric and poetic" and its meaning typically "veiled and allusory" (McWilliam 2007, 76). Metaphors of heating (*maputu*) and cooling (*manikin*) are also important, given that a balance of heating and cooling are considered to be optimal for the "proper order" (*atolan*). As a consequence, transgressive behaviour (including conflict) involves "excessive and dangerous uncontrolled heat (*maputu*) which require ritualised containment and 'cooling' (*haniki*) to render them benign" (McWilliam 2007, 77). McWilliam (2007, 85–86) describes conflicts when prospective marrying couples elope together, often to the house of the man's maternal uncle. This is described as an "abduction" (*mnaenat*). In such cases the women's family are spoken of as having "hot hearts and angry heads" (*nekan maputu, nakan natoh*). Under such circumstances, local mediators (*nete lanan* – "bridge path") may be appointed to seek to lessen tensions and to conduct a ceremony known as "shutting the two and three gates (*ek eno nuam tenu*)", involving ritual exchange, shared eating and drinking and appropriate "formal" speech with which speakers allude to the need to "honour the aggrieved party and wipe away their shame" (*ta fuf sin, ma kaus mae*). The reference to the gates relates to the idea of the man entering the house yard and stealing the girl and to the implied sexual violation of the woman's body.

6. Ibibio (Nigeria)

Sociologist Daniel Offiong (1997) provides an account of *esop isöñ* ("elders council" or "village council") among the Ibibio of south-eastern Nigeria. The task of the elders council is to restore solidarity and "eliminate disharmony" (Offiong 1997, 425). Central to this process is a belief that *ikan* (departed elders, who are all male) will bring misfortune, such as no male children, poor crops and constant illness, if there is a departure from "socially approved norms" (Offiong 1997, 425). Living elders act as intermediaries between the living and the ancestors, thus "when elders preside over cases, they do so with the full weight of the supernatural powers of the ancestors behind them" (Offiong 1997, 426). Cases before the *esop isöñ* include conflicts between husband and wife that involve a threat to life, accusations of

34 "Traditional" conflict management mechanisms

witchcraft and land disputes. Once a case is reported to the village head the chair of the *esop isöñ* sets a day for the hearing. When the supporters of the litigants are present, the chair, with the assistance of the elders, appoints one of their number to be the presiding elder for the case. A libation of palm wine (poured out as an offering to the ancestors) is made, followed by a prayer which "enables all to focus attention on the need for maintaining harmony" (Offiong 1997, 434). First, the person who brought the case is asked to present his/her case and is then "aggressively and thoroughly questioned" by the defendant, the elders and then members of the audience (Offiong 1997, 434). Witnesses are also called and their testimonies scrutinised through questioning in a "lively and heated, but orderly" procedure (Offiong 1997, 434). When all answers and questions have been exhausted, the elders deliberate on the evidence, issue a verdict (arrived at by consensus) and state the fine (usually meat and beer). The person who brought the case and the defendant are then required to swear an oath (*mbian uwöñ*) that they will not attempt to hurt their opponent or their loved ones (Offiong 1997, 435). This will ensure what the elders call *ate emen* ("real peace").

7. Tolai (Papua New Guinea)

Anthropologist Arnold Epstein (1971) describes *varkurai* on the island of Matupit in Papua New Guinea. When someone wishes to raise a complaint, he or she informs the councillor who represents the village on the Native Local Government Council who will summon the village to assemble by blowing a conch shell (Epstein 1971, 167). The process is overseen by *tena varkurai*, consisting of the councillor and two or three men of prominence who are not immediately party to the dispute under consideration (Epstein 1969, 185). The *tena varkurai* consider cases concerned with land, marriage, theft, debt and breach of kinship obligations, although, as Epstein (1971, 166) notes, given the small size of the community, a specific complaint leads to the airing of a "series of grievances and counter-grievances" indicating a more general deterioration in relationships. Before the "committee" and the assembled village, the person who brought the case describes his or her grievance, those involved can retort and observers can make statements (Epstein 1971, 165). The aim of the *varkurai*, therefore, is "the full airing of grievances" (Epstein 1971, 169). During such exchanges the councillor and members of the "committee" only intervene if the argument shows signs of straying too far afield (Epstein 1969, 185). Avoiding "any appearance of seeking to dominate or monopolize proceedings" (Epstein 1971, 165), the primary role of the "committee" is to "allow the disputants to make their arguments before the assembly and then, by discreet intervention at appropriate moments, to try and persuade or prevail upon one or other of the parties to yield gracefully" (Epstein 1969, 185). This is done by appealing to "moral values to which all in the audience could be expected to subscribe and respond" (Epstein 1971, 168). If agreement is reached, "reconciliation will probably be marked with a meal" (Epstein 1969, 186).

Comparison of the case studies

Following Fry (2000, 334), we must recognise each of these seven cases as distinct and "highly specific to the particular cultural system within which they operate". On the other hand, it is legitimate to search for "recurring cultural patterns [and] underlying principles" (Fry & Bjorkqvist 1996, 5) as long as we remain aware of the dangers of essentialism and denying change and that we do not sacrifice an appreciation of difference by only seeking what is the same.

i. Restoring the "harmony" of the group

Fry (2000, 348) notes that the emphasis on "restoring relationships and promoting group harmony is noteworthy for its pervasiveness from one cultural setting to the next". This is evident in the cases discussed above. In the Kpelle "moot", the "blessing focuses attention on the concern with maintaining harmony and the well-being of the group as a whole" (Gibbs 1963, 4). Likewise in the context of the Ibibio, the fines are always minimal (beer and meat), because the main aim "is to make peace and re-establish harmony between the conflicting parties" (Offiong 1997, 438). Whether or not "harmony ideology" (Nader 1991, 53; see Introduction) was introduced by colonial authorities in the contexts described above, the twin aspects of "harmony ideology" are apparent. On the one hand, conflict management mechanisms that employ "harmony ideology" are a "technique of control to keep the state out" (Nader 1997, 713). As discussed above, in Indonesia people chose *paresa dou* ("to investigate an individual") over going to the police because involving "outsiders is to relinquish a share of control over the outcome of a dispute" (Just 1991, 109). Likewise in Nigeria, cases are brought before the *esop isöñ* ("elders council") rather than the formal courts because of the corruption of police officers (Offiong 1997, 430).

But the other aspect of "harmony ideology" is also present, a "coercive harmony" used to repress conflict by sacrificing the needs of the individual to those of the group (Nader 1997, 715). This is most apparent in the case of the Dou Donggo. As noted above, conflict management among the Dou Donggo is not principally concerned with punishment, deterrence or individual rights, but with restoring the proper social relations and status between individuals. As a consequence, the "acceptability of a solution may take precedence over assessing actual responsibility" (Just 1991, 116). The result of this is that in some cases "readily available conclusive evidence is not sought or is ignored while in other cases evidence widely known and (privately) admitted to be false is accepted without dispute" (Just 1986, 44). Among the Dou Donggo, elders construct a representation of the "truth" that may not necessarily correspond to what actually happened but which will be an "accurate portrayal of the relevant social relationships, communal interests and moral principles" (Just 1986, 48). In other words, the objective of "harmony", achieved through "the restoration of damaged status relationships" (Just 1991, 117), is prioritised over the "truth". Put another way, "harmony ideology" is employed to subordinate the needs of the, potentially innocent, individual over the needs of the community.

36 "Traditional" conflict management mechanisms

Bearing in mind Avruch's (2000, 341) and Zechenter's (1997, 334) warnings about those who would claim homogeneous agreement regarding norms of behaviour by members of a group, it is important to acknowledge that conflict management mechanisms arise at moments of transgression and lend themselves, therefore, to reasserting the fiction of group consensus. The *bcaraa'*, for example, is an opportunity to reaffirm an idealised image of the community by restating and reaffirming the paramount values of "interdependence, generosity, and mutual aid" (Robarchek 1979, 113). The *bcaraa'* begins and ends with speeches by senior relatives of the disputants that "stress the interdependence of the group and the necessity of maintaining mutual assistance and harmony within it" (Robarchek 1979, 108). A principal purpose of *bcaraa'* is, therefore, "the restatement and reaffirmation of the paramount values of the group" (Robarchek 1979, 122). Likewise, in the context of Papua New Guinea, Epstein (1971, 185) notes that the aim of *varkurai* is "to restore harmony where social relations have become embittered". This is achieved by common agreement and mutual consent rather than personal authority, because an appeal is made to "certain norms and values recognised and accepted throughout the community" (Epstein 1971, 169). As a consequence, settlement can only be reached when "the parties are persuaded that their behaviour was not in conformity with the norms to which they themselves subscribe" (Epstein 1971, 169). Just (1991, 45 59) also demonstrates that a *paresa* is not only concerned with specific conflicts but is an occasion "for the rediscovering, representing, and acting out of those principles that constitute a society's moral foundations" and to "affirm the social solidarity of the community". This conforms with my discussion in the Introduction to this book of Lewis A. Coser (1956, 128) and his view that the management of a conflict is a means by which a group's values are reaffirmed and dormant norms made explicit. While conflicts may, as a consequence, be resolved, the question remains as to who benefits from such a reaffirmation and who may be disadvantaged (Zechenter 1997, 334).

ii. Reintegrating the "wrongdoer"

I have just suggested that conflict management mechanisms can subordinate the interests of the individual to "the restatement and reaffirmation of the paramount values of the group" (Robarchek 1979, 122). On the other hand, all seven case studies indicate the importance of reintegrating the individual "wrongdoer" into the group. I have placed "wrongdoer" in inverted commas as in a number of the case studies the responsibility of the person considered the initiator of the conflict is downplayed and relativised. In the case of the *Ho'oponopono*, for example, the wronged party must also ask forgiveness from the "wrongdoer" for their negative retaliation in order "to release (*kala*) and cut ('*oki*) the entangling negative bonds" (Ito 1985, 206). No individual, therefore, emerges as righteous from *Ho'oponopono*. Rather, the double-forgiveness re-establishes the relationship on an equal footing. Likewise, in giving his "judgement" in the *bcaraa'*, the headman may lecture both parties concerning their guilt in the matter and he may fine both disputants (Robarchek 1979, 110).

The same features are seen in the case of the Kpelle moot, in which the mediator and other participants point out not only the faults of the "wrongdoer" but also the aggrieved party. There is, therefore, "no unilateral ascription of blame, but an attribution of fault to both parties" (Gibbs 1963, 5; see Nader 1969, 76–78). This relativisation of blame is further emphasised by the fact that in the Kpelle moot the "wrongdoer" is required to apologise and provide token gifts to the aggrieved party, but it is also customary for the wronged party to give, in return, a small token to show his or her good will (Gibbs 1963, 4). As a consequence, the "wrongdoer" is "not singled out and isolated as being labelled deviant" (Gibbs 1963, 8). This relativisation is also seen in the *bcaraa'* in the "seemingly paradoxical practice" of imposing a fine on the "wrongdoer" and "then returning all or part of it to him" (Robarchek 1979, 113).

Regarding the *esop isön* of the Ibibio, Offiong (1997, 434) notes that the elders "do not want to isolate the guilty party because this could turn him or her into a danger for the community". As with the Kpelle moot, the penalty imposed (some beer and meat) is not extravagant and so avoids generating bitterness and resentment. Furthermore, the need for the "guilty" party to provide a shared feast at the end of the case is not a penalty but allows the "guilty" party to act as a host, thereby transforming him or her from a dishonourable to an honourable status (Offiong 1997, 437). As a consequence, the "guilty" party "is pulled back into a relationship with the wider community" (Offiong 1997, 438). In the cases of the *Ho'oponopono, bcaraa'*, Kpelle moot and the *esop isön*, rather than being ostracised, the "wrongdoers'" responsibility is relativised to facilitate instant rehabilitation.

iii. Sharing food and drink

As indicated above, the restoration of the solidarity of the group and the rehabilitation of the "wrongdoer" is often symbolised by the parties and spectators sharing a drink together, as among the Kpelle, the *Ho'oponopono* in Hawaii, the Meto and the Tolai. In the Kpelle moot, for example, following a prayer for restoration of harmony in the group all present drink together "to symbolize the restored solidarity of the group and the rehabilitation of the offending party" (Gibbs 1963, 5). Related to the reintegration of the individual "wrongdoer" into the group, all in attendance at the Kpelle moot consume the rum or beer paid for by the "wrongdoer" as a "fine" (Gibbs 1963, 4), while the meat and beer paid for by the losing party at the *esop isön* in Nigeria is shared with the other party and all those who have been present (Offiong 1997, 437).

The case studies considered above indicate that a common feature of conflict management mechanisms is commensality (eating and drinking together), be it "drinking coffee together in a Lebanese village or a massive village feast financed by the loser as a public apology, as in pre-revolutionary China" (Merry 1982, 30; see Finnström 2010, 153; Koch et al. 1977, 272–273). This resonates with the discussion in the Introduction of this book regarding the importance of sharing food and drink in the reconstruction of relationships in Bosnia-Herzegovina (see Jansen 2013, 234; Strupinskienė 2016, 13). When Bert Ingelaere (2016, 148) asked

38 "Traditional" conflict management mechanisms

Rwandans how they defined "living with" one another (*kubana*), they described "the sharing of food and drinks, ceremonies of conviviality". Likewise, in the case of East Timor, Lia Kent (2016, 47) describes how, following the repair of the *uma lulik* (sacred house), pigs, chickens and goats were slaughtered and the family shared a meal together, an important form of communication that "the family was united again and that it would no longer be divided". Eating and drinking together are, therefore, "relational and embodied forms of communication" (Kent 2016, 42). Stephanie Hobbis Ketterer (2014, 11), in her study of a grassroots Japanese–Korean reconciliation project and the part played by food in the activities of the organisation, draws on the work of David Sutton (2001) to argue that, because we consume food on a daily basis and regularly with others, the seemingly mundane act of eating serves the purpose of reproducing our social relations. As a consequence, the "food events" that conclude the conflict management mechanisms described above allow for "a new inclusivity based on largely non-verbal interactions, and by so doing, can alter perceptions of the other in a more comprehensive manner than verbal-only exchanges ever could" (Ketterer 2014, 11).

iv. The active participation of the community

With the exception of *Ho'oponopono* in Hawaii, all of the case studies involve the wider community, who are not only present as spectators but as active participants. The Kpelle moot takes place before an assembled group which includes kin of the litigants and neighbours who "sit in a mixed fashion, pressed closely upon each other, often overflowing on to a veranda" (Gibbs 1963, 3–4). All of those present must participate in the blessing chanted by one of the oldest men at the start of the moot. As the elder chants a series of imperatives, the spectators must respond in unison *e ka ti* ("so be it") (Gibbs 1963, 4). The effect of this is "to unite those attending in common action before the hearing begins" (Gibbs 1963, 4; see Offiong 1997, 433).

The same active participation of those present is seen in the *bcaraa'*, which involves calling together not only those in dispute and their male kin but also "any interested spectators" for "a debate and discussion of the entire affair" (Robarchek 1979, 106–108). Describing the *bcaraa'*, Robarchek (1979, 108) notes that "Women, children, and other spectators, including kinsmen not taking direct part in the *bcaraa'* sit around … talking, sleeping, or listening to the discussions." Kinsmen who do take part argue their case for their kinsman and can question him to bring out particular points (Robarchek 1979, 109). The same inclusiveness is reported by Offiong (1997, 425), who notes that nobody (man or woman) is excluded from the *esop isöñ* and that everybody present can ask questions of those in dispute or provide information pertinent to the conflict.

In the case of the Dou Donggo, Just (1991, 133) also notes that "from the very outset a *paresa* is a public event, attended not only by kinsmen of both accuser and accused as well as witnesses and neighbours". Among the Dou Donggo the "ulti-mate audience is a general communal one", the *doumatuatua* (the *ad hoc* panel of village elders) being "in a dialogue with the community at large, both shaping and reflecting public opinion" (Just 1991, 138). The proceedings, therefore, are "directed as much to the observing community as at the litigants" (Just 1986, 58). Just (1986, 47 57) emphasises that *paresa* is a performance, "a noisy, theatrical, emotional, even violent affair" in which "evidence" (possibly fabricated) was displayed to the audience so that they were "provided with a ready counter to any future protestations of innocence" (Just 1986, 57). Also drawing on the theatrical metaphor, Epstein (1971, 167) states that although the assembled villagers:

> appear at first glance simply as an attentive audience immersed in the play unfolding before them, they are themselves actors in the piece, and by their reactions offer from time to time a judgement on the behaviour of the parties. Seizing on such signals, Councillor and "committee" intervene at appropriate moments to try and persuade one or other parties to yield gracefully and so open the way to a settlement.

In all of the cases considered above (with the exception of *Ho'oponopono* in Hawaii) the wider community are active participants in the conflict management mechanism. While this appears egalitarian, it is also necessary if such mechanisms are to act as opportunities for instructing members of the group on the group's norms and values and the associated questions of who benefits from such a reaffirmation and who may be disadvantaged (Zechenter 1997, 334).

v. The airing of comprehensive information

In all seven cases the emphasis is placed on airing information in as comprehensive a way as possible. In the case of *Ho'oponopono* in Hawaii, Ito (1985, 209) describes how the person conducting the process constantly questions and restates what each person says in order to clarify interpretations with the purpose of making "everything, even the implicit and covert, explicit and understandable for both the speaker and the other family members". The same feature is evident in the Kpelle moot, in which both parties are "thoroughly quizzed" not only by the mediator and one another but by anyone present (Gibbs 1963, 4). As a consequence, "hardly anything mentioned is held to be irrelevant", leading to "a more thorough ventilation of the issues" so that in "a familiar setting, with familiar people, the parties to the moot feel at ease and free to say all that is on their minds" (Gibbs 1963, 5–7). The same freedom is seen in the example from Papua New Guinea, where the role of the *tena varkurai* is to create conditions in which "parties may wrangle with one another" (Epstein 1971, 167). Reflecting on this, Epstein (1971, 167) suggests that the "underlying assumption appears to be that only when grievances have been properly aired on all sides can the path be opened up to reconciliation". Such an underlying assumption is in contrast to truth commissions (see Chapter 4) which, although claiming to be an opportunity for individuals to "ventilate" their truth (see Verdoolaege 2006, 67), actually restrict testimony as commissioners constantly

40 "Traditional" conflict management mechanisms

interrupt those giving testimony and prevent them from talking about unanticipated topics (Verdoolaege 2002, 11). Likewise, in international criminal courts (see Chapter 5) it is the lawyer's questions that "organise the story, deciding which parts can be told, and in what order" (Eades 2008, 210). In both contexts the emphasis is placed on generating a restricted "close-edited diagram" (Geertz 1983, 173) of the real world rather than as comprehensive an account as possible.

This comprehensive search for information is taken to extremes in the case of *bcaraa'*, which cannot end "while anyone still has anything to say about the issue" (Robarchek 1979, 110). Robarchek (1979, 110) describes how:

> All the events leading up to and surrounding the dispute are examined and re-examined from every conceivable perspective over and over again, ad nauseam. Every possible explanation is offered, every imaginable motive laid bare, every mitigating circumstance examined ... finally a point is reached where there is simply nothing more to say ... a *bcaraa'* does not end when all the arguments have been logically rebutted; it ends when no one had anything more to say.

Robarchek (1979, 113) suggests that the objective is to remove "much of the motivation for individual, idiosyncratic action by dissipating the emotional content of disputes". In other words, the *bcaraa'* provides a procedure that "drains the emotion out of conflict situations" (Robarchek 1979, 112). By incessantly retelling the events from every conceivable angle "the issues no longer have the capacity to elicit any emotional reaction from anyone", so that "the conflict has been 'talked to death'" (Robarchek 1979, 112). In Nigeria, Offiong (1997, 438) also found that in order for the solution to a dispute to be lasting "it is essential that nothing be held in or left unsaid that will embitter either party and undermine the decision", while Gibbs (1963, 7) notes that in the Kpelle moot nothing should be left unsaid that could "embitter and undermine the decision". As Marilyn Strathern (1974, 271–272) observes in the context of conflict management in Papua New Guinea, "an issue should be so thoroughly aired that not even the most minor factor relating to it remain to foster further grievances in the hearts of the disputants".

Conclusion

The management of conflict through "traditional" means has been a long-standing concern of anthropologists. It is a concern, however, that brings with it a number of dangers. These include essentialising the "cultures" with which such mechanisms are associated in ways that misrepresent a "culture" as "free of dissensions, of internal contradictions or paradoxes" (Avruch 2000, 341). Likewise, describing such mechanisms as "traditional" may lend them an aura of prestige when, in reality, they are a "product of the colonial encounter" (Falk Moore 1989, 289) and continue to change over time. Taken together, these two dangers may allow conflict management mechanisms to be used to enforce a "coercive harmony"

(Nader 1997, 715) that subordinates the interests of certain members of a community (as I will discuss in Chapter 2 in relation to *mato oput* in Uganda).

Alongside the need to be cautious about how we assess accounts of conflict management mechanisms is the question of comparison. On the one hand, the seven cases I considered are "intimately related to other aspects of personality, society and culture" (Robarchek 1979, 104). This does not mean, however, that they should only be considered in isolation. To do so would be to misunderstand ethnography. All of the authors summarised above employ comparison with other ethnographic accounts, not only to demarcate their focus but also to assist in the analysis of what they observed during fieldwork. From this perspective, comparison is integral to ethnographic accounts in the first place. Having said that, the five common features I identified from the case studies are inevitably provisional, as different readers of the same ethnographies or different ethnographies would generate alternative common features. Provisionally "identifying recurring cultural patterns and isolating underlying principles is essential", however, as this allows us to "expand the number of options to consider in approaching conflict" (Fry & Bjorkqvist 1996, 5).

Bibliography

Al-Krenawi, Alean, and John R. Graham. 1999. "Conflict Resolution through a Traditional Ritual among the Bedouin Arabs of the Negev", *Ethnology* 38 (2): 163–174.

Avruch, Kevin. 1998. *Culture and Conflict Resolution*. Washington, DC: United States Institute of Peace Press.

Avruch, Kevin. 2000. "Culture and negotiation pedagogy", *Negotiation Journal* 16 (4): 339–346.

Avruch, Kevin. 2007. "A Historical Overview of Anthropology and Conflict Resolution", *Anthropology News*: 4813–4814.

Avruch, Kevin and Peter W. Black. 1991. "The Culture Question and Conflict Resolution", *Peace & Change* 16 (1): 22–45.

Avruch, Kevin and Peter W. Black. 1993. "Conflict resolution in intercultural settings – problems and prospects". In *Conflict Resolution Theory and Practice: Integration and Application*, edited by Dennis J. D. Sandole and Hugo Van Der Merwe, 131–145. Manchester, UK: Manchester University Press.

Bohannan, Paul. 1969. "Ethnography and Comparison in Legal Anthropology". In *Law in Culture and Society*, edited by Laura Nader, 401–418. Chicago, IL: Aldine.

Chanock, Martin. 1987. *Law, Custom and Social Order: The Colonial Experience in Malawi and Zambia*. Cambridge, UK: Cambridge University Press.

Clifford, James. 1988. *The Predicament of Culture: Twentieth Century Ethnography, Literature and Art*. Cambridge, MA: Harvard University Press.

Colson, Elizabeth. 1995. "The Contentiousness of Disputes". In *Understanding Disputes: The Politics of Argument*, edited by Pat Caplan, 65–82. Oxford: Berg Publishers.

Comaroff, John L. and Simon Roberts. 1977. "The Invocation of Norms in Dispute Settlement: The Tswana Case". In *Social Anthropology and Law*, edited by Ian Hamnett, 77–112. London: Academic.

Comaroff, John L. and Simon Roberts. 1981. *Rules and Processes: The Cultural Logic of Dispute in an African Context*. Chicago, IL: University of Chicago Press.

Coser, Lewis A. 1956. *The Functions of Social Conflict*. London: Routledge and Kegan Paul.

42 "Traditional" conflict management mechanisms

Cowan, Jane K., Marie-Benedicte Dembour and Richard A. Wilson (eds.). 2001. "Introduction". In *Culture and Rights: Anthropological Perspectives*, 1–26. Cambridge, UK: Cambridge University Press.

Eades, Diana. 2008. "Telling and Retelling Your Story in Court: Questions, Assumptions and Intercultural Implications", *Current Issues in Criminal Justice* 20 (2): 209–230.

Epstein, Arnold L. 1969. *Matupit: Land, Politics, and Change Among the Tolai of New Britain.* Canberra: Australian National University Press.

Epstein, Arnold L. 1971. "Dispute Settlement among the Tolai", *Oceania* 41 (3): 157–170.

Falk Moore, Sally. 1977. "Individual Interests and Organisational Structures: Dispute Settlements as 'Events of Articulation'". In *Social Anthropology and the Law*, edited by Ian Hammett, 159–188. London: Academic Press.

Falk Moore, Sally. 1989. "History and the Redefinition of Custom in Kilimanjaro". In *History and Power in the Study of Law: New Directions in Legal Anthropology*, edited by J. Starr and J.F. Collier, 277–301. Ithaca, NY: Cornell University Press.

Falk Moore, Sally. 2000. *Law as Process: An Anthropological Approach* (2nd edition). Oxford: James Currey.

Finlay, Andrew. 2006. "Anthropology Misapplied? The Culture Concept and the Peace Process in Ireland", *Anthropology in Action* 13 (1–2): 1–10.

Finnström, Sverker. 2010. "Reconciliation Grown Bitter?: War, Retribution, and Ritual Action in Northern Uganda". In *Localizing Transitional Justice: Interventions and Priorities after Mass Violence*, edited by Rosalind Shaw, Lars Waldorf and Pierre Hazan, 135–156. Stanford, CA: Stanford University Press.

Fry, Douglas P. 2000. "Conflict Management in Cross-Cultural Perspective". In *Natural Conflict Resolution*, edited by Filippo Aureli and Frans de Waal, 334–351. Berkeley, CA: University of California Press.

Fry, Douglas P. and Kaj Bjorkqvist (eds.). 1996. "Introduction: Conflict Resolution Themes". In *Cultural Variation in Conflict Resolution: Alternatives to Violence* 3–8. London: Routledge.

Geertz, Clifford (ed.). 1983. "Local Knowledge: Fact and Law in Comparative Perspective". In *Local Knowledge*, 167–234. New York: Basic Books.

Gibbs, James L.Jr. 1963. "The Kpelle Moot: A Therapeutic Model for the Informal Settlement of Disputes", *Africa: Journal of the International African Institute* 33 (1): 1–11.

Gluckman, Max. 1963. *Custom and Conflict in Africa*. Oxford: Basil Blackwell.

Gluckman, Max. 1969. "Concepts in the Comparative Study of Tribal Law". In *Law in Culture and Society*, edited by Laura Nader, 349–373. Chicago, IL: Aldine.

Gulliver, Philip H. 1979. *Disputes and Negotiations: A Cross-Cultural Perspective*. New York: Academic Press.

Hoebel, E. Adamson. 1954. *The Law of Primitive Man: A Study in Comparative Legal Dynamics.* Cambridge, MA: Harvard University Press.

Ingelaere, Bert. 2016. *Inside Rwanda's Gacaca Courts: Seeking Justice after Genocide*. Madison, WI: University of Wisconsin Press.

Ito, Karen L. 1985. "Ho'oponopono, 'to make right': Hawaiian conflict resolution and metaphor in the construction of a family therapy", *Culture, Medicine and Psychiatry* 9 (2): 201–217.

Jansen, Stef. 2013. "If reconciliation is the answer, are we asking the right questions", *Studies in Social Justice* 7 (2): 229–243.

Just, Peter. 1986. "Let the Evidence Fit the Crime: Evidence, Law, and 'Sociological Truth' among the Dou Donggo", *American Ethnologist* 13 (1): 43–61.

Just, Peter. 1991. "Conflict Resolution and Moral Community among the Dou Donggo". In *Conflict resolution: Cross-cultural perspectives*, edited by Kevin Avruch, Peter W. Black and Joseph A. Scimecca 107–143. New York: Greenwood Press.

Kent, Lia. 2016. "Sounds of Silence: Everyday Strategies of Social Repair in Timor-Leste", *Australian Feminist Journal* 42 (1): 31–50.

Ketterer, Stephanie Hobbis. 2014. "'Love Goes through the Stomach': A Japanese–Korean Recipe for Post-conflict Reconciliation", *Anthropology in Action* 21 (2): 2–13.

Koch, Klaus-Friedrich, Soraya Altorki, Andrew Arno and Letitia Hickson. 1977. "Ritual Reconciliation and the Obviation of Grievances: A Comparative Study in the Ethnography of Law", *Ethnology* 16 (3): 269–283.

Mader, Laura. 1997. "Controlling Processes: Tracing the Dynamic Components of Power", *Current Anthropology* 38 (5): 711–737.

Malinowski, Bronislaw. 1926. *Crime and Custom in Savage Society*. London: Kegan Paul.

McWilliam, Andrew. 2007. "Meto Disputes and Peacemaking: Cultural Notes on Conflict and its Resolution in West Timor", *The Asia Pacific Journal of Anthropology* 8 (1): 75–91.

Merry, Sally Engle. 1982. "The Social Organization of Mediation in Nonindustrial Societies: Implications for Informal Community Justice in America". In *The Politics of Informal Justice*, edited by Richard L. Abel, 17–45. Cambridge, MA: Academic Press.

Merry, Sally Engle. 1988. "Legal Pluralism", *Law and Society Review* 22 (5): 869–896.

Merry, Sally Engle. 2001. "Law: Anthropological Aspects". In *International Encyclopedia of the Social and Behavioral Sciences*, edited by Neil J. Smelser and Paul B. Baltes, 8489–8492. New York: Elsevier.

Merry, Sally Engle. 2003. "Human Rights Law and the Demonization of Culture (And Anthropology Along the Way)", *PoLAR: Political and Legal Anthropology Review* 26 (1): 55–76.

Nader, Laura (ed.). 1969. "Styles of Court Procedure: To Make the Balance". In *Law in Culture and Society*, 69–91. Chicago, IL: Aldine.

Nader, Laura. 1991. "Harmony Models and the Construction of Law". In *Conflict Resolution: Cross-Cultural Perspectives*, edited by Kevin Avruch, Peter W. Black and Joseph A. Scimecca, 41–59. New York: Greenwood Press.

Nader, Laura. 1997. "Controlling Processes: Tracing the Dynamic Components of Power", *Current Anthropology* 38 (5): 711–737.

Nader, Laura and Harry F. Todd (eds.). 1978. *The Disputing Process: Law in Ten Societies*. New York: Columbia University Press.

Offiong, Daniel A. 1997. "Conflict Resolution among the Ibibio of Nigeria", *Journal of Anthropological Research* 53 (4): 423–441.

Robarchek, Clayton A. 1979. "Conflict, emotion and abreaction: Resolution of conflict among the Semai Senoi", *Ethos* 7 (2): 104–123.

Rose, Laurel L. 1992. *The Politics of Harmony: Land Dispute Strategies in Swaziland*. Cambridge, UK: Cambridge University Press.

Scott, James C. 1998. *Seeing like a State: How Certain Schemes to Improve the Human Condition Have Failed*. New Haven, CT: Yale University Press.

Shaw, Rosalind. 2007. "Memory Frictions: Localizing the Truth and Reconciliation Commission in Sierra Leone", *The International Journal of Transitional Justice* 1 (2): 183–207.

Snyder, Francis G. 1981. "Colonialism and Legal Form: The Creation of 'Customary Law' in Senegal", *The Journal of Legal Pluralism and Unofficial Law*, 19 49–90.

Strathern, Marilyn. 1974. "Managing Information: The Problems of a Dispute Settler (Mount Hagen)". In *Contention and Dispute*, edited by A.L. Epstein, 271–316. Canberra: Australian National University Press.

Strupinskienė, Lina. 2016. "What is reconciliation and are we there yet? Different types and levels of reconciliation: A case study of Bosnia and Herzegovina", *Journal of Human Rights* 16 (4): 1–21.

Summerfield, Derek. 1999. "A critique of seven assumptions behind psychological trauma programmes in war-affected areas", *Social Science & Medicine* 48 (10): 1449–1462.

Sutton, David E. 2001. *Remembrance of Repasts: An Anthropology of Food and Memory*. Oxford: Berg Publishers.

United Nations. 2004. *The Rule of Law and Transitional Justice in Conflict and Post-Conflict Societies*. New York: United Nations.

Verdoolaege, Annelies. 2002. The Human Rights Violations Hearings of the South African TRC: A Bridge Between Individual Narratives of Suffering and a Contextualizing Master-Story of Reconciliation. Department of African Languages and Cultures, Ghent University, Belgium.

Verdoolaege, Annelies. 2006. "Managing reconciliation at the human rights violations hearings of the South African TRC", *The Journal of Human Rights* 5 (1): 61–80.

Waldorf, Lars. 2006. "Mass Justice for Mass Atrocity: Rethinking Local Justice as Transitional Justice", *Temple Law Review* 79 (1): 1–88.

Wilson, Richard A. 2000. "Reconciliation and Revenge in Post-Apartheid South Africa: Rethinking Legal Pluralism and Human Rights", *Current Anthropology* 41 (1): 75–98.

Zechenter, Elizabeth M. 1997. "In the Name of Culture: Cultural Relativism and the Abuse of the Individual", *Journal of Anthropological Research* 53 (3): 319–347.

2

RE-TRADITIONALISING CONFLICT MANAGEMENT

In recent years, "indigenous" or "traditional" conflict management practices have been promoted as more effective responses to the aftermath of violent conflict than "external" models such as truth commissions (see Chapter 4) and international criminal trials (see Chapter 5). Scholars have argued that the transition from violent conflict to "peace" needs to be "localised" by incorporating "traditions" that are designed and implemented by local communities (see Arriaza & Roht-Arriaza 2008; Lundy & McGovern 2006; McEvoy & McGregor 2008). Within this movement, "locally situated measures are lauded for their authenticity and presumed efficiency" (Horne 2014, 18; see Betts 2005). Such an approach has been popular with policymakers, as is evident in a report issued by the office of the United Nations Secretary General on the subject of post-conflict societies:

> we must learn better how to respect and support local ownership, local leadership and a local constituency for reform, while at the same time remaining faithful to United Nations norms and standards … due regard must be given to indigenous and informal traditions for administering justice or settling disputes, to help them continue their often vital role.
>
> *(United Nations 2004, paras 17 36)*

This statement displays a "fascination with locality" (Shaw & Waldorf 2010, 4), reflecting the belief that embedding post-conflict interventions in the "local" will "enhance their legitimacy and efficacy [by] providing an authentic and familiar environment through which popular participation might begin to flourish" (Allen & Macdonald 2013, 3). The "re-traditionalisation" movement has, however, come under criticism from anthropologists, criticism that I will consider in the first section of the chapter. While acknowledging that critique, the chapter will then consider whether there are degrees of "re-traditionalisation" and whether there are ways in

46 Re-traditionalising conflict management

which "local" responses can still be promoted whilst avoiding the pitfalls identified by anthropologists. Three sub-Saharan African contexts (Rwanda, Uganda and Mozambique) will be considered in detail to illustrate this debate.

The dangers of re-traditionalisation

In general, anthropologists have been cautious about the claims made for "local tradition" in response to violent conflict. Kimberly Theidon (2009, 9), for example, warns of "the facile embrace of the local community" as a solution. Part of the reason for anthropologists' cynicism can be explained by the discipline's long-standing study of how "indigenous" groups struggle for legal recognition and protection. These studies have demonstrated how "indigenous" groups have strategically (re)presented themselves (and their "traditions") in ways that correspond with "Western" fantasies of the "noble savage" (see Conklin 1997; Englund 2004; Hodgson 2011; Igoe 2006; Kuper 2003; Lynch 2011; Turner 1991). While some anthropologists have argued, on the one hand, that groups which gain benefits by strategically (re)presenting themselves in this manner should be applauded, others recognise that such groups have been forced to conform to a caricature of "authentic indigenous group" that is not of their own making. This suggests that once "locals" become aware of criteria of "authenticity" dictated by "external authorities" (the United Nations, non-governmental organisations, national government, etc.) they choose to represent themselves in terms that correspond to such stereotypes, although not all will succeed in gaining recognition (see Li 2000; Hodgson 2002, 1040). The form in which "locals" strategically represent their "authentic, local culture" in order to conform to external caricatures should be seen, therefore, as "artefacts or inventions", as "products of positioning and the articulation of local and global discourses and dynamics" (Sylvain 2014, 253). I would suggest that those who survive violent conflict may also find themselves being required to represent their "traditions" in a manner that conforms to caricatures promoted by "external authorities".

A further reason for caution among anthropologists regarding the promotion of "tradition" is that although the report by the United Nations (2004, 7) quoted above speaks with approval of "local ownership", UN human rights bodies have tended to talk of "local culture" as a "barrier to progress", implying "culture" belongs "to the domain of the primitive or backward, in contrast to the civilisation of the coloniser" (Merry 2003, 60). Regarding issues as diverse as child marriage in Kenya (Archambault 2011), child prostitution in Thailand (Montgomery 2001) and female genital circumcision (FGC) in East Africa (Koomen 2014), anthropologists have demonstrated how "culture" has been demonised and employed as an explanation for human rights violations that, in reality, have far more diverse explanations (child marriage and prostitution are responses to socio-economic insecurity, contemporary forms of FGC are a response to heavy handed attempts at eradication, etc.). While it could be argued that such selectivity is legitimate (some "local culture" is in line with human rights, other "local culture" is not), it also suggests that the criteria used by external authorities such as the UN to choose which "traditions" meet with their approval are not entirely transparent.

There is also a question of what the word "local" refers to (the reason why I have been putting it in inverted commas). The report by the United Nations (2004, 7) quoted above uses the word "local" as if its meaning is self-evident, such as "we must learn better how to respect and support local ownership, local leadership and a local constituency for reform". On one hand it has been argued that "local" is an improvement on the word "traditional" as it avoids the idea of unchanging "tradition" and, instead, recognises that socio-economic conditions change (Baines 2007, 96n20; see Chapter 1). Anthropologists, however, remain wary of the term "local" and the way it may be used to serve the interests of external authorities such as national governments and international aid agencies. For example, government officials, academics and NGO workers based in the Indonesian capital, Jakarta, celebrate the use for conflict resolution of *hibualamo* (the "big meeting house") on the island of Halmahera (eastern Indonesia) as a "local", "bottom-up approach". The anthropologist Christopher Duncan (2016, 469) notes, however, that most North Halmaherans see the promotion of *hibualamo* "as another example of a top-down initiative … designed and promoted by an elite circle of North Halmaherans and their supporters". Duncan (2016, 468) suggests this illustrates that while the word "local" implies "bottom-up" approaches coming from local communities (in contrast to "top-down" ones coming from the state and international or national NGOs), "what exactly constitutes the 'top' and the 'bottom' depends on your vantage point".

This is not to suggest that anthropologists dismiss the potential of "traditional" conflict management out of hand. Writing in the context of the Meto people in West Timor (see Chapter 1), anthropologist Andrew McWilliam (2007, 88–90) argues that there are "distinct advantages in utilising culturally accepted practices for mediating disputes", including shared understandings that convey shared sentiments and shared social and spiritual sanctions which make non-compliance or failure to find resolution less likely. McWilliam (2007, 89) notes, however, that such customary processes tend to be "strategic improvisations", rather than a set of fixed rules, and change depending on the given circumstances. As such, their efficacy would be undermined if they were formally codified by external authorities such as national governments.

McWilliam's observation that "traditional" conflict management processes tend to be "strategic improvisations" rather than a fixed set of rules relates to the discussion of "culture" in Chapter 1. To recap, "culture" is not a set of fixed rules but "a field of creative interchange and contestation … and continuous transformation" (Cowan et al. 2001, 5). While "tradition" may, of course, be "inspired by a group's past", it is "constantly being adapted to meet new social and political circumstances, and is capable of synthesising external elements" (Stovel 2008, 306). As a consequence, "traditional" conflict management processes do not follow a "stable body of rules but [are] rather a body of rules continually undergoing transformations in separate cases" (Rose 1992, 191). Anthropologists Tim Allen and Anna Macdonald (2013, 19) suggest a paradox if such processes are codified and promoted by "external authorities":

48 *Re*-traditionalising conflict management

> They will lose their flexibility and will no longer have the many resonances and associations of lived ritual actions. But crucially, they will have a status that is at least partly based on their externally supported authority. They will become privileged rites and most likely the preserve of certain figures of male authority recognised by the international community or by the government.

The concern voiced by Allen and Macdonald also suggests that what is presented as being "local" is, in reality, reliant on promotion by "external authorities". In his reflection on the way that the "local" has become a feature of the reports and websites of peacebuilding and conflict resolution organisations, Roger Mac Ginty (2015, 846) argues that while projects "may have a local face, and be enacted by local personnel in local communities, the real power may come from donors and administrators in New York, London, Geneva or elsewhere". The political scientist Cynthia Horne (2014) provides an illustration of this in relation to the Aceh region (Indonesia) and East Timor (occupied by Indonesia 1975–1999), both of which were involved in protracted separatist conflicts involving an armed independence movement fighting the government of Indonesia. Horne notes that both the post-conflict responses in Aceh (from 2005) and East Timor (from 1999) have been characterised by "internationals" as "bottom-up" initiatives that employ "local" reconciliation and conflict resolution processes, such as the use of *adat* ("customary law") in Aceh (see Braithwaite et al. 2010; DeShaw Rae 2009). Horne (2014, 21–24), however, challenges the portrayal of *adat* as "local tradition", given that it was intentionally revived by the Indonesian government in the 1990s (see Duncan 2009) and that both the design phase and the bulk of the implementation stage in Aceh and East Timor were strongly influenced by international actors. In East Timor, for example, Horne (2014, 27) describes how local groups were instructed by the Comissão de Acolhimento, Verdade e Reconciliação de Timor Leste (Commission for Reception, Truth and Reconciliation, CAVR, see Chapter 4) in how to use "traditional" methods, including the typical seating arrangements for *lisan* (a regional *adat* variant), the structure of *nahe biti boot* ("spreading of the mat") ceremonies (Commission for Reception, Truth and Reconciliation 2006, Section 9.3.5; see Babo-Soares 2004) and how hearings should be concluded with "a moral teaching presented on the theme of togetherness" (Commission for Reception, Truth and Reconciliation 2006, Section 9.3.5). In other words, international actors in both Aceh and East Timor were integral to the design and implantation of processes otherwise portrayed as "local".

The way in which national governments can manipulate "local" conflict management processes is also illustrated by Duncan's (2016) discussion of *adat*-based reconciliation efforts in North Maluku (eastern Indonesia) following violence between Muslims and Christians (1999–2000) in which several thousand people died and more than 230,000 were displaced. The *adat*-based reconciliation efforts have been hailed by government officials, the media and scholars as a successful example of "grassroots" reconciliation (Duncan 2016, 461; see Bräuchler 2015). Duncan (2016, 464–465) notes, however, that it was political leaders, high-ranking civil servants and customary law experts who promoted the revitalisation of *adat* as a means of shifting people's identification from their religion (Christianity or Islam) to their common ethnicity (Tobelo). The primary form this revitalisation of *adat* took was the *hibualamo*, the "big meeting house" that has traditionally been the centre of Tobelo villages and had been used in the past for the mediation of conflict within the village, with other villages or between people of different religions (Duncan 2016, 465). While no surviving *hibualamo* existed, the district head of North Halmahera, Hein Namotemo, made *adat* a tool of reconciliation during his two terms in office. Duncan (2016, 466) notes that the ritual celebrations of *hibualamo* promoted by Namotemo were officially sanctioned events reflecting "reconciliation as spectacle" and encouraging the forgetting of the past, rather than "an actual practice in which various factions or individuals meet to discuss their differences or to reconcile". As a consequence, the population considered *hibualamo* celebrations to be "little more than public displays stage-managed by a handful of elites [that had] little to do with people's actual views on inter-faith relations or issues of reconciliation" (Duncan 2016, 467). While communities did take part in "reconciliation ceremonies", they did it only for reasons of economic survival, as community members had little interest in repairing inter-group relations (Duncan 2016, 468; see Introduction). Duncan (2016, 469) concludes that, although presented as "local", this was, in reality, an elite-managed version of "reconciliation" which ignored issues important to local communities, including truth and accountability.

While Horne (2014) and Duncan (2016) demonstrate how international agencies and national governments may use the idea of the "local" to serve their own interests, the promotion of "tradition" may also strengthen the position of "traditional" leaders (usually older men) and strengthen discrimination based on gender and age. Writing in the context of the war (1987–2005) in Uganda between government forces and the Lord's Resistance Army (LRA, predominantly recruited from among the Acholi people), the political scientist Adam Branch (2014, 662) warns that calling on "tradition" may legitimise the power of "male elders, who are presented as the privileged repositories and guardians of tradition and the exclusive mediators with the spiritual world". Branch (2014, 623) reports how, in interviews following the end of the insurgency of the LRA in 2005, Acholi men and male elders explained to him that the revival of their traditional authority would require "imposing discipline at the family and clan levels through warnings, fines, corporal punishment and, if all else fails, expulsion from the clan and curses". This would, Branch (2014, 624) argues, potentially erase women's and youth's public space and social and economic opportunities, thereby "reinforcing the very forms of inequality and domination that helped drive on the conflict". There is a danger, therefore, that such promotion of "traditional" conflict management mechanisms can also "end up reinforcing the very injustices and modes of domination and inequality that gave rise to episodes of violence in the first place" (Branch 2014, 613). As noted in Chapter 1, we must always ask why some "traditions" are resurrected and by whom (Zechenter 1997, 334).

50 *Re*-traditionalising conflict management

Sierra Leone provides a further illustration of Branch's observation that promoting "tradition" may reinforce the injustices that gave rise to the conflict in the first place. The civil war in Sierra Leone (1991–2002) was, in part, a response by youth to oppressive social obligations demanded by male elders (see Richards 1996). The use by chiefs (a creation of colonial authorities) of their power to reinforce hierarchies of class, gender and age meant that young men bore the brunt of such abuse, which made them willing recruits when war broke out (see Fanthorpe 2001; 2006). While acknowledging that "traditional" approaches may have "romantic and practical appeal" in Sierra Leone, sociologist Laura Stovel (2008, 306) warns that they "may reinforce the very tensions that contributed to the war in the first place". Stovel (2008, 307) illustrates this with the use by officials and civil society leaders in post-war Sierra Leone of the Krio proverb (Krio is the English-based creole spoken in the capital and to a lesser degree elsewhere in the country) "There's no bad bush to throw away a bad child" (i.e., no matter what a child has done, the community always has a place for him or her). Stovel (2008, 318) suggests that, while the proverb promotes a vision of "African Society being inherently conciliatory and inclusive", there is an assumption implicit in the proverb that returning to the pre-war situation is the ideal and that it may uncritically:

> reinforce the pre-war status quo … and ignore the fact that Sierra Leoneans primarily integrate through age-old relations of dependency, many of which are tremendously exploitative, and leave many women, children and other marginalised groups extremely vulnerable to abuse.

Examples such as this led Allen and Macdonald (2013, 15) to ask whether it is appropriate to reinstate a "traditional" social order if "that social order was linked to the outbreak of the violent conflict".

In this section I have considered how anthropologists (and other ethnographers) have sounded a note of caution regarding the "re-traditionalisation" movement for a number of reasons: that international and national authorities can caricature "tradition" to serve their own interests; that the "local" is presented as being intrinsically good, when what is "local" is, in reality, a matter of perspective; that promoting "tradition" may codify and thereby rigidify mechanisms whose efficacy depends on flexibility; and that it may reinforce the exploitative authority of "traditional" leaders. Such caution does not mean, however, that anthropologists reject outright any promotion of "local traditions" in the aftermath of violent conflict. As noted above, McWilliam (2007, 88–90) notes that while we should avoid essentialising traditional processes, we should also recognise that there are "distinct advantages in utilising culturally accepted practices for mediating disputes", including shared understandings that convey shared sentiments and shared social and spiritual sanctions which make non-compliance or failure to find resolution less likely. Given this potential, are there ways in which "local tradition" can be harnessed whilst avoiding the pitfalls outlined above? I will consider this question through case studies from Rwanda, Uganda and Mozambique.

Inkiko-Gacaca (Rwanda)

Between 7 April and mid-July 1994 an estimated 937,000 Rwandans (according to a 2001 census; IRIN 2001), the vast majority of whom were Tutsi, were murdered in massacres committed by militia and elements of the army, often with the participation of the local population (see Des Forges 1999; Eltringham 2004). In his report of 31 May 1994 the UN Secretary General declared genocide had been committed (United Nations 1994, 36), paving the way for the creation of the International Criminal Tribunal for Rwanda (ICTR), which would go on to indict ninety-three high-ranking individuals apprehended outside of Rwanda for war crimes (mistreatment of civilians or prisoners of war); crimes against humanity (a widespread or systematic attack on a civilian population, whether or not in a time of war); and genocide (the intent to destroy, in whole or in part, a national, ethnical, racial or religious group) (see Eltringham 2019; Chapter 5). In Rwanda itself, with more than 120,000 imprisoned for alleged participation in the genocide by 2000, the Rwandan government passed a law creating 11,000 *Inkiko-Gacaca* (*gacaca* tribunals) staffed by nearly 260,000 lay judges to try lower level genocide perpetrators for murder, manslaughter, assault and property offences and to hand down sentences from five to thirty-five years, but also offering reduced sentences and community service for those who confessed (Waldorf 2010, 187–188).

A pilot phase of the new *Inkiko-Gacaca* from 2002 to 2004 was followed by a nationwide roll out in January 2005, in which the "entire population" was enlisted to "prosecute, defend, testify and judge" an estimated 761,000 suspects and hear 1.1 million cases (see Burnet 2008, 173). Before the public hearings, a panel of nine judges (*inyangamugayo*) compiled a dossier of evidence against which oral testimony was assessed as witnesses were called on to corroborate, revise or correct the evidence in the dossier (Thomson 2011, 380). During the *Inkiko-Gacaca* process officials constantly reminded people of the need to "unify and reconcile" (Thomson 2011, 377). According to Rwanda's President Paul Kagame, the purpose of *Inkiko-Gacaca* was to "end impunity", promote reconciliation and "establish the real truth of what happened during the genocide" (Burnet 2010, 96), with the billboards promoting *Inkiko-Gacaca* reading *Inkiko Gacaca: Ukuri, Ubutabera, Ubwiyunge* ("Gacaca Courts: Truth, Justice, Reconciliation") (Waldorf 2010, 192).

Human rights scholar Lars Waldorf (2010, 188) argues that, despite claims by the Rwandan government that *Inkiko-Gacaca* was "traditional", it "bore no resemblance to customary dispute resolution other than the name". In its "traditional" form, *gacaca* brought together *inyangamugayo* ("people of integrity"), the parties to a dispute and the local community to establish the facts of a conflict and find a resolution to disputes involving property, inheritance, personal injury and marital relations (Burnet 2008, 175). Taking its name from a patch of grass found in the inner courtyard of a traditional homestead, the most private place in the family home, *gacaca* was a private affair, the deliberations confidential, the "judgement" only reported publicly if that was a deliberate decision of the *gacaca* process (Burnet 2008, 175). Sanctions imposed by *gacaca* were restitutive and not individualised; for example, family and clan members had to pay a gift of livestock (Waldorf 2010, 186). The intention of *gacaca* in this "traditional" form was "not to determine individual guilt ... but to restore harmony and social order ... and to reintegrate the person who was the source of the disorder" (Reyntjens & Vandeginste 2005, 118; see Chapter 1). Although *gacaca* sessions were still being held by local officials in the 1980s to resolve quarrels between family members and immediate neighbours (see Reyntjens 1990), *gacaca* was never codified by Rwandan law, "so the exact format and function of *gacaca* varied widely from community to community" (Burnet 2008, 176). In contrast to "traditional" *gacaca*, *Inkiko-Gacaca* proceedings were codified; considered serious crimes rather than minor disputes; were not private; were punitive rather than restorative; and the testimony of confessed prisoners was placed centre stage (in the past the aggrieved party gave testimony first, followed by witnesses and then by the accused, who would be cross-examined by other witnesses) (Burnet 2008, 176–177; see Waldorf 2010, 188).

While there can be no doubt that *Inkiko-Gacaca* reflects Sally Merry's (1988, 882) observation that governments "promote new state judicial institutions with traditional symbolic trappings, claiming to reinstitute traditional law", if *Inkiko-Gacaca* was effective, was its divergence from "traditional" *gacaca* a problem? Unfortunately, research indicates that *Inkiko-Gacaca* did not "end impunity", promote reconciliation or "establish the real truth of what happened during the genocide", as Rwanda's president had hoped (Burnet 2010, 96). Research found that the

FIGURE 2.1 An *Inkiko-Gacaca* hearing in 2006. (Photo courtesy of Karen Brounéus)

centrality of confession in *Inkiko-Gacaca* was an obstacle to establishing the truth (Burnet 2010, 96). Given that only prisoners who had confessed were eligible to appear before *Inkiko-Gacaca*, this created "a perverse incentive for those prisoners who believe[d] themselves innocent, to invent something to confess to" (Zorbas 2009, 139). Alternatively, prisoners who knew themselves to be guilty confessed to lesser crimes in order to receive lighter sentences (Burnet 2008, 178–179; Ingelaere 2016, 155) or even paid someone else to confess to crimes they themselves had committed (known as *kugura umusozi*, or "buying the hill") (Waldorf 2010, 194).

In general, anthropologist Bert Ingelaere (2016, 117) found that a "pragmatic" rather than an "objective" truth was pursued in *Inkiko-Gacaca,* with many confessions, accusations and witnessing being "partial or false" (see Waldorf 2010, 193–194). Ingelaere (2016, 118) explains this in relation to Kinyarwanda (the language spoken in Rwanda) and the notion of *kumenya Kinyarwanda* ("speaking (knowing) Kinyarwanda"). This implies not just the ability to speak Kinyarwanda but "knowing when to speak, when not to speak, how to speak, and what to speak" and the notion of *ubwenge,* which refers to "wisdom and trickery, caution, cleverness, and prudence". When combined, people used these notions to navigate the space of *Inkiko-Gacaca* to achieve "the most optimal outcome in the given circumstances" in terms of basic survival and an increase in well-being (Ingelaere 2016, 120). Regarding the issue of "when not to speak", Ingelaere (2016, 128) suggests there was also an "unwillingness to 'denounce one's own blood' expressed as *ceceka* ('keeping quiet') and *kuitvamo* ('not denouncing oneself')" (see Waldorf 2010, 195). While this could be due to ethnicity (a Hutu would not denounce a Hutu), it could also be the case that Hutu defendants were members of the extended families of Tutsi survivors. Such reticence was not due to simple loyalty, but because denunciation could have negative consequences for a person's social and economic existence in a precarious subsistence economy (Ingelaere 2016, 129; see Introduction). This meant that *Inkiko-Gacaca* could not, necessarily, "establish the real truth of what happened during the genocide".

Another reason why the "truth" revealed by *Inkiko-Gacaca* was "pragmatic" rather than "objective" was that it was used as a means of extracting revenge for animosity that preceded the 1994 genocide (especially conflicts over land) and to get rid of a "long-standing enemy, an annoying neighbour, an untrustworthy husband, or an avaricious parent" (Ingelaere 2016, 124–125 138; see Burnet 2008, 179 183–187). Material gain was also pursued through *Inkiko-Gacaca* (see Burnet 2008, 186–187; Ingelaere 2016, 125–128). Susan Thomson (2011, 383) provides the example of Esther, a Tutsi survivor, who was instructed on how to deliver testimony against a prisoner by a local official who had business dealings with her brother. Esther told Thomson (2011, 383), "My brother was in business with [the local official]; they knew [the accused] had a house and a good job … [The official] told me to denounce him. [The official] said if I didn't I would end up dead or in prison."

A final reason why *Inkiko-Gacaca* could not necessarily "establish the real truth of what happened during the genocide" was that it was based on a pre-determined "truth" that did not correspond to people's experience. Thomson (2011, 379) notes that, for "ordinary Rwandans", the 1994 genocide was more complex than

54 *Re*-traditionalising conflict management

simply Hutu killing Tutsi. Rather, "some Tutsi killed Hutu, some Hutu protected Tutsi; Twa also participated; and just as some from each group joined in the killing, others stood by" (Thomson 2011, 379; see Mironko 2006; Straus 2006). The Rwandan government's policy of "national unity and reconciliation", however, employed essentialist categories in which survivors were Tutsi and perpetrators were Hutu (see Eltringham 2004, 97), implying that all Hutu were "guilty until proven innocent" (Thomson 2011, 278; see Jaji 2017; Waldorf 2010, 200). Thomson (2011, 384), for example, quotes Anselme, a sixteen-year-old boy whose three uncles were in prison on allegations of genocide crimes, saying that, "For me, *gacaca* is just a way for the government to put us Hutu in prison." *Inkiko-Gacaca*, therefore, produced "a particular version of justice and reconciliation that reinforce[d] the power of the post-genocide government at the expense of individual processes of reconciliation" (Thomson 2011, 374). Seen from this perspective, *Inkiko-Gacaca* was a means for the Tutsi-dominated post-genocide government to strengthen its authority in line with Branch's (2014, 662) warning that calling on "tradition" may legitimise the power of elites. This supports the fear that "local dispute-resolution mechanisms will be driven in new – often problematic – directions where they are captured and co-opted by the state" (Waldorf 2010, 202).

Regarding "reconciliation", *Inkiko-Gacaca* hearings could not consider the alleged killing of Hutu by the Rwandan Patriotic Army/Front (RPA/F) during and after the 1994 genocide of Tutsi (see King 2010, 303). Evidence had been presented to UN officials in the Rwandan capital, Kigali, on 19 September 1994 of "calculated, preplanned, systematic atrocities and genocide against Hutus by the RPA"; claiming that 30,000 had been massacred; that the "methodology and scale" suggested a "plan implemented as a policy from the highest echelons of the government" (ICTR 2006, para 5; see Eltringham 2019, 38–41). Given that *Inkiko-Gacaca* only considered the crime of genocide against Tutsi in 1994 (war crimes were removed from the law in 2004), it could not consider the alleged killing of Hutu by the RPA/F, or crimes allegedly committed by the RPA/F during the insurgency (1994–1996) in the north-west (Jackson 2004) or in the Democratic Republic of Congo in 1996 (Office of the United Nations High Commissioner for Human Rights 2010). As a consequence, some Hutu considered *Inkiko-Gacaca* to be a form of "institutionalised injustice" (Ingelaere 2016, 130; see Thomson 2011, 384; Waldorf 2010, 197). Genocide survivors also indicated dissatisfaction with *Inkiko-Gacaca*, as Ingelaere (2016, 131) reports:

> For some survivors, testifying against a defendant was useless because it was not going to bring back their loved ones, it was not going to bring them any material compensation for their loss, and it might even generate bad relationships with the accused and their families with whom they had to live on a daily basis.

Having outlined the weaknesses of *Inkiko-Gacaca* in relation to its stated objectives, it is important to acknowledge that *Inkiko-Gacaca* progressed in different ways depending on community characteristics and histories and that the laws underpinning

Inkiko-Gacaca changed over seven years (see Waldorf 2010, 189–192). Ingelaere (2016, 133–146), for example, compares two different communities. In Rukoma, where the genocide was "unimaginably devastating" (almost the whole of the Tutsi population of 12,758 was killed), *Inkiko-Gacaca* proceedings were, initially at least, "organized as collective vengeance", with survivors using false testimony to get as many Hutu as possible convicted. In contrast, the genocide in Ntabona had alternated between violence and resistance, with both Hutu and Tutsi considering those who resorted to violence as a "group of bandits". In Ntabona, Tutsi women married to Hutu men had been protected by their extended Hutu families while Hutu families saved unrelated Tutsi. In Ntabona, *Inkiko-Gacaca* generally operated in the way it had been envisaged, demonstrating that "local strategies and histories reshaped *gacaca* in diverse ways in different localities" (Ingelaere 2016, 145).

While acknowledging the influence of context, an overall assessment of *Inkiko-Gacaca* suggests that the stated aim of promoting reconciliation and establishing "the real truth of what happened during the genocide" (Burnet 2010, 96) was impaired by the centrality of confession; "cultural" norms that gave rise to a "pragmatic" rather than an "objective" truth; opportunities for revenge and material gain; the exclusion of alleged crimes committed against Hutu; and the lack of comfort the process brought to Tutsi survivors. Despite claims by the Rwandan government that *Inkiko-Gacaca* reflected Rwandan "tradition", it bore little resemblance to "traditional" *gacaca* and, according to the research considered above, failed to achieve its stated objectives. *Inkiko-Gacaca* appears, therefore, to be an example of how a national government can appropriate "local tradition" but fail to achieve the intended results (Merry 1988, 882).

Mato Oput (Uganda)

In 1986 the National Resistance Army (NRA), led by Yoweri Museveni (current President of Uganda) violently unseated President Tito Okello, an ethnic Acholi from northern Uganda (Okello had overthrown President Milton Obote the previous year). Pursuing the retreating Acholi army into northern Uganda, NRA soldiers took revenge against civilians, giving rise to the Holy Spirit Army (HSA) led by Alice Kakwena, a female spirit medium (Baines & Stewart 2011, 6). Despite attracting mass support from the Acholi population who had suffered at the hands of the NRA, the HSA faced a series of military defeats (see Behrend 1999). Parts of the HSA regrouped in 1988 as the Lord's Resistance Army (LRA), led by Joseph Kony (Baines 2007, 99). Kony proclaimed himself a messianic prophet, vowing to overthrow Museveni and rule Uganda according to the Ten Commandments (Apuuli 2011, 118). Operating in northern Uganda and South Sudan, the LRA forcibly recruited people, including 30,000 children and youth, who were used as human shields, porters, labourers and fighters (see Apuuli 2004). Ninety per cent of the population of Acholiland was displaced by the fighting and, at one point, there was a death rate of 1,000 persons per week from violence, disease and extreme poverty (Baines 2010, 410).

56 *Re*-traditionalising conflict management

Partly as a result of lobbying by the Acholi Religious Leaders Peace Initiative, the Ugandan government passed an act in 2000 that granted amnesty to LRA rebels who voluntarily returned home, a policy supported in Acholiland as many LRA combatants had been abducted as children (Apuuli 2011, 122). In January 2004, however, the prosecutor of the International Criminal Court (ICC; see Chapter 5) announced that the situation had been referred to the court by the Ugandan government, and in October 2005 arrest warrants were issued for Kony and four of his commanders for crimes against humanity and war crimes (see Apuuli 2006). Subsequent peace talks between the LRA and the Ugandan government in Juba, South Sudan, between 2006 and 2008 discussed ways in which the ICC warrants could be revoked or sidestepped. Meanwhile, the ICC prosecutor was criticised for failing to issue warrants regarding alleged crimes committed by the Uganda People's Defence Force (the government army) and for ignoring the potential of "local" mechanisms for conflict resolution and reconciliation (Allen 2010, 242).

Drawing on extensive fieldwork in northern Uganda, the anthropologist Sverker Finnström (2010, 141–143) describes one "local" mechanism based on the principle of *culo kwo* ("to pay an unreconciled killing"), in which the clan of a murdered person is compensated by the murderer's clan. Following protracted negotiations, compensation is given to a young man (chosen by a spirit medium) from the offended clan to meet bride wealth expenses, so that he can marry and father a child who will be named after the deceased (see Baines 2007, 105). An all-day ritual, called *mato oput* ("drinking the bitter herb or root"), is then held on neutral ground, in the uncultivated bush, where both the offending and offended parties drink a concoction made from the blood of a sacrificed sheep and a bitter root of the *oput* tree, symbolising the swallowing of bitterness (Finnström 2010, 153; see Apuuli 2011, 123). Without *mato oput* "a barrier of bad atmosphere (*ojebu*) develops between the two clans" so that they cannot socialise, trade or intermarry and misfortune affects the offending clan (Finnström 2010, 143). Having attended a number of *mato oput* rituals (although none related to the war), Finnström (2010, 142) considers the ritual to be an important way in which to achieve "the restoration of social relations" among the Acholi people. Finnström (2010, 145) also describes *gomo tong* ("the bending of the spears"), at which spears from both parties are bent and exchanged. *Gomo tong* "is not about remembering and assessing every detail of a long and violent conflict", but "finding a consensual understanding about what the conflict was essentially about, and how to coexist" (Finnström 2010, 145).

During fieldwork in 2004, Allen (2010, 244) found that urban-based "opinion leaders" in Gulu, the largest town in the war-affected region, rejected the ICC warrants and argued that "justice" had to be "locally grounded to have meaning" and that *mato oput* should be promoted. Around the same time, an influential report (see Liu Institute for Global Issues and Gulu District NGO Forum 2005) proposed collecting and writing down practices, rituals and ceremonies to be promoted by a recently created body of Acholi chiefs and elders (*Ker Kwaro Acholi* – "authority of Acholi grandfathers/elders") (see Allen 2010, 248; Branch 2014, 619). The support

FIGURE 2.2 *Mato oput* in Gulu, northern Uganda, January 1998. (Photo courtesy of Sverker Finnström)

for such an approach culminated in the June 2007 Agreement on Accountability and Reconciliation (AAR) between the LRA and the Ugandan government, which proposed that mechanisms such as *mato oput* be officially recognised and incorporated into Ugandan law.

Erin Baines (2007, 105–106) outlines a number of problems with adopting *mato oput* in the way envisaged by the AAR. First, which clan would perform *mato oput*, given it was difficult to trace who had killed whom in the war; while *mato oput* could be straightforwardly adapted to killing in the war, what about rape, sexual violence and abduction; would Acholi government soldiers accused of atrocities also have to undergo rituals; and could the clans of high-ranking LRA commanders pay the required compensation? Allen (2010), who has been conducting ethnographic fieldwork in Acholiland since the 1980s, was also sceptical. Allen (2010, 245) notes that *mato oput* had been singled out as a possible remedy because of a report entitled "The Bending of Spears", commissioned by the UK-based NGO International Alert and written by the former head of Oxfam in Uganda, Dennis Pain (1997). Pain proposed that the traditional chiefs (*Rwodi-mo*) be reinvigorated and *mato oput* (combined with *gomo tong*) promoted, with international donors providing funds to pay compensation. Pain holds a Ph.D. in Political and Social Anthropology from the University of Cambridge and had conducted fieldwork in Gulu in the late 1960s. Despite Pain's credentials, a report commissioned by the Agency for Cooperation and Research in Development criticised his recommendations, noting that traditional structures were

58   *Re*-traditionalising conflict management

weak; few people considered the traditional structures to be a priority; "elders" were not sure how to carry out the rituals; and there was disagreement on who were "real" traditional leaders (Allen 2010, 247; see Dolan 2000). Despite this, the notion of Acholi traditional leaders promoting "traditional reconciliation" proved popular with international agencies, Ugandan Christian leaders and Ugandan human rights campaigners (Allen 2010, 248; see Apuuli 2011). Local support could not, however, deny the instrumental involvement of an international NGO (International Alert) in the initial promotion of *mato oput*, nor the later involvement of international donors in promoting "traditional justice" (Allen 2010, 248; see discussion of Horne 2014 above), confirming Mac Ginty's (2015, 846) observation that, while projects "may have a local face", the "real power may come from donors and administrators in New York, London, Geneva or elsewhere".

On the other hand, if *mato oput* proved effective, would the involvement of "internationals" matter? Allen (2010, 252) remained sceptical for a number of reasons. When Allen had observed rituals in Acholi villages in the 1980s it was the action that was described ("we have cleansed a spirit from the compound") rather than the name of a particular ritual, thereby allowing for flexible adaptation to specific circumstances, reflecting the observation that such mechanisms are "strategic improvisations" (McWilliam 2007, 89). To codify such practices, Allen (2010, 253) argued, would mean rituals losing flexibility and becoming the "preserve of certain figures of male authority recognised by the government", echoing colonial efforts to incorporate "tribal" customs into British rule through government-appointed chiefs (see Chapter 1). From this perspective, those attempting to institutionalise "local rituals" could be accused of neo-colonialism (Allen 2010, 259). Allen (2010, 255–256) also warned that such rituals could be used in ways that "outsiders" would not deem appropriate, pointing out that ritual cleansing can be very violent, especially "witch-cleansing", and that "there are serious risks in local customs and rituals being interpreted as inherently benign". Such rituals could strengthen gender- and age-based structures of domination, thereby worsening the domination by older Acholi men of women and youth (see Branch 2014, 615). Finally, Allen (2010, 258–261) noted that promoting Acholi "rituals" would give the impression that the Ugandan government and the rest of the country had nothing to do with the violence and would also reinforce the view that people in northern Uganda are "primitive", "innately violent" and not ready for "modern" justice, perpetuating an image of the Acholi as "preoccupied with war" that was promoted as part of a British colonial policy of "divide and rule" (Apuuli 2011, 119).

While Allen is largely dismissive of the promotion of "traditional" mechanisms in northern Uganda, Finnström (2010, 146) takes a more positive, albeit cautious, approach to the potential of *mato oput* as a means for people to "cope with a difficult situation". For Finnström (2010, 146) rituals are "situated socially" and remain "a way of addressing present concerns" precisely because they shift "in meaning and appearance over time". For Finnström (2010, 153), therefore, it is not really a question of whether rituals are "authentic" and "traditional" or "inauthentic" and "recently invented"; rather, they are a flexible, evolving means to achieve "social solidarity".

Re-traditionalising conflict management 59

In a similar vein to Finnström, Baines (2010, 411) suggests that the process of social reconstruction in northern Uganda takes place not in formal institutions (including formalised "traditional justice mechanisms" such as *mato oput*) but through the way in which conflict-affected communities employ existing socio-cultural resources to acknowledge and move past the wrongs committed. Baines (2010, 415) sees potential in this "messy territory" of the "social processes that order morality and relationships among persons located in the day-to-day" (see Introduction for a discussion on reconstructing mundane relationships).

To illustrate her position, Baines (2010, 413) provides an account of how Acholi invoke the spirit world to "help right wrongs committed by them against others, or by others against them". This involves *jogi* (singular: *jok*) who are ancestral spirits linked to the geographic location of a particular clan and who maintain the moral order by sending misfortune until clan unity is restored. A particular spirit is a *cen* (a free *jok;* i.e., not related to specific clan ancestors or locations), which is a "vengeful spirit of persons who either died badly (murder or neglect) or were treated badly in death (failure to give a proper burial or treating a corpse without respect)" (Baines 2010, 420). Baines (2010, 420) recounts how possession by *cen* was a frequent explanation among returned LRA abductees for why they were unable to reintegrate into their communities, as the spirits of those they had killed were "choking them at night, forcing them … to try to kill others or themselves". Only by paying *culo kwo* ("to pay an unreconciled killing") and reconciling with the clan of the dead can one escape the *cen* (Baines 2007, 93n95).

Baines (2010, 426) provides the example of Joska, a returned LRA abductee who was tormented at night by the spirits of a boy and girl she had killed while in the LRA. After Joska's elders had consulted three *ajwaki* (singular: *ajwaka*, usually barren women possessed by a spirit who are consulted to determine the cause of misfortune and avenues of redress) without success, her parents consulted a fourth *ajwaka* who drew up a list of demands for compensation from the two spirits. Having agreed to pay the compensation, Joska performed a ritual cleansing (transferring each of the spirits to a sacrificial goat) and, on a later occasion, drank the *oput* root (symbolising swallowing one's anger). Following this, Joska was no longer troubled. Baines (2007, 97) suggests that this illustrates how abductees such as Joska did not wait for *mato oput* to be codified, but, using her own means, sought to "put her world, and that of her community, in order through traditional healers and spirit mediums".

The important feature of this case was that, because Joska did not know the clan of the boy and girl she had killed, the "traditional" form of *mato oput* could not be applied (Baines 2010, 428; see Finnström 2010, 141–143). Despite this, Joska and other abductees could flexibly adapt "tradition" to their specific circumstances so that the spirit world became a "recourse for social reconstruction" (Baines 2010, 430; see Allen 2010, 252). The example of Joska demonstrates that mechanisms such as *mato oput* were being used in Uganda, but "without any inducement by any" external authority (Baines 2007, 113).

Unlike the example of *Inkiko-Gacaca* in Rwanda, *mato oput* in Uganda did correspond closely to practices actually being used by Acholi, as witnessed by Finnström

60 *Re*-traditionalising conflict management

(2010, 153). Despite this, the adoption of these practices as a formalised response to the conflict was in doubt, given that traditional structures were weak; "elders" were not sure how to carry out the rituals; and there was disagreement on who were "real" traditional leaders (Allen 2010, 247). This did not mean, however, that "traditional" mechanisms were not being used effectively. Baines' (2010, 426) example of Joska demonstrates that mechanisms could alleviate the aftermath of the conflict, but that *mato oput* had to be understood as part of a wider Acholi spirit world and was performed in a way different to "tradition" as the identities of the victims were not known. This demonstrates that rituals such as *mato oput* are "situated socially" and are "a way of addressing present concerns" precisely because they shift "in meaning and appearance over time" (Finnström 2010, 146).

Baines (2010) concludes that, in northern Uganda, rituals were being used in an organic, adaptive way "out of sight" (Finnström 2010, 146), rather than being formally codified and promoted, as in the case of *Inkiko-Gacaca* discussed above. This raises the question of whether mechanisms such as *mato oput* can or should be formalised, given that "internationals" may be wary of endorsing the spirit world in which such mechanisms are embedded. As Baines (2010, 414) suggests, one reason why recourse to the spirit world is not promoted by "internationals" is that they tend to search for "mechanisms that resonate with western norms" (see Igreja & Skaar 2013, 169). Furthermore, formalisation could rob mechanisms of the flexibility that made them effective for abductees like Joska.

Gamba spirits (Mozambique)

While the example of *Inkiko-Gacaca* illustrates how "traditional" mechanisms can be appropriated and codified by national governments (often with "international" support) in ways that fail to achieve the intended results, the example of *mato oput* is a more complex picture in which codification is proposed but, in the meantime, the mechanism is being creatively adapted "out of sight" (Finnström 2010, 146) by those for whom it is effective. My final example, Mozambique, further illustrates how "traditional" mechanisms are "a way of addressing present concerns" precisely because they shift "in meaning and appearance over time" (Finnström 2010, 146). The example of Mozambique further supports what Baines (2010) found in Uganda, that "traditions" are used creatively but that their efficacy relies on their flexibility – a flexibility that would be lost if the mechanism was codified (Allen 2010, 253).

The Mozambique civil war (1977–1992), fought between the Frente de Libertação de Moçambique (Mozambique Liberation Front, FRELIMO) government and the rebel group Resistência Nacional Moçambicana (Mozambican National Resistance, RENAMO), resulted in the death of one million people (half of whom were children), with one quarter of the population fleeing their homes (see Nordstrom 1998, 104). Writing on post-war Mozambique, the anthropologist Carolyn Nordstrom (1998, 116) notes the belief that the souls of those killed by soldiers followed them back to their homes and families and caused them problems. As a consequence, when, following the end of the war, soldiers, children

Re-traditionalising conflict management   **61**

and refugees returned home to their families they were believed to be potential contaminators of the community as they might be haunted by spirits of the dead (Honwana 2005, 92). Alcinda Manuel Honwana (1997, 300) provides the example of Paulo, a nine-year-old boy who had been kidnapped by RENAMO soldiers and held captive for eight months before escaping. When he arrived home he was taken to the *ndomba* ("house of the spirits") where he was presented to the ancestral spirits, who were thanked by Paulo's grandfather for his return. A few days later Paulo took part in a purification ritual as described by his father (Honwana 1997, 300–301):

> We took him to the bush (about 2 km away from our house). There we built a small hut covered with dry grass in which we put the child dressed with the dirty clothes he came back with from the RENAMO camp. Inside the hut the child was undressed. Then we set fire to the hut, and Paulo was helped out by an adult relative. The hut, the clothes, and everything else that the individual brought from the camp has to be burned. This symbolises the rupture with that past. Then the child had to inhale the smoke of some herbal remedies, as well as be bathed with water treated with medicine to cleanse his body internally and externally. Finally, we vaccinated him to give him strength.

The "vaccination" (*ku thlavela*), involving making small cuts in the body and filling them with herbal remedies, was considered essential to "cleanse the individual and heal trauma" (Honwana 1997, 301). Such rituals mark a break with the past traumatic experience that caused the state of pollution. Honwana (1997, 293–295) argues that because "traditional institutions" are embedded in a "shared system of meanings that regulate the social life of rural communities", such mechanisms function as the "means through which healing and order" can be re-established in the aftermath of the civil war.

Victor Igreja and Elin Skaar (2013) also recognise the "ongoing vitality of local cultural practices of justice and healing". Drawing on fieldwork carried out in Mozambique between 2011 and 2012, they note that while among urban political elites and civil society organisations there has been a tendency to avoid accountability for actions during the civil war, in rural areas "silence was not an effective way to deal with the legacies of the past violence" (Igreja & Skaar 2013, 175). The need for accountability was expressed in the Gorongosa (a district in the central province of Sofala) language with the phrase *micero ai vundi* ("a conflict does not rot"), indicating that, over time, unresolved conflicts increase in intensity, disturbing social life as the spirits of dead victims afflict perpetrators or their relatives until there is a resolution (Igreja & Skaar 2013, 152 170).

In the aftermath of the civil war, *gamba* spirits (the spirits of soldiers that died during the conflict) became both the principal harmful spirits and also evolved to enable healing. Igreja and Skaar (2013, 171) explain that by possessing perpetrators (or their kin), *gamba* spirits demanded justice through a public hearing of accusations. An example described by Igreja and Skaar (2013, 172–174) involved a young woman, Zabeta, who had suffered various afflictions, including the death of her two babies, divorce and violent nightmares. Zabeta claimed that a *gamba* spirit possessed her at night and accused her uncle, Languisse, of being responsible for two violent deaths during the civil war. Having taken her case to a community court, Zabeta was possessed during the hearing and the judges transferred the case to a *gamba* healer. On two occasions Zabeta was possessed, with the aid of the *gamba* healer, by the spirits of a RENAMO soldier and a civilian neighbour who had died following a false accusation by Languisse that they were conspiring with FRELIMO against RENAMO. Confronted with this evidence, Languisse acknowledged his guilt. The *gamba* healer ordered the spirits to demand their reparations, which for the soldier was the return of his possessions and for the civilian that Languisse's youngest daughter be used in work as a *gamba* healer. The case of Zabeta illustrates that revelations, acknowledgement and accountability were conditions for appeasing the spirits and reunifying families and the communities (Igreja 2012, 419).

In Igreja and Skaar's (2013, 175) account, the spirits of the dead played a role in breaking the post-conflict silence in favour of accountability, not only articulating calls for justice but also creating an "appropriate language and social spaces to determine responsibility for a given violation". In this process, perpetrators were not cut off from social and economic relations; rather, the culprit initially lost face when his or her misdeeds were revealed, but then gradually rebuilt relations of trust with the community (see Chapter 1). For Igreja and Skaar (2013, 175) this was "an important form of justice that is consistent with local practices and paves the way for reconciliation and renewal". People took part in the *gamba* sessions because the "spirits have set the norms of conflict resolution and people believe that this is an effective way to speak out and address the crimes of the civil war" (Igreja 2012, 419). Such rituals are aimed at "asking for forgiveness, appeasing the souls of the dead, and preventing any future afflictions (retaliation) from the spirits of the dead, closing in this way the links with the 'bad' past" (Honwana 2005, 97; see Englund 1998).

Igreja and Skarr's (2013, 170–171) examples illustrate that traditional practitioners were "using the means available to them to restore peace and stability in their communities" (Honwana 1997, 304). Whereas before the war *gamba* spirits were

FIGURE 2.3 AND 2.4 A *gamba* healing session at night. (Photos courtesy of Victor Igreja)

believed to possess people to protect the hosts from wartime suffering, after the war *gamba* spirits became associated with reckoning with perpetrators of violence and, ultimately, as a means of reconciliation and renewal. As Igreja (2012, 412) notes, the change undergone by *gamba* spirits from being a means of protection to a means of reckoning indicates that "tradition" changes as people use "their own ways and means to restore peace and stability to their communities" (Honwana 2005, 98).

Conclusion

In recent years "traditional" conflict management mechanisms have been "lauded for their authenticity and presumed efficiency" (Horne 2014, 18). Anthropologists have sounded a note of caution regarding the "re-traditionalisation" movement: that international and national authorities can caricature "tradition" to serve their own interests; that the "local" is presented as being intrinsically good, when what is "local" is, in reality, a matter of perspective; that re-traditionalisation may codify and thereby rigidify mechanisms whose efficacy depends on flexibility; and that it may reinforce the exploitative authority of "traditional" leaders. The case studies I considered above illustrate some of these points. *Inkiko-Gacaca* in Rwanda was not even a caricature of "traditional" *gacaca*, given that it "bore no resemblance to customary dispute resolution other than the name" (Waldorf 2010, 188) and that it "reinforce[d] the power of the post-genocide government at the expense of individual processes of reconciliation" (Thomson 2011, 374).

Uganda and Mozambique, however, present a more complicated picture which, in part, supports McWilliam's (2007, 88–90) argument that there are "distinct advantages in utilising culturally accepted practices". In Uganda there were moves akin to those in Rwanda to formalise and promote *mato oput*. Such formalisation would have potentially robbed the mechanism of its flexibility and strengthened gender- and age-based structures of domination (Allen 2010). When left to operate "out of sight" (Finnström 2010, 146), however, spirit divination and *mato oput* were used in a creative way to reintegrate LRA abductees into their communities, as in the case of Joska. Likewise in Mozambique, ways of working with the spirit world were modified to restore peace and stability to communities, emphasising that "tradition" is effective because it is "flexible, fluid and enduring" (Nordstrom 1998, 114). This suggests a need to "highlight the creativity and resolution-finding ability of local actors" (Bräuchler & Naucke 2017, 428). The problem, however, is that such mechanisms, embedded in the spirit world, do not correspond to "mechanisms that resonate with western norms" and do not lend themselves to codification and promotion by national governments and international aid agencies (Igreja & Skaar 2013, 169).

Bibliography

Allen, Tim. 2010. "Bitter Roots: the 'invention' of Acholi traditional justice". In *The Lord's Resistance Army: Myth and Reality*, edited by Tim Allen and Koen Vlassenroot, 242–261. London: Zed Books.

64 *Re*-traditionalising conflict management

Allen, Tim and Anna Macdonald. 2013. *Post-conflict Traditional Justice: A Critical Overview.* London: London School of Economics and Political Science.

Apuuli, Kasaija Phillip. 2004. "The International Criminal Court (ICC) and the Lord's Resistance Army (LRA) insurgency in Northern Uganda", *Criminal Law Forum* 15 (4): 391–409.

Apuuli, Kasaija Phillip. 2006. "The ICC Arrest Warrants for the Lord's Resistance Army Leaders and Peace Prospects for Northern Uganda", *Journal of International Criminal Justice* 4 (1): 179–187.

Apuuli, Kasaija Phillip. 2011. "Peace over Justice: The Acholi Religious Leaders' Peace Initiative (ARLPI) vs. the International Criminal Court (ICC) in Northern Uganda", *Studies in Ethnicity and Nationalism* 11 (1): 116–129.

Archambault, Caroline S. 2011. "Ethnographic Empathy and the Social Context of Rights: 'Rescuing' Maasai Girls from Early Marriage", *American Anthropologist* 113 (4): 632–643.

Arriaza, Laura and Naomi Roht-Arriaza. 2008. "Social Reconstruction as a Local Process", *The International Journal of Transitional Justice* 2 (2): 152–172.

Babo-Soares, Dionísio. 2004. "Nahe biti: The philosophy and process of grassroots reconciliation (and justice) in East Timor", *The Asia Pacific Journal of Anthropology* 5 (1): 15–33.

Baines, Erin K. 2007. "The Haunting of Alice: Local Approaches to Justice and Reconciliation in Northern Uganda", *International Journal of Transitional Justice* 1 (1): 91–114.

Baines, Erin K. 2010. "Spirits and social reconstruction after mass violence: Rethinking transitional justice", *African Affairs* 109 (436): 409–430.

Baines, Erin and Beth Stewart. 2011. "'I cannot accept what I have not done': Storytelling, Gender and Transitional Justice", *Journal of Human Rights Practice* 3 (3): 245–263.

Behrend, Heike. 1999. *Alice Lakwena and the Holy Spirits: War in Northern Uganda 1986–97.* Oxford: James Currey.

Betts, Alexander. 2005. "Should Approaches to Post-conflict Justice and Reconciliation be Determined Globally, Nationally or Locally?" *European Journal of Development Research* 17 (4): 735–752.

Braithwaite, John, Valerie Braithwaite, Michael Cookson and Leah Dunn. 2010. *Anomie and Violence: Non-truth and Reconciliation in Indonesian Peacebuilding.* Canberra: Australian National University E Press.

Branch, Adam. 2014. "The Violence of Peace: Ethnojustice in Northern Uganda", *Development and Change* 45 (3): 608–630.

Bräuchler, Birgit. 2015. *The Cultural Dimension of Peace: Decentralization and Reconciliation in Indonesia.* London: Palgrave Macmillan.

Bräuchler, Birgit and Philipp Naucke. 2017. "Peacebuilding and conceptualisations of the local", *Social Anthropology* 25 (4): 422–436.

Burnet, Jennie E. 2008. "The Injustice of Local Justice: Truth, Reconciliation, and Revenge in Rwanda", *Genocide Studies and Prevention* 3 (2): 173–193.

Burnet, Jennie E. 2010. "(In)justice: Truth, Reconciliation and Revenge in Rwanda's Gacaca". In *Transitional Justice: Global Mechanisms and Local Realities after Genocide and Mass Violence*, edited by Alexander Laban Hinton, 95–118. New Brunswick, NJ: Rutgers University Press.

Commission for Reception, Truth and Reconciliation. 2006. *"Chega!" Final Report of the Commission for Reception, Truth and Reconciliation in East Timor.* Dili: CAVR.

Conklin, Beth. 1997. "Body paint, feathers, and VCRs: Aesthetics and Authenticity in Amazonian Activism", *American Ethnologist* 24 (4): 711–737.

Cowan, Jane K., Marie-Benedicte Dembour and Richard A. Wilson (eds.). 2001. "Introduction". In *Culture and Rights: Anthropological Perspectives*, 1–26. Cambridge, UK: Cambridge University Press.

Des Forges, Alison Liebhafsky. 1999. *"Leave none to tell the story": Genocide in Rwanda*. New York: Human Rights Watch.

DeShaw Rae, J. 2009. *Peacebuilding and Transitional Justice in East Timor*. Boulder, CO: First Forum Press.

Dolan, Christopher. 2000. *Inventing traditional leadership? A critical assessment of Denis Pain's "The Bending of the Spears"*. COPE Working Paper 31. London: ACORD.

Duncan, Christopher R. 2009. "Reconciliation and Revitalization: The Resurgence of Tradition in Postconflict Tobelo, North Maluku, Eastern Indonesia", *The Journal of Asian Studies* 68 (4): 1077–1104.

Duncan, Christopher R. 2016. "Coexistence not Reconciliation: From Communal Violence to Non-Violence in North Maluku, Eastern Indonesia", *The Asia Pacific Journal of Anthropology* 17 (5): 460–474.

Eltringham, Nigel. 2004. *Accounting for Horror: Post-Genocide Debates in Rwanda*. London: Pluto.

Eltringham, Nigel. 2019. *Genocide Never Sleeps: Living Law at the International Criminal Tribunal for Rwanda*. Cambridge, UK: Cambridge University Press.

Englund, Harri. 1998. "Death, Trauma and Ritual: Mozambican Refugees in Malawi", *Social Science & Medicine* 46 (9): 1165–1174.

Englund, Harri. 2004. "Introduction". In *Rights and the Politics of Recognition in Africa*, edited by Harri Englund and Francis B. Nyamnjoh, 1–29. London: Zed Books.

Fanthorpe, Richard. 2001. "Neither citizen nor subject? 'Lumpen' agency and the legacy of native administration in Sierra Leone", *African Affairs* 100 (400): 363–386.

Fanthorpe, Richard. 2006. "On the limits of liberal peace: Chiefs and democratic decentralization in post-war Sierra Leone", *African Affairs* 105 (418): 27–49.

Finnström, Sverker. 2010. "Reconciliation Grown Bitter?: War, Retribution, and Ritual Action in Northern Uganda". In *Localizing Transitional Justice: Interventions and Priorities after Mass Violence*, edited by Rosalind Shaw, Lars Waldorf and Pierre Hazan, 135–156. Stanford, CA: Stanford University Press.

Hodgson, Dorothy L. 2002. "Introduction: Comparative Perspectives on the Indigenous Rights Movement in Africa and the Americas", *American Anthropologist* 104 (4): 1037–1049.

Hodgson, Dorothy L. 2011. *Being Maasai, Becoming Indigenous: Postcolonial Politics in a Neoliberal World*. Bloomington, IN: Indiana University Press.

Honwana, Alcinda Manuel. 1997. "Healing for Peace: Traditional Healers and Post-War Reconstruction in Southern Mozambique", *Peace and Conflict: Journal of Peace Psychology* 3 (3): 293–305.

Honwana, Alcinda Manuel. 2005. "Healing and Social Reintegration in Mozambique and Angola". In *Roads to Reconciliation*, edited by Elin Skaar, Siri Gloppen and Astri Suhrke, 83–100. Lanham, MD: Lexington Books.

Horne, Cynthia M. 2014. "Reconstructing 'Traditional' Justice from the Outside In: Transitional Justice in Aceh and East Timor", *Journal of Peacebuilding & Development* 9 (2): 17–32.

ICTR. 2006. Military I – Defence Exhibit DK112 – UN Code Cable "The 'Gersoni' Report Rwanda. Admitted as evidence 16 November.

Igoe, Jim. 2006. "Becoming Indigenous Peoples: Difference, Inequality, and the Globalization of East African Identity Politics", *African Affairs* 105 (420): 399–420.

Igreja, Victor. 2012. "Multiple Temporalities in Indigenous Justice and Healing Practices in Mozambique", *The International Journal of Transitional Justice* 6 (3): 404–422.

Igreja, Victor and Elin Skaar. 2013. "'A conflict does not rot': state and civil society responses to civil war offences in Mozambique", *Nordic Journal of Human Rights* 31 (2): 149–175.

Ingelaere, Bert. 2016. *Inside Rwanda's Gacaca Courts: Seeking Justice after Genocide*. Madison, WI: University of Wisconsin Press.

66 *Re*-traditionalising conflict management

IRIN. 2001. Government puts genocide victims at 1.07 million. Integrated Regional Information Network for Central and Eastern Africa. https://reliefweb.int/report/rwanda/rwanda-government-puts-genocide-victims-107-million

Jackson, Paul. 2004. "Legacy of Bitterness: The Insurgency War in North West Rwanda", *Small Wars and Insurgencies* 15 (1): 19–37.

Jaji, Rose. 2017. "Under the Shadow of Genocide: Rwandans, Ethnicity and Refugee Status", *Ethnicities* 17 (1): 47–65.

King, Elisabeth. 2010. "Memory Controversies in Post-Genocide Rwanda: Implications for Peacebuilding", *Genocide Studies and Prevention* 5 (3): 293–309.

Koomen, J. 2014. "Global governance and the politics of culture: campaigns against female circumcision in East Africa", *Gender, Place & Culture* 21 (2): 244–261.

Kuper, Adam. 2003. "The Return of the Native", *Current Anthropology* 44 (3): 389–402.

Li, Tania Murray. 2000. "Articulating Indigenous Identity in Indonesia: Resource Politics and the Tribal Slot", *Comparative Studies in Society and History* 42 (1): 149–179.

Liu Institute for Global Issues and Gulu District NGO Forum. 2005. *RocoWat I Acholi: Restoring Relationships in Acholi-land: Traditional Approaches to Justice and Reintegration.* Vancouver: University of British Columbia Press.

Lundy, Patricia and Mark McGovern. 2006. "Participation, Truth and Partiality: Participatory Action Research, Community-based Truth-telling and Post-conflict Transition in Northern Ireland", *Sociology* 40 (1): 71–88.

Lynch, Gabrielle. 2011 "Becoming Indigenous in the Pursuit of Justice: The African Commission on Human and Peoples' Rights and the Endorois", *African Affairs* 111 (442): 24–45.

Mac Ginty, Roger. 2015. "Where is the local? Critical localism and peacebuilding", *Third World Quarterly* 36 (5): 840–856.

McEvoy, Kieran and Lorna McGregor (eds.). 2008. *Transitional Justice from Below: Grassroots Activism and the Struggle for Change.* London: Hart Publishing.

McWilliam, Andrew. 2007. "Meto Disputes and Peacemaking: Cultural Notes on Conflict and its Resolution in West Timor", *The Asia Pacific Journal of Anthropology* 8 (1): 75–91.

Merry, Sally Engle. 1988. "Legal Pluralism", *Law and Society Review* 22 (5): 869–896.

Merry, Sally Engle. 2003. "Human Rights Law and the Demonization of Culture (And Anthropology Along the Way)", *PoLAR: Political and Legal Anthropology Review* 26 (1): 55–76.

Mironko, Charles. 2006. "Ibitero: Means and Motive in the Rwandan Genocide". In *Genocide in Cambodia and Rwanda: New Perspectives*, edited by Susan E. Cook, 163–190. New Brunswick, NJ: Transaction Publishers.

Montgomery, Heather. 2001. "Imposing Rights? A Case Study of Child Prostitution in Thailand". In *Culture and Rights: Anthropological Perspectives*, edited by Jane K. Cowan, Marie-Benedicte Dembour and Richard A. Wilson, 80–101. Cambridge, UK: Cambridge University Press.

Nordstrom, Carolyn. 1998. "Terror Warfare and the Medicine of Peace", *Medical Anthropology Quarterly* 12 (1): 103–121.

Office of the United Nations High Commissioner for Human Rights. 2010. *Report of the Mapping Exercise documenting the most serious violations of human rights and international humanitarian law committed within the territory of the Democratic Republic of the Congo between March 1993 and June 2003.* Geneva: Office of the United Nations High Commissioner for Human Rights.

Pain, Dennis. 1997. *"The Bending of Spears": Producing Consensus for Peace and Development in Northern Uganda.* London: International Alert.

Reyntjens, Filip. 1990. "Le gacaca ou la justice du gazon au Rwanda", *Politique Africaine* 40: 31–41.

Reyntjens, Filip and Stef Vandeginste. 2005. "Rwanda: An Atypical Transition". In *Roads to Reconciliation*, edited by Elin Skaar, Siri Gloppen and Astri Suhrke, 101–127. Lanham, MD: Lexington Books.

Richards, Paul. 1996. *Fighting for the Rain Forest: War, Youth and Resources in Sierra Leone*. London: Heinemann.

Rose, Laurel L. 1992. *The Politics of Harmony: Land Dispute Strategies in Swaziland*. Cambridge, UK: Cambridge University Press.

Shaw, Rosalind and Lars Waldorf. 2010. "Introduction: Localizing Traditional Justice". In *Localizing Transitional Justice: Interventions and Priorities after Mass Violence*, edited by Rosalind Shaw, Lars Waldorf and Pierre Hazan, 3–26. Stanford, CA: Stanford University Press.

Stovel, Laura. 2008. "'There's no bad bush to throw away a bad child': 'tradition'-inspired reintegration in post-war Sierra Leone", *The Journal of Modern African Studies* 46 (2): 305–324.

Straus, Scott. 2006. *The Order of Genocide: Race, Power, and War in Rwanda*. Ithaca, NY: Cornell University Press.

Sylvain, Renée. 2014. "Essentialism and the Indigenous Politics of Recognition in Southern Africa", *American Anthropologist* 116 (2): 251–264.

Theidon, Kimberly. 2009. "Editorial Note", *International Journal of Transitional Justice* 3 (3): 295–300.

Thomson, Susan. 2011. "The Darker Side of Transitional Justice: The Power Dynamics Behind Rwanda's Gacaca Courts", *Africa* 81 (3): 373–390.

Turner, Terence. 1991. "Representing, Resisting, Rethinking: Historical Transformations of Kayapo Culture and Anthropological Consciousness". In *Colonial Situations: History of Anthropology*, edited by George W. Stocking, 285–313. Madison, WI: University of Wisconsin Press.

United Nations. 1994. *Report of the Secretary-General on the situation in Rwanda*. S/1994/640. 31 May. New York: United Nations.

United Nations. 2004. *The Rule of Law and Transitional Justice in Conflict and Post-Conflict Societies*. New York: United Nations.

Waldorf, Lars. 2006. "Mass Justice for Mass Atrocity: Rethinking Local Justice as Transitional Justice", *Temple Law Review* 79 (1): 1–88.

Waldorf, Lars. 2010. "'Like Jews Waiting for Jesus': Posthumous Justice in Post-Genocide Rwanda". In *Localizing Transitional Justice: Interventions and Priorities after Mass Violence*, edited by R. Shaw, L. Waldorf and Pierre Hazan, 183–204. Stanford, CA: Stanford University Press.

Zechenter, Elizabeth M. 1997. "In the Name of Culture: Cultural Relativism and the Abuse of the Individual", *Journal of Anthropological Research* 53 (3): 319–347.

Zorbas, Eugenia. 2009. "What does reconciliation after genocide mean? Public transcripts and hidden transcripts in post-genocide Rwanda", *Journal of Genocide Research* 11 (1): 127–147.

3

MEMORY AND TESTIMONY IN THE AFTERMATH OF VIOLENT CONFLICT

Writing in the context of the Spanish civil war (1936–1939), Madeleine Davis (2005, 866–867) distinguishes between "personal memory" (of an individual), "historical memory" (official records and the writing of history) and "collective memory" (public, social and cultural practices for narrating the past). "Collective" or "social memory" is "the means by which information is transmitted among individuals and groups and from one generation to another" (Crumley 2002, 40; see Connerton 1990, 37). "Personal memory" of violent conflict never exists in isolation from "collective memory", which is itself in an on-going, evolving relationship with "historical memory", produced by, among others, historians, journalists, truth commissioners (see Chapter 6) and judges (see Chapter 5).

This relationship is illustrated by testimony about the Northern Irish "Troubles" (1969–1997) given by Protestants living in the predominantly Roman Catholic/republican county of South Armagh. Anthropologists Hastings Donnan and Kirk Simpson (2007, 22) provide three accounts of the killing of a part-time soldier in the early 1970s by republican paramilitaries. The first account is an eyewitness testimony given by the man's widow in 2001; the second an account given in 2004 by a member of a support group for Protestant victims of the "Troubles"; and the third an account published in a local newspaper in 2006. All three accounts are almost identical despite being narrated three years apart by different people in different places. The account shifts from being "personal memory" (of the widow) to "historical memory" (the newspaper article) while also being "collective memory", having become an emblematic "account that others can tell" in order to communicate "group belonging" (Donnan & Simpson 2007, 22; see Jessee 2016).

In addition to investigating the three forms of memory (personal, collective, historical), anthropologists have also concerned themselves with the way in which there is "implicit transmission" (Wajnryb 1999, 84) of memory through embodiment (see Green 1994; Kleinman and Kleinman 1994; Samuels 2016) and how this relates to the inter-generational transmission of memory (see Argenti & Schramm 2010). Embodiment and inter-generational transmission are illustrated by anthropologist Julia Dickson-Gomez's (2002) description of survivors of state violence during the Salvadoran civil war (1979–1992) between the military-led government and the Farabundo Martí National Liberation Front (a coalition of five left-wing guerrilla groups). Dickson-Gomez describes how survivors displayed *nervios*, a catch-all term for illness caused by trauma (including headaches, stomach problems and insomnia). Dickson-Gomez (2002, 420 428) suggests that the embodied memory of the parents is "transmitted implicitly to children as parents' *nervios* creates an environment of distrust, confusion, and resentment in the family". Whilst I acknowledge that personal, historical and collective memory (with inter-generational and embodied expressions) are interconnected, I have chosen in this chapter to concentrate on the initial verbal narration and dissemination of personal memory (see Quesada 1998).

The chapter begins by considering the evolution of what Rosalind Shaw (2007b, 189) describes as a global paradigm of "redemptive remembering through truth-telling" and the critique of this perspective from anthropologists. The remainder of the chapter considers insights from anthropologists and other ethnographers regarding how memory operates in the aftermath of violent conflict, asking what the relationship is between "forensic truth" and the "narrative truth" of the survivor and what status should be given to testimonies that are always "co-productions" with others.

The "age of testimony"

The contemporary period has been described as an "age of testimony" (Felman & Laub 1992, 201) in which a "charismatic victim" has emerged and become the "basis for dealing with past atrocities" (Bonacker 2013, 115 101). In this "age of testimony" the "victim's word can no longer be doubted" (Fassin & Rechtman 2009, 29). The origins of the "age of testimony" can be traced to the aftermath of the Holocaust, the genocide of more than six million Jews by the government of Nazi Germany between 1941 and 1945 (see Rees 2017). While the International Military Tribunal (Major War Criminals) at Nuremberg (1945–1946) relied on documents to prosecute twenty-four high-ranking Nazis, the trial of Adolf Eichmann (German SS-Obersturmbannführer and a key organiser of the Holocaust) in Jerusalem in 1962 for "crimes against the Jewish people" relied on the testimonies of victim-witnesses. Although the Israeli prosecutor, Gideon Hausner (1967, 291–292) knew that only a fraction of the Nazi archives "would have sufficed to get Eichmann sentenced ten times over", Hausner believed that only "the various narratives of different people about diverse experiences would be concrete enough to be apprehended" (see Landsman 2012). As a consequence, 112 witnesses, many of them Holocaust survivors, were called to give testimony in the trial (Cesarani 2005, 262). Up to that point, survivors had been reticent to talk of their experiences because of a desire to (re)integrate in the USA and Europe (see Novick 2001, 121) and because the new Israeli state only celebrated "valiant partisan fighters", while "personal tales of non-combatant survivor suffering were derided" (Kidron 2010, 433).

70   Memory and testimony

The decision by Hausner to place witness testimony at the heart of a "testimonial theatre" (Bachmann 2010, 109) that would "reach the hearts of men" (Hausner 1967, 291) transformed the way the Holocaust was remembered in that it "came to be defined as a succession of individual experiences with which the public was supposed to identify" (Wieviorka 2006a, 88; see Galchinsky 2010, 9). As the "advent of the witness" (Wieviorka 2006b, 389), the Eichmann trial bequeathed a paradigmatic template for the contemporary "Era of the Witness" (Wieviorka 2006a), in which the individual experiences of those affected by violence are collected and used in human rights reporting, truth commissions (see Chapter 4) and criminal trials (see Chapter 5).

The privileged position now given to the "charismatic victim" is reflected in the constant call for the collection and preservation of survivor memory (see Ley-desdorff 2009, 23), that survivors' experiences of death and loss should be gathered, preserved and acknowledged lest survivors be "condemned to dwell alone and nameless in the ruins of memory" (Das 1996, 69). Given the argument that the experience of violence defies language (see Green 1994, 230; Morris 1997, 27–28; Scarry 1985), the opportunity to tell one's story is promoted as the means to re-establish "a sense of self in time and place" (Ross 2003b, 330; see Agger & Jensen 1990). The "telling of truth", it is argued, "turns the survivors from objects to subjects" (Mertus 2000, 149), thereby enabling "healing" and future peace. Such an approach is reflected in a poster of the Sierra Leone Truth and Reconciliation Commission written in Krio (the English-based creole spoken in the capital and to a lesser degree elsewhere in the country) which read *Tru at fo tok, but naim nomo go bring pis* ("It's hard to speak the truth, but only this will bring peace") (Shaw 2007b, 199) and a poster at the public hearings of the Human Rights Violation Committee (HRVC) of the South African Truth and Reconciliation Commission (SATRC) which read "Revealing is healing" (Ross 2003a, 79).

Anthropologists have been sympathetic to the proposal that telling one's experience of violent conflict is a means to recovery. Veena Das and Arthur Kleinman (2001, 6), for example, argue that "Finding one's voice in the making of one's history" is necessary to "generate new contexts through which everyday life may become possi-ble". As noted in the Introduction, John Borneman (2002, 289 296) argues that "witnessing", as a form of "cultivated listening" for "truth" by a third party, will enable "truth-telling" and that giving victims a voice will create a "sense of ending, rupture, and break with the past". Likewise, Michael Jackson (2002, 245) writes:

> To relate a story is to retrace one's steps, going over the ground of one's life again, reworking reality to render it more bearable. … In this way we gain some purchase over events that confounded us, humbled us and left us helpless. In telling a story we renew our faith that the world is within our grasp.

While anthropologists clearly see value in "truth-telling", they (and other scholars) have also voiced concern about what Shaw (2007b, 189) describes as a global paradigm of "redemptive remembering through truth-telling". It has been argued, for example, that survivor testimony has become embedded in a parasitic "Human

Rights Industry" (Hopgood 2013) in which the testimony of victims allows those in Europe and North America to represent themselves as "saviours", thereby recreating a colonial, civilising "international hierarchy of race and colour" (Mutua 2001) and reproducing disempowering caricatures that serve to obscure individual biography (see Kennedy 2002; LaCapra 2001; Ticktin 1999). Likewise, anthropologist Christopher Colvin (2006, 172) describes a "global political economy of traumatic storytelling" in which "the memories of victimhood are commoditized: the remembrance of pain is commercialised" to satisfy jaded "westerners" in search of experience (see Linke 2009, 155; Schaffer & Smith 2004, 13–14 27 32 36–37). It is suggested that this perpetuates "geopolitical and institutional privilege" (Madlingozi 2010, 210), the consumption of "sad sentimental stories" (Rorty 1982) strengthening the structural superiority of audience(s) in the Global North in relation to victims in the Global South (see Razack 2007, 376 384). As political scientist Adam Branch (2011, 127) warns, the desire for collecting and preserving testimony of violent conflict can reduce "the victim of violence to a natural resource, grist for the advocacy mills ... to be exported and processed abroad by Western human rights organisations into human rights reports".

Writing in the context of the Khulumani ("Speak Out") Support Group that represents victims and survivors of gross human rights violations committed under apartheid in South Africa (1948–1994), the legal sociologist Tshepo Madlingozi (2010) sees a relationship between the collection of testimonies for human rights reporting and the "rescuing" mission of colonialisation (see Abu-Lughod 2002; Spivak 1988, 297). Madlingozi (2010, 210) suggests that the "practice of speaking for and about victims further perpetuates their disempowerment and marginality", given that those who "mine" the stories of victims do so "by dint of our geopolitical and institutional privilege". Madlingozi (2010, 210) suggests that those who collect and disseminate testimonies (what he terms "transitional justice entrepreneurs") get to speak on behalf of victims:

> not because the latter invited and gave her a mandate but because the entrepreneur sought the victim out, categorized her, defined her, theorized her, packaged her, and disseminated her on the world stage. Having "mined" the story in order to use it in the First World ... the entrepreneur reinforces her status as the authoritative knower who is ordained to teach, civilize and rescue the benighted, hapless victim.

A consequence of testimonies being "mined" (Madlingozi 2010, 210) and treated as a "natural resource" (Branch 2011, 127) is that those who give testimony may become alienated from their testimony. This occurs because elements are either "edited in" or "edited out" of testimony. The legal scholar Michelle McKinley (1997, 74) illustrates "editing in" with the case of a Zimbabwean asylum seeker who was able to recount her experience of rape with "emotional detachment" but whose lawyers wanted her to inhabit the subject position of a "deeply disturbed and traumatised" person in order to present a story of persecution. Working on the

72 Memory and testimony

case as a law student, McKinley (1997, 75) admits that in order to create a statement that the judge would believe she found herself "'editing in' sentiments of resentment, vulnerability and loss which completely contravened everything [the asylum seeker] said and certainly contradicted her attitude". The asylum seeker was initially furious when the statement was read back to her, although she eventually conceded and was granted asylum.

While McKinley's example illustrates how elements of a testimony can be "edited in", aspects of testimony can also be "edited out". Anthropologist Fiona Ross (2003b, 335) notes how testimonies given at the SATRC would circulate beyond the control of those who had testified, as the testimonies were "reported and repeated in the media, on the internet, reproduced and analysed by scholars and others" (Ross 2003b, 335; see Henri 2003). To illustrate the consequences of this, Ross (2003a) provides the example of Yvonne Khutwane, an ANC activist who had been arrested and detained (1985–1986) for political activities and who was one of the few women activists to testify before the HRVC of the SATRC. In the course of her testimony, and in response to persistent questions from a member of the commission, Mrs Khutwane described being sexually molested by two white police officers, an event not mentioned in her original statement to the SATRC. At the time of the public hearing of the HRVC in 1996, both Mrs Khutwane and the SATRC presented her story as emblematic of the experience of political activists. Newspaper reports, however, focused on the sexual assault and omitted to mention that she only described it in response to persistent questions from commissioners. Ross (2003a, 93) argues that the manner in which Mrs Khutwane's testimony was reported meant that, rather than being recognised as a political activist who had suffered different forms of violence (solitary confinement, torture, beating), her experience was reduced to being a victim of sexual molestation. This illustrates how testimonies tend to pass through a "collage of intervening presences – witness, editor, transcriber, translator, reader" so that the text "reflects the different voices, styles of expression, perceptions of 'truth', and political agendas of each and every participant in its chain of production" (Douglass 2003, 68).

Caroline Williamson's (2016) study of the testimony of female survivors of the 1994 Rwandan genocide of the Tutsi who gave testimony to the Genocide Archive of Rwanda illustrates the effect of such "intervening presences". Williamson (2016, 34) notes how the women in their video testimonies given in Kinyarwanda actively contest the dominant perception of Rwandan survivors as "passive, voiceless victims of inevitable, unstoppable violence" by highlighting the complicity of certain foreign nations in the genocide and the failure of the international community to prevent the genocide or stop it once it was underway (see Dallaire & Beardsley 2004). Despite this, "interventions by translators and editors" end up reinforcing the very perception the women wished to contest (Williamson 2016, 36). By comparing the original Kinyarwanda interview with the French or English translations, Williamson (2016, 37) demonstrates that the "translator's overall tendency is to portray the Rwandan woman as more accepting of their situation and less critical of the West", presenting them as "stoical victims, rather than outspoken critics". Furthermore, some of the translated testimonies have been collated in a book in which Williamson (2016, 41 45) detects "systematic alterations" of the testimonies that perpetuate the "stereotypes of Western heroes saving poor, helpless African victims by omitting survivor's criticisms of the West". Given that the book contains no information about the translation and editing process, readers may be deceived into believing that it contains the "unrestricted voices of Rwandan survivors" (Williamson 2016, 46). The material considered by Williamson (2016) is an example of the process described by anthropologist Brigittine French (2009, 97) as "entextualisation", in which oral testimony is translated from one language to another, is then transcribed and then extracts are taken from the transcript and inserted in a report or book which may, in turn, be selectively quoted in other reports. The examples provided by Ross and Williamson suggest that those who are encouraged to give testimony must face the possibility that their private memory is transformed by the way the media present it, or by the way it is presented in an academic publication (including the book you are reading) (see Byrne 2004; Donnan & Simpson 2007, 24; Eltringham 2003).

In addition to the way in which "intervening presences" (Douglass 2003, 68) distort testimonies, anthropologists have argued, more generally, that Eurocentric assumptions underpin the notion of "redemptive remembering through truth-telling" (Shaw 2007b, 189). Shaw (2007b, 193) provides an account of the development of the "hegemonic, historically constituted Western memory discourse". Drawing on Talal Asad's genealogy of discipline and power in the church (Asad 1993, 83–167), Shaw (2007b, 192) notes how the medieval Church made the practice of verbal confession a universal discipline, whereby verbalising "what lay hidden within the conscience was to produce the truth that restored the confessing sinner to spiritual health". In addition, since the 19th century, psychoanalytical ideas regarding the "cathartic release" of "repressed memories" have "all seeped into American and European consciousness through the development of 'therapy culture'" (Shaw 2007b, 192; see Moon 2009). This has converged with the psychiatric condition of post-traumatic stress disorder (PTSD) and its treatment by narrating traumatic events from the past (Shaw 2007b, 192). Combined, these three developments, principally in North America and Europe, have naturalised the idea that "explicit verbal recounting" will lead to healing (Shaw 2007a, 67).

Shaw's argument that the "universal" value placed on speaking about the past may be particular to Europe and North America is supported by Derek Summerfield (formerly the principal psychiatrist for the Medical Foundation for the Care of Victims of Torture). Like Shaw, Summerfield (1999, 1449–1451) notes how in the last fifty years the "Western trauma discourse" has "come to be experienced as natural and self-evident". Summerfield (1999, 1455) warns, however, that what "constitutes psychological knowledge is the product of a particular culture at a particular point in time". Summerfield (1999, 1452–1454) notes that psychological responses are not the same as physical trauma (such as the universal consequences of being hit by a bullet in the leg). This means that suffering is context-specific in that it "arises from, and is resolved in, a social context, shaped by meanings and understandings applied to events" (Summerfield 1999, 1454). In other words,

74 Memory and testimony

people engage with memories of violent conflict within a particular social context and "speaking the truth" may not be a chosen response because "many non-Western cultures have little place for the revelation of intimate material outside the family circle and consider 'active forgetting' as a normative means of coping" (Summerfield 2000, 429).

Summerfield (1999, 1456) notes that, despite the "received wisdom" that victims must "emotionally ventilate" and "work through" what has happened to them, "there is no objective evidence of the efficacy of psychological debriefing after trauma" and "little empirical knowledge of these processes" (see Mendeloff 2004). The clinical psychologist Karen Brounéus (2008, 52) sought to rectify the lack of knowledge by exploring *Inkiko-Gacaca* (*gacaca* tribunals) in Rwanda which "leaned heavily on the modern (and largely western) notion that truth telling is therapeutic for individuals as well as for local and national communities" (Waldorf 2010, 198) (see Introduction and Chapter 2). Brounéus (2008) conducted interviews with sixteen female genocide survivors who had given evidence in *Inkiko-Gacaca* following the 1994 genocide of the Tutsi in Rwanda. Brounéus (2008, 71) found that giving testimony involved intense psychological suffering for all of the women and none of them considered it a "healing experience". Part of the reason for this, Brounéus (2008, 62) suggests, is that therapy normally takes place over the longer term in a safe and controlled environment in a trusting relationship with a trained therapist. In contrast, giving testimony in *Inkiko-Gacaca* (or a truth commission; see Chapter 4) is analogous to "one-session psychological debriefing", a practice discredited among psychologists as it may increase the risk of PTSD and depression. In addition to the negative experience of testifying, Brounéus (2008, 71–72) also found that the women had been harassed before, during and after giving testimony; that several had no family left; and many lived with chronic health problems due to having been subjected to sexual violence during the 1994 genocide. Brounéus (2008, 72) argues that this wider environment must also be taken into account when promoting "talking cures" and concludes that "assumptions about truth-telling may be more based on theoretical thinking than on reality".

So far I have suggested that privileging "truth-telling" as a response to violent conflict may be based on European and North American assumptions that reflect and strengthen "geopolitical and institutional privilege" (Madlingozi 2010, 210). While this suggests caution in promoting "redemptive remembering through truth-telling" (Shaw 2007b, 189), such "truth-telling" may also be resisted by survivors. As I discussed in the Introduction, anthropologists have argued that survivors of violent conflict may avoid talking about the past because of "cultural" beliefs or socio-economic survival (see Millar 2011). In Mozambique, for example, the reintegration rituals described by Alcinda Manuel Honwana (2005, 95) did not involve "verbal exteriorisation" because to "talk and recall the past is not necessarily seen as a prelude to healing or diminishing pain", but is often "believed to open the space for the malevolent forces to intervene". In Banja Luka, the capital of Republika Srpska in Bosnia-Herzegovina, Anders Stefansson (2010, 66) reports that economic interdependence required "silencing sensitive political and moral questions related to the recent war". Also speaking of Bosnia-Herzegovina, Marita Eastmond and Johanna Mannergren Selimovic (2012, 522) note that "livelihood concerns tend to compel people towards the pragmatic, putting aside the conflicting narratives of the war to focus on managing the present, rather than scrutinizing the past".

While "cultural beliefs" or "economic" reconciliation (Strupinskienė 2016, 3–5) may prevent people testifying about the past, there is also "the ethics of inciting people to talk about things that we cannot repair" (Shaw & Waldorf 2010, 13). Anthropologist Jennie Burnet (2008, 181) quotes a Rwandan Tutsi survivor widowed in the 1994 genocide, "We cannot forget the wounds we have in our hearts, but the *Gacaca* [process] has warned us to be patient and courageous [But in] everything I do I am reminded that I am alone." Reflecting on this, Burnet (2008, 182) suggests that:

> The fundamental message here is that there can be no justice for genocide survivors. Whether through Gacaca or any other judicial process, genocide survivors will never have justice, because the gaping holes in their lives cannot be filled. No one can bring their dead family members back to life.

Anthropologist Kimberly Theidon (2007, 461) provides a similar example in the context of the Peruvian Truth and Reconciliation Commission (CVR, Comisión de la Verdad y Reconciliación del Perú) established in 2000. When a testimony-taking unit of the CVR asked a focus group of peasant women about Sendero Luminoso ("Shining Path", a communist organisation that fought the government from 1980 to 2000), one woman stated, with affirmative murmurs from other women in the group, "When I forget, I'm well. Remembering – even now, I just go crazy. I can hardly stand it. But I'm so-so when I forget" and, later, "We just want to forget". If giving testimony in *Inkiko-Gacaca* or the CVR brought so little benefit to survivors (and may have been detrimental in terms of their physical and economic security, as Brounéus suggests), is it ethical to insist that such individuals can only "move on" if they tell their story?

In this section I have suggested that in the "age of testimony" (Felman & Laub 1992, 201) a global paradigm of "redemptive remembering through truth-telling" (Shaw 2007b, 189) has asserted that survivors of violent conflict must "emotionally ventilate" and "work through" what has happened to them (Summerfield 1999, 1456). Research suggests, however, that, despite claims to universality, this approach is culturally specific; may be contrary to "cultural" assumptions; may not actually help survivors and tends to portray them as abject victims. In the discussion so far I have considered criticism of the promotion of "truth-telling" in the aftermath of violent conflict. I shall now consider what is meant by the term "truth".

Forensic vs narrative truth

The global paradigm of "redemptive remembering through truth-telling" (Shaw 2007b, 189) claims that those who have experienced violent conflict should seek "to construct narrative plots with a beginning and an end in order to get necessary

76 Memory and testimony

continuity in their lives" (Mannergren Selimovic 2015, 233). This can lead to an assumption that testimony is a "kind of 'pure' utterance and 'authentic' transmission of experience" (Douglass 2003, 56). Memory, however, is "inherently revisionist" (Samuel 1994, 236). Cornelia Sorabji (2006, 4) notes, for example, how, over time, the narratives of those who had survived the siege of Sarajevo (1992–1996) by the army of Republika Srpska took on a "more organized, 'story-like' form", that survivors of violent conflict "impose narrative structure on memories" (see Das & Kleinman 2001, 6; Godfrey & Richardson 2004, 144; Vansina 1980, 262). This development over time is summarised by the anthropologist Michael Jackson (2002, 15): "To reconstitute events in a story is no longer to live those events in passivity, but to actively rework them, both in dialogue with others and in one's own imagination." As a consequence, memory is transformed "as it is replayed, recited, reworked and reconstrued in the play of intersubjective life" (Jackson 2002, 41).

Given such changes over time, testimonies are not straightforwardly "objective truth". Nora Strejilevich (2006, 703) a survivor of the "Dirty War" (1976–1983) in Argentina in which up to 30,000 people suspected of opposing the military government were killed, argues that testimony after violent conflict gives voice to an "intimate, subjective, deep" account of that experience and that this purpose is overlooked when testimony is only defined "as a means to provide information and knowledge based on facts". In other words, survivor testimony is not simply a matter of recounting "objective facts", but entails "an amount of forgetting, of readjusting history in relation to a changing present and reenvisioned future" (Eastmond & Mannergren Selimovic 2012, 506). Reflecting on the difference between survivor testimony and a factual report, the final report of the SATRC distinguished between "factual or forensic truth" and "personal or narrative truth" (Truth and Reconciliation Commission 1998, 1:112; see Felman & Laub 1991, 59–60; Leydesdorff 2009, 23; Payne 2008, 197–228; Wilson 2001, 37). Echoing Strejilevich, archivist scholar Eric Ketelaar (2012, 210) defines narrative truth as a testimony that "does not strive at factual truth, but attempts to explain why, according to the narrator, things happened and to give meaning to these events, both to the individual narrator and to society".

Erin Baines and Beth Stewart (2011) illustrate "narrative truth" with the example of Ajok, an Acholi women who, having been abducted by the Ugandan rebel group the Lord's Resistance Army (LRA; see Chapter 2), was forced to become a co-wife to a commander and bear him two children before she escaped and returned to her community. Baines and Stewart organised monthly storytelling sessions facilitated and attended by twenty-seven formerly abducted women over a period of eighteen months, replicating the Acholi communal practice of *wang-o* ("telling stories around the fire pit") (Baines & Stewart 2011, 4). The stories Ajok told at the *wang-o* concerned the cultural norms that had been transgressed in the bush, especially being forced to marry before she was socially or culturally ready (Baines & Stewart 2011, 3). Ajok recounted how she sought "to preserve her girlhood at great cost" when forced to marry; that she was "a good and honest wife and co-wife"; and that, on her return to her community, she strove to be a "productive and independent member of society" (Baines & Stewart 2011, 8–12). Ajok's stories were designed to reject the shame thrust upon her as a "bush wife" by her suspicious family and community by emphasising her innocence and reaffirming her self-worth, asserting that she is, and always had been, *dano adana* (a "human person"; a legitimate Acholi woman). (Re)constructing life stories in this way allowed survivors such as Ajok to restore their humanity and to "renegotiate their social marginalization and insist on their innocence" (Baines & Stewart 2011, 3). Baines and Stewart (2011, 16) suggest that because the principal purpose of Ajok's story was to "make sense of the experiences and reclaim her status and self-worth", "facts and information" were secondary. What is important in testimony by survivors such as Ajok, therefore, is "not an objective truth, but rather how the participants observe their lives and the environment in which they struggle to survive" (Baines & Stewart 2011, 5).

That "facts and information" may be secondary to the purpose of testimony is also apparent when the speaker chooses to speak of the collective, rather than solely individual, experience of violent conflict. This is the case for *testimonio*, a form of testimony that originated in Latin America in the 1970s and 1980s which is concerned with collective accountability and the need for social change (see Douglass 2003, 61–62; Maclean 2008). The literary and cultural critic John Beverley (1996) defines *testimonio* as "a novel or novella-length written narrative … told in the first person by a narrator who is also the real protagonist or witness of the

FIGURE 3.1 A neighbour walking home past a *wang-o* ("telling stories around the fire pit") set up for the evening in Pabo, northern Uganda. (Photo courtesy of Erin Baines)

78 Memory and testimony

events he or she recounts, and whose unit of narration is usually a 'life' or a significant life experience". The distinction with autobiography is that the narrative of *testimonio* is "always linked to a group or class situation marked by marginalisation, oppression and struggle" (Gelles 1998, 16). The purpose of *testimonio*, therefore, is not restricted to the individual experience of violence; rather, "*testimonios* tend to speak of collective experience and resist Western obsessions with individuality" (Hanlon & Shankar 2000, 267).

That *testimonio* is less a "factual or forensic truth" and more of a "personal or narrative truth" (Truth and Reconciliation Commission 1998, 1:112) is evident in the controversy surrounding Rigoberta Menchú's (1984) account of violence (including genocide) perpetrated against Mayan indigenous peoples in Guatemala by government forces (1960–1996). The factual veracity of Menchú's account was challenged by the anthropologist David Stoll (1999; see Sanford 1999). Reflecting on the controversy, Ana Douglass (2003, 80–81) suggests that "Menchú's conscious manipulation of the facts ... reveals more about her level of awareness of the expectations of her readership and international politics than about her own character". Douglass (2003, 81) argues that Menchú, by deliberately claiming to have witnessed things that she did not see, was able to make "'an unbelievable story' believable to the otherwise detached Western readership". Menchú chose to claim other people's experiences as her own in order to influence her intended audience.

The case of Rigoberta Menchú suggests that the intended audience envisaged by the person giving testimony may result in embellishment of the "factual truth". Not only do survivors tailor testimony according to anticipated audiences in this way, but this may give rise to multiple versions of a testimony because survivors interact with multiple audiences, including other "survivors in the local community, perpetrators in the local community ... national government officials, and international human rights advocates" (French 2009, 98; see Portelli 1998, 30). Diana Eades (2008, 213) notes that story-telling involves "different emphases for different audiences", including the choice of different words and expressions and the "omission of details from the original telling of the story, or inclusion of details not found in its original telling". In other words, as a "performed event" a testimony is "differently realized each time it is told" (Jackson 2002, 358). Testimonies are not, therefore, static and unchanging, but "particular instances ... told at particular times for particular audiences in specific contexts" (Ross 2003b, 332).

A final way in which survivor testimony is not simply a matter of recounting "objective facts" but is "reworked and reconstrued" (Jackson 2002, 22) in the "changing present" (Eastmond & Mannergren Selimovic 2012, 506) is what Primo Levi (an Italian–Jewish survivor of the Nazi extermination and labour camp Auschwitz-Birkenau in Poland) calls "foreign material" (Levi 1986, 130; see Douglas 2001, 142). "Foreign material" refers to information that survivors encounter after the fact, be it from other survivors, from the media and so on. This new information is then incorporated into and revises survivor testimony, leading to a "blurring of source distinctions" as "one cannot know from reading [a testimony] under what conditions a given piece of information had been introduced" (Jönsson & Linell 1991, 434). This was apparent in the trial of Adolf Eichmann mentioned above, at which Hannah Arendt (1994 [1963], 224) noted, having observed the trial, that almost none of the witnesses in the trial possessed the "capacity for distinguishing between things that had happened ... more than sixteen, and sometimes twenty, years ago, and what [they] had read and heard and imagined in the meantime" (see Eltringham 2013). The incorporation of "foreign material" into testimony was apparent in my own research at the International Criminal Tribunal for Rwanda (ICTR) (see Eltringham 2019, 147–149; see Chapter 5). For example, a protected Rwandan prosecution witness:

PROSECUTION LAWYER: Is there anything about any aspect of your testimony over the past two weeks that you wish to correct or amend?

WITNESS: Thank you. Regarding my testimony, what I would like to correct is what I said regarding the rally at Ruhengeri. I thought I said that I had seen [the accused] in Ruhengeri, but when the video footage of that rally was shown to me [in the courtroom] I realised that I had been mistaken. I saw somebody else, but he was not the one.

From that moment on the witness's testimony would have been altered by exposure to the video and it is unlikely that the reason for that alteration (viewing a video as part of giving testimony at the ICTR) would be acknowledged if the witness were to give testimony in the future.

In this section I have reflected on the way in which, rather than being an "authentic" transmission of experience (Douglass 2003, 56), testimony changes over time in order to give meaning to events in relation to a "changing present" (Eastmond & Mannergren Selimovic 2012, 506). This suggests that while giving testimony in the aftermath of violent conflict may benefit survivors, as in the case of Ajok, survivor testimony is not a static, factual account but a "personal or narrative truth" (Truth and Reconciliation Commission 1998, 1:112) that will change over time as it is delivered to different audiences and incorporates "foreign material".

The co-production of testimony

The previous section placed emphasis on the way in which survivors of violent conflict fashion a "personal or narrative truth" in order to restore their humanity. Placing the emphasis solely on individual authorship may, however, be deceptive. While oral testimonies are described as allowing "survivors to speak for themselves" (Hartman 1995 192) so that their testimonies almost "appear to tell themselves" (Wilson 1997, 143), testimonies of violent conflict are not "intact and awaiting only the opportunity to be told" (Ross 2003a, 6). Rather, as indicated above, testimonies are "authored and authorised dialogically and collaboratively in the course of sharing one's recollections with others" (Jackson 2002, 22). In other words, testimonies are produced in dialogue with "elicitors", be they journalists, human rights researchers, academics, judges and so on (see Clark 2005; Eastmond 2007; Felman & Laub 1991, 57; Jackson 2002, 22; Maclean 2014; Vansina 2006 [1961], 29).

80 Memory and testimony

Testifying about the experience of violent conflict almost always relies on an elicitor who asks questions, so that testimony is the "result of a relationship, a common project in which both the informant and the researcher are involved together" (Portelli 1981, 103; see Vansina 2006 [1961], 29). For example, Rigobertu Menchú's narrative was fundamentally shaped by the questions put to her by Burgos (a comrade in arms), questions later removed from the final text (see Eltringham 2014, 203; Gelles 1998, 16; Spivak 2006, 22). This implies that testimonies are not simply "intact and awaiting only the opportunity to be told" (Ross 2003a, 6), but only come into existence when called forth by another person (see Laub 1992, 57).

The suggestion that it is the elicitor who "establishes the basis of narrative authority" (Portelli 1998, 28) is supported by the way in which commissioners of the HRVC at the SATRC often interrupted the testimony of witnesses (see Blommaert et al. 2006, 46; Chapter 4). Jan Blommaert, Mary Bock and Kay McCormick (2006, 47) give the example of a Nomonde Tyali who testified about the killing of her nephew by the South African Defence Force in 1989. Of the 1,680 words in the text of her hearing, her contribution amounted to only 657 words, in contrast to 1,023 words spoken by the HRVC chairperson. This indicates that "the commissioners wanted to have full control over the testimonies, not only by asking certain questions and by interrupting the testifiers, but also by preventing them from talking about unanticipated topics" (Verdoolaege 2002, 11).

The example of Nomonde Tyali suggests that, whereas many testimonies are co-productions, the elicitor can come to dominate the process. This is illustrated by Michele Langfield and Pam Maclean (2009, 199) who argue that while it is claimed that the collection of video testimonies of Holocaust survivors provides "'direct' access to the memories of survivors", such testimonies are, in reality, the products of a complex process of construction in which the witness and interviewer make choices that shape the final structure and content of the video testimony. Langfield and Maclean examined a selection of video testimonies held at the Jewish Holocaust Museum and Research Centre (JHMRC) in Melbourne, Australia. The JHMRC collection is a community project that arose out of the need for Holocaust survivors to speak after decades of silence. By 2007, 1,700 testimonies had been recorded (Langfield & Maclean 2009, 202). The interviewers are unpaid, non-academic volunteers, some of whom are survivors themselves. Interviewers use a standard chronology of the Holocaust in order to "make sense of first-person accounts by placing them within a chronology and ordering them into a comprehensible narrative structure" (Langfield & Maclean 2009, 204). This is done in order that the narratives are accessible to future viewers of the video testimony.

The standard chronology used at the JHMRC reflects the experience of Jews in western Poland (Langfield & Maclean 2009, 205). Problems arise, however, when a survivor's account deviates from this standard chronology and interviewers, unfamiliar with alternative Holocaust narratives, fail to understand what they are being told (Langfield & Maclean 2009, 205). Langfield and Maclean (2009) discuss the example of Rosa, who was deported from Hungary to Auschwitz-Birkenau in 1944. In Hungary, the ghettoisation and deportation process happened over a few weeks in 1944 and was, therefore, very different to the experience of Jews in Poland (Langfield & Maclean 2009, 205). Although the lack of awareness by Hungarian Jews of the Holocaust is well-documented, the non-survivor interviewer, unfamiliar with what happened in Hungary, challenged Rosa's narrative, "Well, you would have heard – this is the middle of 1944 – that the Germans were killing the Jews" (Langfield & Maclean 2009, 213). The interviewer's unwillingness to deviate from the standard, Poland-centric chronology meant that he tried to reconcile Rosa's testimony with the incompatible standard chronology (Langfield & Maclean 2009, 205). There is a need to be aware, therefore, that in using standardised questions to ensure that material is accessible and comparable, elicitors may suppress hitherto unrecorded experiences and, in the process, belittle the survivor (see discussion of SATRC statement-taking in Chapter 4).

The way in which the JHMRC's standard chronology suppresses hitherto unrecorded experiences is even more apparent in courtrooms (see Chapter 5) or activities that adopt legal fact-finding procedures, such as human rights reporting and truth commissions (see Chapter 4). Drawing on research in trials involving Aboriginal people in Australia, Eades (2008, 210) notes how there are "fundamental contradictions between everyday storytelling … and the expectations and interpretations of storytelling and retelling in court", because "the ways in which you tell your story in the legal process is very strange", delivered in "very short bits, segmented by lawyer questions". It is the lawyer's questions that "organise the story, deciding which parts can be told, and in what order, as well as what parts can't be told" (Eades 2008, 210). All of this relies on an arrangement that limits some speakers (lawyers) to ask questions, while others (witnesses) may only answer questions they are asked. As legal scholar Michael Conley and anthropologist William O'Barr (2005, 21) observe:

> The special rules of the courtroom are highly unusual from a conversational point of view. From an everyday perspective, it would be very peculiar to limit some speakers so that their only type of turn is asking questions, while restricting others to giving answers to whatever questions they are asked.

Research has also shown that a large number of questions put to witnesses in trials require a minimal response and that narrative answers are often avoided, with the result that "witnesses can hardly be thought to tell their stories in their own words" (Luchjenbroers 1997, 501; see Danet et al. 1976). Furthermore, given that witnesses can only speak when answering the question that has most recently been asked of them and that only lawyers and judges are permitted to ask questions, witnesses are prevented from "participating in meaningful negotiation on anything but the smallest point of clarification on this most immediate question" (Eades 2008, 212). What this means is that witnesses cannot "tell their own story in their own way" (Eades 2008, 212). The narrative sought by lawyers, human rights investigators and truth commissions does not correspond to the unmediated narrative witnesses would tell given the opportunity.

82 Memory and testimony

Another way in which the survivors lose control over their testimony is that they are not aware what the lawyer, human rights investigator or truth commissioner considers important. This can be illustrated by an example from my own research at the ICTR. A prosecution lawyer explained to me:

> We only need ten or fifteen minutes out of their whole lifetime. We're only interested in a tiny little part. We're not interested in the before or the after. They can't understand why this minuscule incident is so important. For example, a woman who was gang raped at four different locations. At the final location she became a "kept woman". When she came to give evidence we tell her that the benevolence of that final person vs. the horrific nature of previous events doesn't really matter because we want her to talk about being a kept woman against her will. We tell her "We just want you to talk about that little bit". But, they don't really want to talk about that, the least of the experiential issues. They want to talk about other things. Therefore, they're frustrated, they're not fulfilled because they haven't told their story.

Survivors of violent conflict may want to tell "whole stories" that reflect their whole lives. These would, however, be "complex and messy stories" (Crosby & Brinton Lykes 2011, 476; see Theidon 2007, 465 468), interweaving the actual event with the emotional aftermath (see Henry 2010, 1106), rather than the "skeletonisation of fact" (Geertz 1983, 170) required by lawyers, human rights investigators and truth commissioners who wish to "strip events of their subjective meanings in a pursuit of objectives legal facts" (Wilson 1997, 139; see Hinton 2016, 34).

In this section I have demonstrated that while it may be convenient to represent testimony as simply a matter of survivors speaking for themselves (see Hartman 1995 192), the decisive role played by those who elicit testimony from survivors of violent conflict needs to be taken into account (see Greenspan & Bolkosky 2006, 436). While the effect of the elicitor may be obscured in published accounts, an examination of video testimony demonstrates the complex process of construction in which the witness and interviewer make choices that shape the final structure and content of the video testimony (Langfield & Maclean 2009, 199). Likewise, lawyers, human rights investigators and truth commissioners use questions to "organise the story, deciding which parts can be told, and in what order, as well as what parts can't be told" (Eades 2008, 210), rather than leaving the survivor to express their testimony "in their own words". While it could be argued that such a process is unavoidable, it draws further attention to the "collage of intervening presences" (Douglass 2003, 68) involved in the production of testimony, and that this may result in those giving testimony experiencing a "loss of voice, of agency, and of self" (Ross 2003b, 335).

Conclusion

The collection and dissemination of testimony has become a naturalised response to violent conflict. Such a process, it is argued, serves those who have experienced violent conflict by creating a "sense of ending, rupture, and break with the past" (Borneman 2002, 289 296). There is concern, however, that such benefits have been elevated to a global paradigm of "redemptive remembering through truth-telling" (Shaw 2007b, 189) despite a lack of supporting evidence (Summerfield 1999, 1456); that the manner in which testimony is taken and disseminated may be detrimental to the person giving testimony (Brounéus 2008); and that the paradigm claims as universal assumptions that originate in Europe and North America.

There is a tension at the heart of the global paradigm of "redemptive remembering through truth-telling" (Shaw 2007b, 189). On one hand, the paradigm places great value on the personal accounts of survivors (which tend to be subjective), while on the other hand the paradigm uses such testimonies as if they are "forensic" accounts in human rights reports, truth commissions and criminal trials. The irony is that while survivors of violent conflict do benefit from giving testimony, in that they "make sense of the experiences and reclaim her status and self-worth" (Baines & Stewart 2011, 16), such testimonies should not be assessed only in terms of providing "information and knowledge based on facts" (Strejilevich 2006, 703). Rather than an "objective truth", such testimony should be understood as a "personal or narrative truth" (Truth and Reconciliation Commission 1998, 1:112) that changes depending on exposure to "foreign material" (Levi 1986, 130), different audiences (French 2009) and the changing needs of the present (see Eastmond & Mannergren Selimovic 2012).

That survivors may benefit from giving testimony should not, however, obscure the fact that testimony is generated in collaboration with an elicitor who co-authors the testimony and who may steer it in ways contrary to the intention of the survivor. There is a further process of "entextualisation"(French 2009, 97) in which oral testimony is translated from one language to another, is transcribed and extracts used in reports or a book which may, in turn, be selectively quoted in other reports or books. This can transform the original testimony in profound ways (see Williamson 2016). Human rights reports, for example, which are predominantly based on eye-witness testimony, "strip events of their subjective meanings in a pursuit of objective legal facts" in order that "the event can be comprehended by readers on the other side of the globe" (Wilson 1997, 135 139). As a consequence, "Subjectivity and information not immediately relevant to the prosecution of the individual case are dismissed" (Wilson 1997, 153) and only the "bare detail" is retained (Strathern 2004, 232; see Hastrup 2003). The "collage of intervening presences" (Douglass 2003, 68) between giving testimony and dissemination may lead those who give testimony to experience a "loss of voice, of agency, and of self" (Ross 2003b, 335).

Bibliography

Abu-Lughod, Lila. 2002. "Do Muslim Women Really Need Saving? Anthropological Reflections on Cultural Relativism and Its Others", *American Anthropologist* 104 (3): 783–790.

Agger, Ingrid and Soren Jensen. 1990. "Testimony as Ritual and Evidence in Psychotherapy for Political Refugees", *Journal of Traumatic Stress*: 3115–3130.

84 Memory and testimony

Arendt, Hannah. 1994 [1963]. *Eichmann in Jerusalem: A Report on the Banality of Evil.* Harmondsworth, UK: Penguin.

Argenti, Nicolas and Katharina Schramm (eds.). 2010. *Remembering Violence: Anthropological Perspectives on Intergenerational Transmission.* Oxford: Berghahn.

Asad, Talal. 1993. *Genealogies of Religion: Discipline and Reasons of Power in Christianity and Islam.* Baltimore, MD: Johns Hopkins University Press.

Bachmann, Michael. 2010. "Theatre and the Drama of the Law: A 'Theatrical History' of the Eichmann Trial", *Law Text Culture* 14 (1): 94–116.

Baines, Erin and Beth Stewart. 2011. "'I cannot accept what I have not done': Storytelling, Gender and Transitional Justice", *Journal of Human Rights Practice* 3 (3): 245–263.

Beverley, John. 1996. "The Margin at the Center: On testimonio (Testimonial Narrative)". In *The Real Thing: Testimonial Discourse and Latin America*, edited by Georg M. Gugelberger, 23–41. Durham, NC: Duke University Press.

Blommaert, Jan, Mary Bock and Kay McCormick. 2006. "Narrative inequality in the TRC hearings: On the hearability of hidden transcripts", *Journal of Language and Politics* 5 (1): 37–70.

Bonacker, Thorsten. 2013. "Global Victimhood: On the Charisma of the Victim in Transitional Justice Processes", *World Political Science Review* 9 (1): 2363–4782.

Borneman, John. 2002. "Reconciliation after ethnic cleansing: Listening, retribution, affiliation", *Public Culture* 14 (2): 281–304.

Branch, Adam. 2011. "Neither Liberal nor Peaceful? Practices of 'Global Justice' by the ICC". In *A Liberal Peace? The Problems and Practices of Peacebuilding*, edited by Susanna Campbell, David Chandler and Meera Sabaratnam, 121–137. London: Zed Books.

Brounéus, Karen. 2008. "Truth Telling as Talking Cure? Insecurity and Retraumatization in the Rwandan Gacaca Courts", *Security Dialogue* 39 (1): 55–76.

Burnet, Jennie E. 2008. "The Injustice of Local Justice: Truth, Reconciliation, and Revenge in Rwanda", *Genocide Studies and Prevention* 3 (2): 173–193.

Byrne, Catherine C. 2004. "Benefit or Burden: Victims' Reflections on TRC Participation", *Peace and Conflict: Journal of Peace Psychology* 10 (3): 237–256.

Cesarani, David. 2005. *Eichmann: His Life and Crimes.* London: Vintage.

Clark, Mary Marshall. 2005. "Resisting Attrition in Stories of Trauma", *Narrative* 13 (3): 294–298.

Colvin, Christopher J. 2006. "Trafficking trauma: Intellectual property rights and the political economy of traumatic storytelling", *Critical Arts: A Journal of South-North Cultural Studies* 20 (1): 171–182.

Conley, John M. and William M. O'Barr. 2005. *Just Words: Law, Language, and Power* (2nd edition). Chicago, IL: University of Chicago Press.

Connerton, Paul. 1990. *How Societies Remember.* Cambridge, UK: Cambridge University Press.

Crosby, Alison and M. Brinton Lykes. 2011. "Mayan women survivors speak: The gendered relations of truth telling in postwar Guatemala", *International Journal of Transitional Justice* 5 (3): 456–476.

Crumley, Carole. 2002. "Exploring Venues of Social Memory". In *Social Memory and History: Anthropological Approaches*, edited by Jacob Climo and Maria Cattell 39–52. Walnut Creek, CA: Altamira Press.

Dallaire, Roméo and Brent Beardsley. 2004. *Shake Hands with the Devil: The Failure of Humanity in Rwanda.* New York: Carroll and Graf.

Danet, Brenda, Kenneth B. Hoffman, Nicole C. Kermish, H. Jeffery Rafn and Deborah G. Stayman. 1976. "An Ethnography of Questioning in the Courtroom". In *Language Use and the Uses of Language*, edited by Roger W. Shuy and Anna Shnukal, 222–234. Washington, DC: Georgetown University Press.

Das, Veena. 1996. "Language and Body: Transactions in the Construction of Pain", *Daedalus* 125 (1).

Das, Veena and Arthur Kleinman. 2001. "Introduction". In *Remaking a World: Violence, Social Suffering, and Recovery*, edited by Veena Das, Arthur Kleinman, Margaret Lock, Mamphela Ramphela and Pamela Reynolds, 1–30. Berkeley, CA: University of California Press.

Davis, Madeleine. 2005. "Is Spain recovering its memory? Breaking the Pacto del Olvido", *Human Rights Quarterly* 27 (3): 858–880.

Dickson-Gomez, Julia. 2002. "The Sound of Barking Dogs: Violence and Terror among Salvadoran Families in the Postwar", *Medical Anthropology Quarterly* 16 (4): 415–438.

Donnan, Hastings and Kirk Simpson. 2007. "Silence and Violence among Northern Ireland Border Protestants", *Ethnos: Journal of Anthropology* 72 (1): 5–28.

Douglas, Lawrence. 2001. *The Memory of Judgment: Making Law and History in the Trials of the Holocaust*. New Haven, CT: Yale University Press.

Douglass, Ana. 2003. "The Menchu Effect: Strategies, Lies and Approximate Truths in Texts of Witness". In *Witness and Memory: The Discourse of Trauma*, edited by Ana Douglass and Thomas A. Vogler, 55–88. New York: Routledge.

Eades, Diana. 2008. "Telling and Retelling Your Story in Court: Questions, Assumptions and Intercultural Implications", *Current Issues in Criminal Justice* 20 (2): 209–230.

Eastmond, Marita. 2007. "Stories as Lived Experience: Narratives in Forced Migration Research", *Journal of Refugee Studies* 20 (2): 248–264.

Eastmond, Marita and Johanna Mannergren Selimovic. 2012. "Silence as Possibility in Postwar Everyday Life", *The International Journal of Transitional Justice* 6 (3): 502–524.

Eltringham, Nigel. 2003. "The Blind Men and the Elephant: The Challenge of Representing the Rwandan Genocide". In *The Ethics of Anthropology*, edited by Pat Caplan, 96–112. London: Routledge.

Eltringham, Nigel. 2013. "'Illuminating the Broader Context': Anthropological and Historical Knowledge at the International Criminal Tribunal for Rwanda", *Journal of the Royal Anthropological Institute*. 19 (2): 338–355.

Eltringham, Nigel. 2014. "Bodies of evidence: Remembering the Rwandan Genocide at Murambi". In *Remembering Genocide*, edited by Nigel Eltringham and Pam Maclean, 200–219. London: Routledge.

Eltringham, Nigel. 2019. *Genocide Never Sleeps: Living Law at the International Criminal Tribunal for Rwanda*. Cambridge, UK: Cambridge University Press.

Fassin, Didier and Richard Rechtman. 2009. *The Empire of Trauma: An Inquiry into the Condition of Victimhood*. Princeton, NJ: Princeton University Press.

Felman, Shoshana and Dori Laub. 1991. *Testimony*. New York: Routledge.

Felman, Shoshana and Dori Laub. 1992. *Testimony: Crises of Witnessing in Literature, Psychoanalysis, and History*. London: Routledge.

French, Brigittine M. 2009. "Technologies of Telling: Discourse, Transparency, and Erasure in Guatemalan Truth Commission Testimony", *Journal of Human Rights* 8 (1): 92–109.

Galchinsky, Michael. 2010. "The Problem with Human Rights Culture", *South Atlantic Review* 75 (2): 5–18.

Geertz, Clifford (ed.). 1983. "Local Knowledge: Fact and Law in Comparative Perspective". In *Local Knowledge*, 167–234. New York: Basic Books.

Gelles, Paul H. 1998. "Testimonio, Ethnography and Processes of Authorship", *Anthropology News* 39 (3): 16–16.

Godfrey, Barry S. and Jane C. Richardson. 2004. "Loss, collective memory and transcripted oral histories", *International Journal of Social Research Methodology* 7 (2): 143–155.

86 Memory and testimony

Green, Linda. 1994. "Fear as a Way of Life", *Cultural Anthropology* 9 (2): 227–256.

Greenspan, Henry and Sidney Bolkosky. 2006. "When Is an Interview an Interview? Notes from Listening to Holocaust Survivors", *Poetics Today* 27 (2): 431–449.

Hanlon, Catherine Nolin and Finola Shankar. 2000. "Gendered Spaces of Terror and Assault: The Testimonio of REMHI and the Commission for Historical Clarification in Guatemala", *Gender, Place & Culture: A Journal of Feminist Geography* 7 (3): 265–286.

Hartman, Geoffrey H. 1995 "Learning from Survivors: The Yale Testimony Project", *Holocaust and Genocide Studies* 9 (2): 192–207.

Hastrup, Kirsten. 2003. "Violence, Suffering and Human Rights: Anthropological Reflections", *Anthropological Theory* 3 (3): 309–323.

Hausner, Gideon. 1967. *Justice in Jerusalem*. London: Nelson.

Henri, Yazir. 2003. "Reconciling Reconciliation: A Personal and Public Journey of Testifying before the South African Truth and Reconciliation Commission". In *Political Transition: Politics and Cultures*, edited by Paul Gready, 262–275. London: Pluto.

Henry, Nicola. 2010. "The Impossibility of Bearing Witness: Wartime Rape and the Promise of Justice", *Violence Against Women* 16 (10): 1098–1119.

Hinton, Alexander Laban. 2016. *Man or Monster? The Trial of a Khmer Rouge Torturer*. London: Duke University Press.

Honwana, Alcinda Manuel. 2005. "Healing and Social Reintegration in Mozambique and Angola". In *Roads to Reconciliation*, edited by Elin Skaar, Siri Gloppen and Astri Suhrke, 83–100. Lanham, MD: Lexington Books.

Hopgood, Stephen. 2013. *The Endtimes of Human Rights*. Ithaca, NY: Cornell University Press.

Jackson, Michael. 2002. *The Politics of Storytelling: Violence, Transgression, and Intersubjectivity*. Copenhagen: Museum Tusculanum Press.

Jessee, Erin. 2016. "The danger of a single story: Iconic stories in the aftermath of the 1994 Rwandan genocide", *Memory Studies* 10 (2): 144–163.

Jönsson, Linda and Per Linell. 1991. "Story generations: From dialogical interviews to written reports in police interrogations", *Text and Talk* 2 (3): 419–440.

Kennedy, David W. 2002. "The International Human Rights Movement: Part of the Problem?", *Harvard Human Rights Journal*: 15 101–15126.

Ketelaar, Eric. 2012. "Truths, Memories and Histories in the Archives of the International Criminal Tribunal for the Former Yugoslavia". In *The Genocide Convention: The Legacy of 60 Years*, edited by Harmen van der Wilt, Jeroen Vervliet, Göran Sluiter and Johannes Houwink ten Cate, 199–221. Leiden: Brill.

Kidron, Carol A. 2010. "Embracing the lived memory of genocide: Holocaust survivor and descendant renegade memory work at the House of Being", *American Ethnologist* 37 (3): 429–451.

Kleinman, Arthur and Joan Kleinman. 1994. "How Bodies Remember: Social Memory and Bodily Experience of Criticism, Resistance, and Delegitimation following China's Cultural Revolution", *New Literary History* 25 (3): 707–723.

LaCapra, Dominick. 2001. *Writing History, Writing Trauma*. Baltimore, MD: Johns Hopkins University Press.

Landsman, Stephan. 2012. "The Eichmann Case and the Invention of the Witness-Driven Atrocity Trial", *Columbia Journal of Transnational Law* 51 (1): 69–119.

Langfield, Michele and Pam Maclean. 2009. "Multiple Framings: Survivor and Non-Survivor Interviewers in Holocaust Video Testimony". In *Memories of Mass Repression: Narrating Life Stories in the Aftermath of Atrocity*, edited by Nanci Adler, Selma Leydesdorff, Mary Chamberlain and Leyla Neyzi, 199–218. Somerset, NJ: Transaction.

Laub, Dori. 1992. "An Event Without a Witness: Truth, Testimony and Survival". In *Testimony: Crises of Witnessing in Literature, Psychoanalysis, and History*, edited by Shoshana Felman and Dori Laub, 75–92. London: Routledge.

Levi, Primo. 1986. "The Memory of Offense". In *Bitburg in Moral and Political Perspective*, edited by Geoffrey Hartman, 131–137. Bloomington, IN: Indiana University Press.

Leydesdorff, Selma. 2009. "When communities fell apart and neighbours became enemies: stories of bewilderment in Srebrenica". In *Memories of Mass Repression: Narrating Life Stories in the Aftermath of Atrocity*, edited by Nanci Adler, Selma Leydesdorff, Mary Chamberlain and Leyla Neyzi, 21–40. New Brunswick, NJ: Transaction.

Linke, Uli. 2009. "The Limits of Empathy: Emotional Anesthesia and the Museum of Corpses in Post-Holocaust Germany". In *Genocide: Truth, Memory, and Representation*, edited by Alexander Laban Hinton and Kevin Lewis O'Neill 147–191. Durham, NC: Duke University Press.

Luchjenbroers, J. 1997. "'In your own words ...' Questions and answers in a Supreme Court Trial", *Journal of Pragmatics* 27 (4): 477–503.

Maclean, Pam. 2008. "Holocaust testimony / 'Testimonio'? An exploration". In *Testifying to the Holocaust*, edited by Pam Maclean, Michele Langfield and Dvir Abramovich, 29–57. Sydney: Australian Association of Jewish Studies.

Maclean, Pam. 2014. "To be Hunted like Animals: Samuel and Joseph Chanesman Remember their Survival in the Polish Countryside during the Holocaust". In *Remembering Genocide*, edited by Nigel Eltringham and Pam Maclean 71–91. London: Routledge.

Madlingozi, Tshepo. 2010. "On Transitional Justice Entrepreneurs and the Production of Victims", *Journal of Human Rights Practice* 2 (2): 208–228.

Mannergren Selimovic, Johanna. 2015. "Challenges of Postconflict Coexistence: Narrating Truth and Justice in a Bosnian Town", *Political Psychology* 36 (2): 231–242.

McKinley, Michelle. 1997. "Life Stories, Disclosure and the Law", *PoLAR: Political and Legal Anthropology Review* 20 (2): 70–82.

Menchú, Rigoberta and Elisabeth Burgos-Debray. 1984. *I, Rigoberta Menchú: An Indian Woman in Guatemala*. London: Verso.

Mendeloff, David. 2004. "Truth-Seeking, Truth-Telling, and Postconflict Peacebuilding: Curb the Enthusiasm?" *International Studies Review* 6 (3): 355–380.

Mertus, Julie. 2000. "Truth in a Box: The Limits of Justice through Judicial Mechanisms". In *The Politics of Memory: Truth, Healing and Social Justice*, edited by Ifi Amadiume and Abdullahi An-Na'im, 142–161. London: Zed Books.

Millar, Gearoid. 2011. "Between Western Theory and Local Practice: Cultural Impediments to Truth-Telling in Sierra Leone", *Conflict Resolution Quarterly* 29 (2): 177–199.

Moon, Claire. 2009. "Healing Past Violence: Traumatic Assumptions and Therapeutic Interventions in War and Reconciliation", *Journal of Human Rights* 8 (1): 71–91.

Morris, David B. 1997. "About Suffering: Voice, Genre, and Moral Community". In *Social Suffering*, edited by Arthur Kleinman, Veena Das and Margaret M. Lock, 25–46. Berkeley, CA: University of California Press.

Mutua, Makua. 2001. "Savages, Victims and Saviours: The Metaphor of Human Rights", *Harvard International Law Journal* 42 (1): 201–245.

Novick, Peter. 2001. *The Holocaust and Collective Memory*. London: Bloomsbury.

Payne, Leigh A. 2008. *Unsettling Accounts: Neither Truth Nor Reconciliation in Confessions of State Violence*. Durham, NC: Duke University Press.

Portelli, Allessandro. 1981. "The Peculiarities of Oral History", *History Workshop* 12 (1): 96–107.

Portelli, Allessandro. 1998. "Oral History as Genre". In *Narrative and Genre*, edited by Mary Chamberlin and Paul Tompson, 23–45. London: Routledge.

Quesada, James. 1998. "Suffering Child: An Embodiment of War and its Aftermath in Post-Sandanista Nicaragua", *Medical Anthropology Quarterly* 12 (1): 51–73.

Razack, Sherene H. 2007. "Stealing the Pain of Others: Reflections on Canadian Humanitarian Responses", *Review of Education, Pedagogy, and Cultural Studies* 29 (4): 375–394.

88 Memory and testimony

Rees, Laurence. 2017. *The Holocaust: A New History*. Harmondsworth, UK: Penguin.

Rorty, Richard. 1982. *Consequences of Pragmatism: Essays, 1972–1980*. Minneapolis, MN: University of Minnesota Press.

Ross, Fiona. 2003a. *Bearing Witness: Women and the Truth and Reconciliation Commission in South Africa*. London: Pluto Press.

Ross, Fiona. 2003b. "On Having a Voice and Being Heard", *Anthropological Theory* 3 (3): 325–341.

Samuel, Raphael. 1994. *Theatres of Memory. Volume 1: Past and Present in Contemporary Culture*. London and New York: Verso.

Samuels, Annemarie. 2016. "Embodied Narratives of Disaster: The Expression of Bodily Experience in Aceh, Indonesia", *Journal of the Royal Anthropological Institute* 22 (4): 809–825.

Sanford, Victoria. 1999. "Between Rigoberta Menchu and La Violencia: Deconstructing David Stoll's History of Guatemala", *Latin American Perspectives* 26 (6): 38–46.

Scarry, Elaine. 1985. *The Body in Pain: The Making and Unmaking of the World*. Oxford: Oxford University Press.

Schaffer, Kay and Sidonie Smith. 2004. *Human Rights and Narrated Lives: The Ethics of Recognition*. Basingstoke, UK: Palgrave Macmillan.

Shaw, Rosalind. 2007a. "Displacing Violence: Making Pentecostal Memory in Postwar Sierra Leone", *Cultural Anthropology* 22 (1): 66–93.

Shaw, Rosalind. 2007b. "Memory Frictions: Localizing the Truth and Reconciliation Commission in Sierra Leone", *The International Journal of Transitional Justice* 1 (2): 183–207.

Shaw, Rosalind and Lars Waldorf. 2010. "Introduction: Localizing Traditional Justice". In *Localizing Transitional Justice: Interventions and Priorities after Mass Violence*, edited by Rosalind Shaw, Lars Waldorf and Pierre Hazan, 3–26. Stanford, CA: Stanford University Press.

Sorabji, Cornelia. 2006. "Managing Memories in Post-War Sarajevo: Individuals, Bad Memories, and New Wars", *Journal of the Royal Anthropological Institute* 12 (1): 1–18.

Spivak, Gayatri Chakravorty. 1988. "Can the Subaltern Speak?" In *Marxism and the Interpretation of Culture*, edited by Cary Nelson and Lawrence Grossberg, 271–313. Urbana, IL: University of Illinois Press.

Spivak, Gayatri Chakravorty. 2006. *In Other Worlds: Essays in Cultural Politics*. London: Routledge.

Stefansson, Anders H. 2010. "Coffee after cleansing? Co-existence, co-operation, and communication in post-conflict Bosnia and Herzegovina", *Focaal* 57: 62–76.

Stoll, David. 1999. *Rigoberta Menchú and The Story of All Poor Guatemalans*. Boulder, CO: Westview Press.

Strathern, Marilyn. 2004. "Losing (Out On) Intellectual Resources". In *Law, Anthropology, and the Constitution of the Social: Making Persons and Things*, edited by Alain Pottage and Martha Mundy, 201–233. Cambridge, UK: Cambridge University Press.

Strejilevich, Nora. 2006. "Testimony: Beyond the Language of Truth", *Human Rights Quarterly* 28 (3): 701–713.

Strupinskienė, Lina. 2016. "What is reconciliation and are we there yet? Different types and levels of reconciliation: A case study of Bosnia and Herzegovina", *Journal of Human Rights* 16 (4): 1–21.

Summerfield, Derek. 1999. "A critique of seven assumptions behind psychological trauma programmes in war-affected areas", *Social Science & Medicine* 48 (10): 1449–1462.

Summerfield, Derek. 2000. "Childhood, War, Refugeedom and 'Trauma': Three Core Questions for Mental Health Professionals", *Transcultural Psychiatry* 37 (3): 417–433.

Theidon, Kimberly. 2007. "Gender in Transition: Common Sense, Women and War", *Journal of Human Rights* 6 (3): 653–678.

Ticktin, Miriam. 1999. "Selling Suffering in The Courtroom and Marketplace: An Analysis of the Autobiography of Kiranjit Ahluwalia", *PoLAR: Political & Legal Anthropology Review* 22 (1): 24–41.

Truth and Reconciliation Commission. 1998. *Truth and Reconciliation Commission of South Africa Report.* 5 vols. Vol. 1. Johannesburg: Palgrave Macmillan.

Vansina, Jan. 1980. "Memory and Oral Tradition". In *The African Past Speaks: Essays on Oral Tradition and History*, edited by Joseph Calder Miller, 262–271. Folkestone, UK: Dawson.

Vansina, Jan. 2006 [1961]. *Oral Tradition: A Study in Historical Methodology.* New Brunswick, NJ: Transaction Publishers.

Verdoolaege, Annelies. 2002. The Human Rights Violations Hearings of the South African TRC: A Bridge Between Individual Narratives of Suffering and a Contextualizing Master-Story of Reconciliation. Department of African Languages and Cultures, Ghent University, Belgium.

Wajnryb, Ruth. 1999. "The Holocaust as Unspeakable: Public Ritual Versus Private Hell", *Journal of Intercultural Studies* 20 (1): 81–93.

Waldorf, Lars. 2010. "'Like Jews Waiting for Jesus': Posthumous Justice in Post-Genocide Rwanda". In *Localizing Transitional Justice: Interventions and Priorities after Mass Violence*, edited by R. Shaw, L. Waldorf and Pierre Hazan, 183–204. Stanford, CA: Stanford University Press.

Wieviorka, Annette. 2006a. *The Era of the Witness.* Translated by Jared Stark. Ithaca, NY: Cornell University Press.

Wieviorka, Annette. 2006b. "The Witness in History", *Poetics Today* 27 (2): 385–397.

Williamson, Caroline. 2016. "Post-traumatic growth at the international level: The obstructive role played by translators and editors of Rwandan Genocide testimonies", *Translation Studies* 9 (1): 33–50.

Wilson, Richard A. (ed.). 1997. "Representing Human Rights Violations: Social Contexts and Subjectivities". In *Human Rights, Culture and Context: Anthropological Perspectives*, 134–160. London: Pluto Press.

Wilson, Richard A. 2001. *The Politics of Truth and Reconciliation in South Africa: Legitimizing the Post-Apartheid State.* Cambridge, UK: Cambridge University Press.

4

SEEKING "TRUTH" IN THE AFTERMATH OF VIOLENT CONFLICT

The anthropologist Rosalind Shaw (2014, 315) notes that, following violent conflict, "truth commissions have become fetish objects to which almost mystical powers of future making are attributed". Part of the reasons for this supposed "mystical power" lies, I would argue, in the ambiguity of the purpose of such institutions. The term "truth" is, for a start, misleading, for, as anthropologist Fiona Ross (2003b, 327) notes, prior to the creation of the South African Truth and Reconciliation Commission (SATRC) in 1995 it was not that there was "silence about the apartheid past"; much was already known through "stories, songs, political rhetoric, magisterial orders, court cases, newspapers, scholarly work, parliamentary debates, [speeches] at funerals and rallies and so on". From this perspective it has been argued that the task of truth commissions is not so much to root out "truth" but to "transform what is widely-known about violent past events – common knowledge – into official acknowledgement" (Bickford 2007, 996; see Laplante 2007, 440). The value of the SATRC, therefore, and thirty or so other truth commissions (see Hayner 2010), lies in "officially confirming and bringing into the public space what was already known" (Wilson 2000, 79).

This raises the question, however, of what purpose such "official acknowledgement" is intended to serve. On their creation, truth commissions tend to be promoted as being at the service of survivors. For example, when, in the aftermath of civil war (1991–2002), the Sierra Leone Truth and Reconciliation Commission (SLTRC) was established in 2002, it was stated that it would "help restore the human dignity of victims and promote reconciliation by providing an opportunity for victims to give an account of the violations and abuses suffered and for perpetrators to relate their experiences" (Government of Sierra Leone 2000, para 62b). Rather than record the experiences of all survivors, truth commissions like the SLTRC record representative exemplars. Reflecting this, the final report of the SATRC states that "Many of those who chose not to come to the Commission heard versions of their stories in the experiences of others. In this way, the Commission was able to reach a broader community" (Truth and Reconciliation Commission 1998, 169). While using exemplars of experience in this way is practical, it has not always satisfied survivors. While Ross (2003a, 337) found that survivors in South Africa described "a sense of comfort derived from recognizing similarities in their experiences to those of testifiers", human rights scholar Lisa Laplante (2007, 446) found that survivors who testified at the Peruvian Truth and Reconciliation Commission (CVR, Comisión de la Verdad y Reconciliación del Perú, established in 2000) still felt frustrated that they "did not have their chance" to tell their story.

Whether or not survivors are ultimately satisfied by truth commissions, the promotion of such institutions as an opportunity for victims to "give an account" reflects the global paradigm of "redemptive remembering through truth-telling" discussed in Chapter 3 (Shaw 2007b, 189). An alternative interpretation of the purpose served by truth commissions is that they are a way by which "a bureaucratic elite seeks to manufacture legitimacy for state institutions" (Wilson 2001, 19); this is also the case for memorial sites (see Chapter 6). Seen from this perspective, the SATRC was primarily "an elite project of nation-building" designed to "forge greater coherence between an established white economic elite and an emergent black political elite" (Wilson 2001, 153). In other words, despite claims to the contrary, truth commissions such as the SATRC do not serve survivors by giving them an opportunity to tell their story but, rather, serve the interests of political and economic elites who require a means of drawing a line under the past in order to get back to "business as usual" (see Connerton 2008, 62).

An indication that truth commissions serve an elite can be seen in the language employed in relation to such institutions that contributes to "psychologising the nation" (Hamber & Wilson 2002, 35). For example, the 1990 decree creating the Chilean National Commission on Truth and Reconciliation (also known as the Rettig Report after the commission's chair, Raúl Rettig) to investigate human rights violations under the military dictatorship of Augusto Pinochet (1973–1990) states "That the moral conscience of the nation demands that the truth about the grave violations of human rights committed in our country between September 11, 1973 and March 11, 1990 be brought to light." Suggesting that the nation of Chile has a "moral conscience" implies "that nations have psyches [and] experience traumas in a similar way to individuals" (Hamber & Wilson 2002, 35). In reality, of course, a "nation" is "an abstract entity that exists primarily in the minds of nation-building politicians" (Hamber & Wilson 2002, 36; see Ignatieff 1998, 169). A possible consequence of "psychologising the nation" in this way is that it forces "premature closure" on survivors, subordinating their "individual needs to the political expediency of national unity and reconciliation" (Hamber & Wilson 2002, 44 36). Psychologist Brandon Hamber and anthropologist Richard Ashby Wilson provide the example of the Madres de Plaza de Mayo in Argentina, the mothers and grandmothers of some of the 30,000 people who were "disappeared" by the government during the Dirty War between 1976–1982 (Hamber & Wilson 2002, 45; see Navarro 1989). Despite a truth commission in Argentina (see Argentine

92 Seeking "truth" in aftermath of conflict

National Commission on the Disappeared 1986), the Madres have continued to repeat their rallying cry that "those who were taken from us alive should be returned to us alive" as a reminder that nothing can be done to replace their missing loved ones. Because of their refusal to accept the "new benevolent political order", marked in part by the 1984 National Commission on the Disappeared, the Madres were denounced as "dinosaurs" by Argentinian politicians, transformed from being the "Mothers of the Nation" to *Las Locas,* "Crazy Little Old Ladies" (Hamber & Wilson 2002, 45). In such a context, a truth commission that claimed to draw a line under the past could be used to silence survivors. As Hamber and Wilson (2002, 36) warn, while a truth commission may "lift an authoritarian regime of denial and public silence", it may also "create a new regime which represses other memories" (see Hackett & Rolston 2009, 362).

The chapter begins by considering two related criticisms of truth commissions by anthropologists and other ethnographers. First, while truth commissions may appear to be concerned with establishing a comprehensive account, their mandates tend to be restrictive, deliberately obscuring parts of the past. Second, while truth commissions appear to be an opportunity for survivors to provide a comprehensive account of their experiences, the manner in which the collection of testimony is organised tends to be restrictive, obscuring certain survivor experiences. In the final section of the chapter I will consider whether community-based truth projects can avoid these two weaknesses and will illustrate this with two examples from Northern Ireland: the Ardoyne Commemoration Project and *Dúchas.*

Restricted mandates of truth commissions

As noted above, truth commissions can paradoxically "create a new regime which represses other memories" (Hamber & Wilson 2002, 36). The way in which a truth commission's mandate may obscure important elements of the past can be illustrated by the SATRC. The commission's mandate was to "provide for the investigation and the establishment of as complete a picture as possible of the nature, causes and extent of gross violations of human rights committed during the period from 1 March 1960 [to 1994]" (Government of South Africa 1995). The term "gross violations of human rights" was defined as "the killing, abduction, torture or severe ill-treatment of any person" by "any person acting with a political motive" (Government of South Africa 1995) and resulted in 21,298 statements, of which 2,400 were heard by the Human Rights Violation Committee (HRVC) (Ross 2003b, 328). This restrictive definition of "gross violations of human rights" meant that many human rights violations committed under apartheid (1948–1994) – including detention without trial, forced removals and "Bantu" education policies (enforcing racially separated educational facilities) – could not be considered by the SATRC (Wilson 2000, 79). Political scientist Mahmood Mamdani (2000, 179) criticises the definition of "gross violations of human rights", given that apartheid was "aimed less at individuals than entire communities" and that the violence was designed to "dispossess people of means of livelihood". In other words, the SATRC's mandate meant it was only concerned with a restricted notion of "personal or direct" violence, rather than "structural or indirect" violence (Galtung 1969, 170; see Introduction), where the latter "is embedded in everyday life and touches on spheres like poverty, hunger, nudity, displacement, loss of dignity" (Honwana 2005, 87). Mamdani (2000, 179) deplores the fact that the testimonies of the 3.5 million people who were forcibly removed between 1960 and 1982, with resulting social and economic hardship, could not be heard at the SATRC. Seen from this perspective, the restrictive mandate of the SATRC meant that it "wrote the vast majority of apartheid's victims out of its version of history" (Mamdani 2000, 183).

By concentrating on direct violence to the body (see Ross 2001, 253), truth commissions tend to be concerned with "negative peace" (the cessation of "direct, personal violence") rather than "positive peace" (the eradication of "indirect, structural violence") (Galtung 1969, 183; see Introduction). Social geographer Joseph Nevins (2003) illustrates this in relation to the UN-sponsored Commission for Reception, Truth and Reconciliation (CAVR: Comissão de Acolhimento, Verdade e Reconciliação de Timor Leste), established in 2002 in East Timor in the aftermath of the 24-year occupation by Indonesia. Prior to the 1975 Indonesian invasion, 60% of coffee production (East Timor's primary export commodity) was in the hands of East Timorese smallholders, the rest produced by Portuguese farmers and a Portuguese company (East Timor was a Portuguese colony until 1975). Following the invasion, East Timorese were required to sell all their coffee to a company owned by the Indonesian military at prices two to three times lower than prices paid to farmers in West Timor (part of Indonesia). This, combined with the collapse of global coffee prices, led to a significant decline in coffee production in East Timor, resulting in a rise in malnutrition in rural areas, a decline in primary school enrolment as families could not afford school fees and long-term impediment to economic development (Nevins 2003, 694). Nevins (2003, 688) argues, therefore, that coffee "embodies the structural violence of Indonesia's crimes" because the control of, access to and distribution of environmental resources are "institutionalised in such a way as to harm human beings". Although the CAVR was mandated to consider the violation of a broad set of human rights (including social and economic rights) by a broad range of actors (including military and police officers, government officials and members of opposition groups, political parties, militias, corporations and other individuals; see Commission for Reception, Truth and Reconciliation 2006, paras 8–16), the emphasis was still on violations of an individual's human rights. Nevins (2003, 697) envisages an alternative approach that would not only consider the violation of individual rights but would also chronicle the losses to the country's coffee sector in order to recognise as violence "institutionalized and indirect practices that contribute to physical injury and/or create, maintain, or exacerbate social injustice" (see Albuja & Cavallaro 2008).

The need for the alternative approach suggested by Nevins is seen in the way that survivors demonstrate an expectation that truth commissions will provide social and economic support in order to tackle structural violence and associated deprivation (see Guthrey 2016b). Writing in the context of the CVR in Peru,

94 Seeking "truth" in aftermath of conflict

anthropologist Kimberly Theidon (2007, 459) reports that "it did not matter how many times people were told they would not necessarily receive reparation for giving testimony … the hope of some economic relief was a very important incentive". Shaw (2007b, 201–202) reports that in Sierra Leone witnesses agreed to testify before the SLTRC because of the expectation that this would lead to material assistance and that they often ended their testimonies with pleas for such help, to which commissioners responded that such assistance was not part of the SLTRC mandate. Shaw (2007b, 203) provides the example of Isatu, who had been shot by the rebel Revolutionary United Front (RUF) during the civil war and cared on her own for her four children. When asked by Shaw why she had wanted to speak to the SLTRC, Isatu indicated that, on one hand, she had embraced the commission's claims regarding speaking the truth, that "I went to clear my chest" to "feel better in my heart". But Isatu also told Shaw that she had expected material assistance and that if she had known it was not to be forthcoming she would have said "Let me no waste my time to go."

Building on Shaw's research, the sociologist Gearoid Millar (2011) conducted ethnographic fieldwork in Makeni (in the Northern Region of Sierra Leone) in 2008–2009 (five years after public hearings had been heard in the community) to further explore local experiences of the SLTRC. Like Shaw, Millar (2011, 524) found that at the time of the hearings people conceived of justice as the provision of "tools and resources to overcome the violations of their needs in the present and the future", rather than concentrating on the past. For example, Amadu, a local chief, argued that the SLTRC should have brought tractors, medicines and help with education "so that peace would be in the country" (Millar 2011, 524). Millar (2011, 526) reports that he rarely heard people demand retribution or truth, but he "constantly heard people ask for assistance with their current situation" (see Robins 2011). In contrast to these tangible requests for material support, the SLTRC's presentation of truth through public hearings "had no discernible impact on the ability of such people to live a better life now or in the future" (Millar 2011, 529). The example of the community described by Millar (2011, 524) demonstrates a "present- and future-oriented justice, one that focuses on survival and moving forward, instead of investigating the past" (see Introduction). Millar and the other research considered in this section suggest that, rather than serving the interests of survivors, the restricted mandates of truth commissions may prevent the inclusion of survivors' past experiences of structural violence (as demonstrated by the examples of South Africa and East Timor) and fail to attend to their immediate needs in the present (as demonstrated by the examples of Peru and Sierra Leone).

It is not a simple task, however, to broaden the focus of truth commissions. This can be illustrated by the Truth and Reconciliation Commission of Canada (TRCC) which, although unlike the other cases I have considered here was not a response to violent conflict, shows how difficult it is to fulfil the twin objectives of establishing a comprehensive account of the past and satisfying survivors. The TRCC was established in 2008 to document the history and impact of the Canadian Indian residential school system, which was attended by approximately 150,00 students from 1884 to

1996. The TRCC's mandate was defined by the Indian Residential School Settlement Agreement (2006), which was the direct result of thousands of individual lawsuits by residential school survivors (Niezen 2016, 921). Anthropologist Ronald Niezen (2016), who conducted ethnographic research at the TRCC, suggests that these origins made the TRCC "victim-centric", its mandate concentrating on the "experiences, impacts and consequences" of the residential schools on individual survivors (Indian Residential School Settlement Agreement 2006). This "victim-centred" approach was bolstered by the lobbying of survivor organisations; the presentation of model survivor testimony (which offered templates for others to follow); guest speakers at events (including survivors of the Holocaust and the 1994 Rwandan genocide of the Tutsi); and exhibits (Niezen 2016, 926–931). As a consequence, the themes that dominated the "Sharing Circles" and "Sharing Panels" at which survivors told their stories were "violence, sadistic regimes of punishment, and sexual abuse of children" (Niezen 2016, 922). By privileging "deeply personal, disturbing narrations", the TRCC "never heard from the government people who ran the schools, the administrators, the inspectors, the school councillors" (Niezen 2016, 926 931). Niezen (2016, 935) argues that as a consequence of the "victim-centric" approach, "our knowledge of the 'perpetrators', their motives, and the institutions that harboured them are left obscured" when it is precisely that knowledge that is needed to prevent similar state policies in the future (see James 2012).

FIGURE 4.1 At a 2011 Truth and Reconciliation Commission of Canada event in Inuvik, Alan and Rosie Kagak weep as they recall their experience as Inuit in Canada's residential school system. (Photo courtesy of Michael Swan)

96 Seeking "truth" in aftermath of conflict

In this section I have considered the way in which the mandates of truth commissions can obscure important parts of a violent past. It is not always the same part of the past that is obscured. In the case of the TRCC in Canada, the accounts of survivors were privileged but the motive and means of perpetrators were neglected. Meanwhile, in South Africa (SATRC), East Timor (CAVR), Peru (CVR) and Sierra Leone (SLTRC), the accounts of survivors of "direct, personal violence" were privileged, while survivors who had suffered "indirect, structural violence" were neglected. These examples place in doubt claims that truth commissions are designed to establish a comprehensive account, and lend credence to the suspicion that they "manufacture legitimacy for state institutions" (Wilson 2001, 19). Having said that, human rights scholar Lisa Laplante (2007, 438) notes how the CVR in Peru, by piecing together thousands of similar stories, was able to show that "human rights violations were not isolated events, but part of a larger pattern," and that these violations were caused by "racist and classist" attitudes towards a particular group of people, those who were "poor, rural, indigenous, minimally educated". In Laplante's opinion, therefore, a truth commission that relied on individual accounts of human rights violations was able to reveal the "structural violence" (rather than just the direct violence) that underpinned the conflict.

Testimony in truth commissions

While the previous section considered how certain experiences of survivors are excluded from consideration by truth commissions, sufficient survivors do, of course, fulfil the criteria and give testimony. The political scientist Louis Bickford (2007, 1033) argues that truth commissions "provide a space for victims to tell their stories. This kind of space is different than a courtroom." Likewise, Catherine Cole (2007, 173) argues that those who testify at truth commissions speak "unimpeded and uninterrupted". Such claims were actively promoted by commissioners at the SATRC. For example, at a hearing in Durban on 16 April 1997, a commissioner informed a testifier, "Now, please be free. This is not a court of law, it's just a place where you want to come and ventilate your truth" (Verdoolaege 2006, 67). Shaw (2007b, 200) encountered the same suggestion of freedom at the SLTRC, with Bishop Humper (Chair of the commission) telling a witness, "Thank you for venting your feelings. That is part of healing."

On one hand, the encouragement to "ventilate your truth" in the aftermath of violent conflict replicates features of "traditional" conflict resolution discussed in Chapter 1. For example, the *bcarra'* among the Semai Sanoi (Malaysia) consists of the incessant retelling of the events from every conceivable angle and continues until "no one wants to say anything else and the conflict has been 'talked to death'" (Robarchek 1979, 112). Likewise, in Chapter 3, I considered the storytelling sessions among Acholi women abducted by the Lord's Resistance Army in which facilitators "would not interrupt the women as they began to talk, nor would they intervene to ask questions, but, following Acholi cultural norms, allowed the speaker to continue until finished" (Baines & Stewart 2011, 4).

However, while these examples appear to support a cross-cultural belief in the value of "venting your feelings", claims made for truth commissions are also part of the global paradigm of "redemptive remembering through truth-telling" (Shaw 2007b, 189), with its culturally specific origins in Europe and North America (see Chapter 3).

"Venting your feelings" may not be a preferred response by survivors. Shaw (2007a, 68) found in Sierra Leone that people "chose not to 'encourage' the return of violence by giving it a public reality". Speaking of testimonies at the SLTRC, Shaw (2007b, 200) reports how:

> the flat, factual tone of testimonies reminded me of the tone of local politicians' speeches. This was not the venting of thoughts and feelings that usually constitutes *blow main* ["blow your mind". Witnesses were testifying] in a way that reduced, as far as possible, the re-entry of that violence as a tangible experience in the present.

Resistance to giving testimony has been recorded in other contexts. Holly Guthrey (2016a) interviewed victims who had given public testimony at the CAVR in East Timor (see above) and at the Solomon Islands Truth and Reconciliation Commission (SITRC), established in 2008 to consider the ethnic conflict known as "the Tensions" (1998–2003) during which at least two hundred people were killed and many others suffered kidnapping, torture and sexual violence (see Vella 2014). About half of Guthrey's respondents in both contexts took issue with what they perceived to be an "incompatibility between their own sociocultural values and expectations and the work of their country's truth commission" (Guthrey 2016a, 2). In both contexts respondents considered speaking about "women's issues" or "sexual violence" in a truth commission as inappropriate. For example, a woman from East Timor who had been sexually abused during the Indonesian occupation stated that to publicly talk of such things "is a disgrace for East Timorese women" and that, having given testimony to the CAVR, "we walked feeling very embarrassed, many people despised us ... I regretted disclosing my sad story in public" (Guthrey 2016a, 15–16). Guthrey (2016a, 19 16) therefore suggests that, rather than "restoring their dignity or facilitating healing", giving testimony may lead to re-victimisation as survivors are left isolated and shunned by their families and communities (see discussion of Brounéus 2008 in Chapter 3). In addition, respondents in the Solomon Islands stated that the past should not be "aired in front of others" (Guthrey 2016a, 3). A respondent told Guthrey (2016a, 17) that "according to *kastom* [custom]", the past is forgotten, otherwise "when I tell the story, I'll say this man did this [to me]; maybe someone will hear and want to take revenge" (see White 1991, 193 197). Guthrey (2016a, 7 19) concludes that "locally ingrained norms of resolving issues" mean that revealing sensitive material outside of the family in a truth commission "can cause some victims to feel worried or distressed, and for some can lead to re-traumatization".

98 Seeking "truth" in aftermath of conflict

The way in which cultural norms could obstruct the giving of testimony of sexual violence suffered by women is also apparent in anthropologist Nayanika Mookherjee's (2006) discussion of *birangonas* (war heroines) in Bangladesh. In 1947 the independence of India from British colonial rule resulted in the creation of a homeland for Muslims, known as East Pakistan (contemporary Bangladesh) and West Pakistan (contemporary Pakistan). West Pakistan's administrative and economic domination, combined with a strategy of forced cultural assimilation, led to a nine-month "war of liberation" in 1971 that resulted in the creation of Bangladesh (Mookherjee 2006, 435). The war left three million dead and 200,000 women raped by the Pakistani army and local collaborators (Mookherjee 2006, 436). An attempt by the Bangladeshi government to prevent the women from being socially ostracised by referring to them as *birangonas* (war heroines) was unsuccessful and the women disappeared from public discourse. In 1992, however, the *Gono Adalat* (People's Tribunal) was established by political activists. "People's tribunals" are a peculiar hybrid of truth commissions, "unofficial truth projects" (UTPs; see below) and international criminal courts (see Chapter 5), given that, like truth commissions, they "draw heavily on truth telling through oral testimony presented to a panel or 'jury of conscience'" (Chinkin 2006, 212), are created by activists rather than governments (as are UTPs), and tend to take the form of a mock trial. The first people's tribunal was the Russell Tribunal, founded in 1966 to investigate and judge American war crimes in Vietnam (see Zunino 2016), followed in 1979 by the Permanent Peoples' Tribunal which, to date, has held forty-six sessions, including on the Armenian genocide (1984), Chernobyl (1996) and Sri Lanka (2013).

Mookherjee (2006) describes the experience of three poor, landless women – Kajoli, Moyna and Rohima – who, as victims of rape in 1971, gave testimony to the *Gono Adalat* in Dhaka in 1992. Back in their home community the women and their families experienced *khota* ("sarcastic scorn") concerning the rapes because, in revealing what had been secret for twenty-one years, they had lost their *man ijjot* (status and honour linked to sexual relationships), making them equivalent to prostitutes (Mookherjee 2006, 439–440). For many in the community the "rightful action of the victim, weak and tabooed, is to be quiet, to remain covered and invisible, and not to protest against the wrongs done to her" (Mookherjee 2006, 441). The paradox, of course, was that in scorning the women for revealing a "secret", people were "always doomed to talk about" the very secret that should have remained concealed (Mookherjee 2006, 444). Both younger men and men who had fought in the 1971 "war of liberation" cast doubt on the veracity of the women's account, relying on the belief that a woman who had actually been raped would not say anything about it (Mookherjee 2006, 440). Mookherjee (2006, 445) suggests that one of the reasons for this response was that, by claiming the mantel of "heroines", the landless, poor, subordinate and otherwise anonymous women challenged local power hierarchies. *Khota* (scorn), therefore, was a means of guaranteeing the continued subordination of the women and their families (Mookherjee 2006, 445).

While Guthrey (2016a) and Mookherjee (2006) suggest that local norms may dissuade survivors from testifying about certain experiences, research indicates that, even if norms do not restrict those who testify, truth commissions do not simply allow survivors to "ventilate" their truth. Even before survivors testified at the SATRC, what they would say was moulded in a particular manner. A survivor had first to give a statement. Those taking statements for the SATRC followed a predetermined protocol which was deliberately designed to control the direction taken by testimony (see discussion of Langfield & Maclean 2009 in Chapter 3). As a consequence, the story was stripped down to its "essential characteristics", with anything outside the "controlled vocabulary" of the protocol being discarded (Wilson 2001, 48). The "controlled vocabulary" by which witness statements were collected and entered into the SATRC's "Information Management System" (IMS) meant that:

> when the TRC went out and "collected" information from people who suffered violations, it did not collect people's stories or narratives as they were told. Stories about violations became coded right from the outset and underwent changes so that they fitted the vocabulary or language of the IMS [which] retrospectively re-framed and re-ordered past experiences.
>
> *(Buur 2001, 45–46)*

In this manner a "new interpretive grid for giving the past meaning was ... imposed" (Buur 2003, 80). Furthermore, because the virtues of forgiveness and reconciliation were "so loudly and roundly applauded" in the hearings of the SATRC, "any expression of a desire for revenge" was excluded from statements (Wilson 2000, 80–81). As a consequence, testimony was prestructured away from survivors' desire for retribution so that "the TRC's message on reconciliation was woven into their written testimonies as the oral testimony of the victim was rendered as text" (Wilson 2000, 82).

While Buur (2001, 2003) and Wilson (2000) demonstrate restrictions placed on survivor statements prior to public testimony at the SATRC, other authors have noted how testimony was further constrained in public hearings. Whereas it may be assumed that giving testimony before the HRVC was a "a simple act, a release of 'stories' of pain that already existed intact", in reality testimonies were "a product of a dialogue between a testifier and member of the HRVC" (Ross 2003a, 79; see Chapter 3 on the co-production of testimony). Ross (2003b, 82–87) illustrates this with the testimony of Yvonne Khutwane, an ANC activist and one of the few women activists who testified before the commission. During Mrs Khutwane's forty-minute public testimony (given in Xhosa) about her detention, torture and sexual molestation, the female psychologist and HRVC member assigned to assist her constantly interrupted to ask questions. In this way Mrs Khutwane's testimony "was not an unmediated flow of words that described her experience, but was marked and shaped by interventions and questions" (Ross 2003a, 88).

Annelies Verdoolaege (2006, 65) also demonstrates how a framework was imposed on witnesses at the oral hearings of the HRVC, whereby commissioners "tried to elicit statements on reconciliation [while seeming] to ignore feelings of retribution, hatred or revenge" (see Wilson 2000, 80–81). Verdoolaege (2002, 11)

100 Seeking "truth" in aftermath of conflict

demonstrates that "the commissioners wanted to have full control over the testimonies, not only by asking certain questions and by interrupting the testifiers, but also by preventing them from talking about unanticipated topics" (see Blommaert et al. 2006, 41). This control was enabled by the commissioners' possession of the witness's statement, which allowed commissioners to refer to the statement to elicit information they deemed relevant (Verdoolaege 2002, 11–14 22–23 26–27). From this perspective, the claim of "ventilating truth" ignores the fact that testimony was a "product of dialogue between a testifier and a member of the HVRC" (Ross 2003a, 79). All testimony is, of course, a co-production between witness and elicitor (see Chapter 3), wherein the elicitor controls the "choice of words in the propositions of questions, the order in which topics are introduced, the ways in which topics are linked, and the topics which are omitted or which the witness is prevented from talking about" (Eades 2008, 215).

The discussion so far in this section suggests the claim that truth commissions "provide a space for victims to tell their stories" (Bickford 2007, 1033) should be treated with caution. And yet it is important to note that while the freedom associated with testifying to a truth commission may be exaggerated, it may be the start of a process which is liberating for survivors in the long term. Laplante (2007, 434–435), for example, argues that in Peru the act of giving testimony to the CVR enabled survivors to break down "entrenched habits of fear and distrust", leading to a "growing, and insatiable, desire among victim-survivors to continue to tell their story". Laplante (2007, 448) provides a number of examples, including the victim–survivor group Asociación Reflexión de Inocentes Liberados and its weekly radio show "*A desalambrar*", which features updated news on the implementation of the CVR's recommendations as well as raising awareness of human rights violations. In this way, Laplante (2007, 449) argues, the CVR has provoked a historically marginalised segment of society to become "vigilant truth-*tellers*", allowing the formerly oppressed to emerge "as political agents with their own political agendas and diverse sites of political struggle" (Feldman 2004, 171). From this perspective, irrespective of the restrictions truth commissions may place on survivors' testimony, "it is the change in personal and political status as truth-tellers" that may make truth commissions worthwhile (Laplante 2007, 435).

Unofficial truth projects

The previous sections have discussed two weaknesses of truth commissions identified by anthropologists and other ethnographers: that mandates may obscure important elements of the past and that what survivors can say in statements and public hearings is constrained. Beyond truth commissions such as those in South Africa, Sierra Leone and Peru, Bickford (2007, 1002) identifies what he calls unofficial truth projects (UTPs) that "seek to replicate the goals, and often the form and content, of formal truth commissions". Bickford (2007, 995) concludes that both UTPs and formal government-sponsored truth commissions have strengths and that neither approach "is inherently superior in terms of truth recovery".

Ultimately, UTPs "achieve legitimacy by combining reasonable ambitions with high levels of professionalism" and should be judged "according to whether they have fairly and accurately portrayed what they have set out to examine, as narrow and specific as that might be" (Bickford 2007, 1027). In other words, it is less to do with the official or unofficial status of the effort than with its professionalism and perceived objectivity (Bickford 2007, 1028). The value of UTPs, according to Bickford (2007, 1035) is that they counter a "one-size-fits-all" approach by being "unique, creative, and appropriate for a local context".

Examples of UTPs include the Proyecto de Recuperación de la Memoria Histórica (Recovery of Historical Memory, or REMHI), an effort led by the Roman Catholic Church to collect testimonies of the survivors of Guatemala's civil war (1960–1996), which left 200,000 dead (see Hanlon & Shankar 2000). Likewise, Laplante (2007, 448) provides the example of Red para el Desarrollo Integral del Niño y la Familia (REDINFA), which has worked with communities in Apurimac, a region greatly impacted by Peru's conflict, to document their own community's memory. Laplante (2007, 435) states that such projects allow survivors to "reject passive telling to third-party authors" and instead to appropriate "their own agency in disseminating memory". This raises the question of whether UTPs such as these are able to fulfil the needs of survivors while avoiding the weaknesses of formal truth commissions identified above.

This question can be explored through the context of Northern Ireland, as a number of informal "storytelling projects" have been established in the aftermath of the conflict (1969–1997) between paramilitaries in favour of remaining part of the United Kingdom (unionist/loyalist, mostly Protestant), paramilitaries in favour of creating a united Ireland (nationalist/republicans, mostly Catholic) and the security forces of the British state (Hackett & Rolston 2009, 366; see Feldman 1991; Sluka 1990). In Northern Ireland, nationalist and republican victims of state violence have had difficulty being acknowledged as victims (Hackett & Rolston 2009, 366). In response, the Ardoyne Commemoration Project (ACP), a community-based "truth-telling" initiative, was established in July 1998 (in the aftermath of the signing of the Good Friday Agreement in April 1998) to record and publish the testimonies of the relatives and friends of the ninety-nine people from the nationalist, working-class Ardoyne area of north Belfast who had died as a result of the conflict. Rather than public hearings, 300 interviews were conducted with the relatives, friends and eyewitnesses of the ninety-nine victims over a four-year period. A book was published, *Ardoyne: The Untold Story*, containing a case study for each of the victims (each made up of two to three oral testimonies) and a series of historical chapters (based on the oral testimonies) that provided context for the deaths (Lundy & McGovern 2006, 75; Ardoyne Commemoration Project 2002). Of the ninety-nine victims, 49% had been victims of loyalist paramilitary groups, 26% had been victims of state security forces (none of these killings had been investigated) and 13% victims of republican paramilitary groups. The latter cases proved among the most challenging for the project as they demonstrated that the "tensions and silences that exist within particular communities" must be addressed

102 Seeking "truth" in aftermath of conflict

as much as antagonism between communities (Lundy & McGovern 2006, 75). The project employed a Participatory Action Research (PAR) approach, in which the researcher becomes a "facilitator" in collecting, validating and disseminating "popular, community-based knowledge in order to challenge social marginalization and structures of oppression" (Lundy & McGovern 2006, 73).

Having been actively involved in the ACP, sociologists Patricia Lundy and Mark McGovern provide an assessment of the strengths and weaknesses of the project. Regarding strengths, as an "insider" project (all of those involved originated in Ardoyne, with one exception) those involved could draw on long-term contacts and social networks, providing a "certificate of honesty" in a context in which state surveillance and the use of informers had created a "culture of secrecy" (Lundy & McGovern 2006, 78). As a founding member of ACP stated, "if it had been a group of people from outside Ardoyne or another country then doors would have been shut and the people would have just put the phone down" (Lundy & McGovern 2006, 76). The development of an "empathetic understanding" between interviewer and interviewee was further enhanced by their shared first-hand experience of traumatic, conflict-related events (Lundy & McGovern 2006, 79). This allowed researchers to "penetrate some of the most impregnable and impenetrable silences" (Lundy & McGovern 2006, 84). Another strength was that an initial, edited version of the interview script was handed back to the interviewee who could then alter his or her testimony (Lundy & McGovern 2006, 76). Furthermore, family interviewees were given access to the complete case study and could raise inaccuracies or issues of concern (Lundy & McGovern 2006, 76). This meant that the survivor was not only the narrator of past experiences but was also "an active participant in the conduct of truth-telling itself" (Lundy & McGovern 2006, 84). This suggests that community-based processes can enable a deeper recognition of survivors because "the storytellers are not reduced to their experience of loss and trauma but are subjects in their own story" (Hackett & Rolston 2009, 369).

Lundy and McGovern, however, do note weaknesses in the ACP. While interviewers and interviewees shared a common experience of conflict-related events, well-established "community narratives" (where the term "community" is used to hide divisions; see discussion of "essentialisation" in Chapter 1) may have impacted on the questions interviewees were asked (see discussion of Langfield & Maclean 2009 in Chapter 3) and may also have affected the willingness of interviewees to challenge dominant narratives (Lundy & McGovern 2006, 80). Another weakness was that while participants in the ACP were adamant that the term "truth" be used to describe their testimonies, rather than "story", Lundy and McGovern (2006, 82–83) recognise that all narratives are partial, constructed and evolving (see Chapter 3). Claiming that a testimony is the "truth" is even more problematic when the project is restricted only to participants from one side of the conflict (see Lundy & McGovern 2006, 74).

Another community-based truth project in Northern Ireland, the Falls Community Council's oral history archive *Dúchas* (Irish for "the experiences that makes us what we are"), provides an example of how dominant "community narratives" could be challenged. Set up in 2000, *Dúchas*, like the ACP, was established to gather memories of the experience of the conflict in a nationalist/republican working-class community in west Belfast, whose members felt "marginalized and alienated from the structures of society" (Hackett 2017, 80). For the first ten years the majority of the interviews, like the ACP, came from within the community. A community partnership (called "Pieces of the Past"), however, was developed with seven other groups, four of whom were from working-class unionist areas. The partnership collected 104 interviews, carried out by those from their own community in order to establish trust (Hackett 2017, 82). The interviews were made available online (http://www.duchasarchive.com/) and ninety-seven of those interviewed agreed to have short extracts from their interviews published in a book, entitled *Living Through the Conflict: Belfast Oral Histories* (Pieces of the Past Project 2014).

Hackett (2003) notes that, like the ACP, the "Pieces of the Past" project had weaknesses. While it was considered essential that interviewers came from the same community as those being interviewed, this replicated the problem noted by Lundy and McGovern (2006, 80), that this adversely affected the willingness of interviewees to challenge a dominant narrative. It was also a missed opportunity for the "educative ... power of memory", wherein "a story might change if told to someone perceived as outside ... the community of the storyteller" (Hackett 2017, 86; see discussion of Eades 2008 in Chapter 3). Despite this weakness, Hackett (2017, 89) argues that "Pieces of the Past" not only contributed to the "official record" but also contributed to positive, cross-community relationships between individuals and groups established through the project itself. While the ACP and the *Dúchas* archives are both valuable as they created a "space for people to tell their story in an overall context of silencing", it remains the case that acknowledgement of those stories "is frequently confined to one's community and can only have a limited effect on the structures of silence and lies often experienced by victims" (Hackett & Rolston 2009, 367 370).

Conclusion

I began the chapter with Wilson's (2001, 19) suggestion that truth commissions are less concerned with "truth" or the needs of victims than with manufacturing "legitimacy for state institutions" in the aftermath of violent conflict. While this is a particularly pessimistic assessment of truth commissions, research by anthropologists and other ethnographers certainly challenges the official claims of truth commissions that they establish an account of the violent past and that this benefits victims. Regarding an account of the past, I considered how the restricted nature of truth commission mandates has resulted in obscuring important parts of the past. Whereas in the case of the TRCC in Canada the accounts of survivors were privileged, but the motive and means of perpetrators were neglected, in the SATRC (South Africa), CAVR (Peru), CVR (East Timor) and SLTRC (Sierra Leone) the accounts of survivors of "direct, personal violence" were privileged, while those who had suffered "indirect, structural violence" were neglected. Not only do

104 Seeking "truth" in aftermath of conflict

restrictive mandates put in doubt the claim that truth commissions are established to generate "as complete a picture as possible" (Government of South Africa 1995, para 23a), the ways in which witness statements are taken prior to hearings and then controlled in hearings suggest that they are not places in which survivors can "ventilate [their] truth" (Verdoolaege 2006, 67). In contrast, the examples of the community-based truth projects in Northern Ireland provide important lessons, especially the value of allowing survivors to edit their testimony so they become active participants in truth-telling, rather than just being involved in "passive telling to third-party authors" (Laplante 2007, 435; see Lundy & McGovern 2006, 84).

Whether the weaknesses of truth commissions can be resolved, the overall claim to create an account of the past must be challenged. While there is no doubt that truth commissions "narrow the range of permissible lies" (Hamber & Wilson 2002, 36–37; see Ignatieff 1996, 113), the final reports and archives of truth commissions never "speak for themselves". As a consequence, "archives are never closed and never complete: every individual and every generation are allowed their own interpretation of the archive, to reinvent and reconstruct its view on and narrative of the past" (Ketelaar 2012, 210). This would suggest that the best a truth commission can hope to achieve is "to present the past as an irresolvable argument that is to be continually debated" (Hamber & Wilson 2002, 36–37). Reflecting this, Laplante (2007, 446) suggests that the final report of the CVR (Peru) "should be viewed as dynamic work, waiting for discussion, exchange and elaboration". From this perspective, perhaps truth commissions should be understood not as a means to "draw a line" under the past but as the impetus for an "insatiable desire among victim-survivors to continue to tell their story" as part of a continuing struggle over representing the past (Laplante 2007, 434–435).

Bibliography

Albuja, Sebastián and James Cavallaro. 2008. "The Lost Agenda: Economic Crimes and Truth Commissions in Latin America and Beyond". In *Transitional Justice From Below, Grassroots Activism And The Struggle For Change*, edited by Kieran McEvoy and Lorna McGregor 121–142. London: Hart Publishing.

Ardoyne Commemoration Project. 2002. *Ardoyne: The Untold Truth*. Belfast: Beyond the Pale Publications.

Argentine National Commission on the Disappeared. 1986. *Nunca Más: Report of the Argentine National Commission on the Disappeared*. New York: Farrar Straus & Giroux.

Baines, Erin and Beth Stewart. 2011. "I cannot accept what I have not done": Storytelling, Gender and Transitional Justice", *Journal of Human Rights Practice* 3 (3): 245–263.

Bickford, Louis. 2007. "Unofficial Truth Projects", *Human Rights Quarterly* 29 (4): 994–1035.

Blommaert, Jan, Mary Bock and Kay McCormick. 2006. "Narrative inequality in the TRC hearings: On the hearability of hidden transcripts", *Journal of Language and Politics* 5 (1): 37–70.

Brounéus, Karen. 2008. "Truth Telling as Talking Cure? Insecurity and Retraumatization in the Rwandan Gacaca Courts", *Security Dialogue* 39 (1): 55–76.

Buur, Lars. 2001. "Making findings for the future: representational order and redemption in the work of the TRC", *South African Journal of Philosophy* 20 (1): 42–65.

Buur, Lars. 2003. "Monumental History: Visibility and Invisibility in the Work of the South African Truth and Reconciliation Commission". In *Commissioning the Past: Understanding South Africa's Truth and Reconciliation Commission*, edited by Deborah Posel and Graeme Simpson, 66–93. Johannesburg: Witwatersrand University Press.

Chinkin, Christine. 2006. "People's Tribunals: Legitimate or Rough Justice", *Windsor Year Book of Access to Justice* 24 (2): 201–220.

Cole, Catherine M. 2007. "Performance, Transitional Justice, and the Law: South Africa's Truth and Reconciliation Commission", *Theatre Journal* 59 (2): 167–187.

Commission for Reception, Truth and Reconciliation. 2006. *"Chega!" Final Report of the Commission for Reception, Truth and Reconciliation in East Timor*. Dili: CAVR.

Connerton, Paul. 2008. "Seven types of forgetting", *Memory Studies* 1 (1): 59–71.

Eades, Diana. 2008. "Telling and Retelling Your Story in Court: Questions, Assumptions and Intercultural Implications", Current Issues in Criminal Justice 20 (2): 209–230.

Feldman, Allen. 1991. *Formations of Violence: The Narrative of the Body and Political Terror in Northern Ireland*. Chicago, IL: University of Chicago Press.

Feldman, Allen. 2004. "Memory Theatres, Virtual Witnessing, and the Trauma-Aesthetic", *Biography* 27 (1): 163–202.

Galtung, Johan. 1969. "Violence, Peace and Peace Research", *Journal of Peace Research* 6 (3): 167–190.

Government of Sierra Leone. 2000. The Truth and Reconciliation Commission Act, Government of Sierra Leone.

Government of South Africa. 1995. Promotion of National Unity and Reconciliation Act 34.

Guthrey, Holly L. 2016a. "Local Norms and Truth Telling: Examining Experienced Incompatibilities within Truth Commissions of Solomon Islands and Timor-Leste", *The Contemporary Pacific* 28 (1): 1–29.

Guthrey, Holly L. 2016b. "Expectations and Promises in the Quest for Truth: Examining Victims' Perceptions of Truth Commission Participation in Solomon Islands and Timor-Leste", *Peace and Conflict: Journal of Peace Psychology* 22 (4): 306–317.

Hackett, Claire. 2003. "Making History: Dúchas, Falls Community Council's Oral History Archive", *Contexts* 2 (1).

Hackett, Claire. 2017. "Struggling with Memory: Oral History and Reconciliation in Belfast Communities". In *Civil War and Narrative*, edited by Karine Deslandes, Fabrice Mourlon and Bruno Tribout 77–90. New York: Springer.

Hackett, Claire and Bill Rolston. 2009. "The Burden of Memory: Victims, Storytelling and Resistance in Northern Ireland", *Memory Studies* 2 (3): 355–376.

Hamber, Brandon and Richard A. Wilson. 2002. "Symbolic Closure Through Memory, Reparation and Revenge in Post-Conflict Societies", *Journal of Human Rights* 1 (1): 35–53.

Hanlon, Catherine Nolin and Finola Shankar. 2000. "Gendered Spaces of Terror and Assault: The Testimonio of REMHI and the Commission for Historical Clarification in Guatemala", *Gender, Place & Culture: A Journal of Feminist Geography* 7 (3): 265–286.

Hayner, Priscilla B. 2010. *Unspeakable Truths: Transitional Justice and the Challenge of Truth Commissions*. London: Routledge.

Honwana, Alcinda Manuel. 2005. "Healing and Social Reintegration in Mozambique and Angola". In *Roads to Reconciliation*, edited by Elin Skaar, Siri Gloppen and Astri Suhrke, 83–100. Lanham, MD: Lexington Books.

Ignatieff, Michael. 1996. "Articles of faith", *Index on Censorship* 25 (5): 110–122.

Ignatieff, Michael. 1998. *The Warrior's Honor: Ethnic War and the Modern Conscience*. London: Vintage.

106 Seeking "truth" in aftermath of conflict

Indian Residential School Settlement Agreement. 2006. "Schedule N", the Mandate of the Truth and Reconciliation Commission, available online at http://www.residentialschool settlement.ca/SCHEDULE_N.pdf

James, Matt. 2012. "A Carnival of Truth? Knowledge, Ignorance and the Canadian Truth and Reconciliation Commission", *The International Journal of Transitional Justice* 6 (2): 182–204.

Ketelaar, Eric. 2012. "Truths, Memories and Histories in the Archives of the International Criminal Tribunal for the Former Yugoslavia". In *The Genocide Convention: The Legacy of 60 Years*, edited by Harmen van der Wilt, Jeroen Vervliet, Göran Sluiter and Johannes Houwink ten Cate, 199–221. Leiden: Brill.

Langfield, Michele and Pam Maclean. 2009. "Multiple Framings: Survivor and Non-Survivor Interviewers in Holocaust Video Testimony". In *Memories of Mass Repression: Narrating Life Stories in the Aftermath of Atrocity*, edited by Nanci Adler, Selma Leydesdorff, Mary Chamberlain and Leyla Neyzi, 199–218. Somerset, NJ: Transaction.

Laplante, Lisa J. 2007. "The Peruvian Truth Commission's Historical Memory Project: Empowering Truth-Tellers to Confront Truth Deniers", *Journal of Human Rights* 6 (4): 433–452.

Lundy, Patricia and Mark McGovern. 2006. "Participation, Truth and Partiality: Participatory Action Research, Community-based Truth-telling and Post-conflict Transition in Northern Ireland", *Sociology* 40 (1): 71–88.

Mamdani, Mahmood 2000. "The Truth According to the TRC". In *The Politics of Memory: Truth, Healing and Social Justice*, edited by Ifi Amadiume and Abdullahi An-Na'im, 176–183. London: Zed Books.

Millar, Gearoid. 2011. "Local Evaluations of Justice through Truth Telling in Sierra Leone: Postwar Needs and Transitional Justice", *Human Rights Review* 12 (4): 515–535.

Mookherjee, Nayanika. 2006. "'Remembering to forget': public secrecy and memory of sexual violence in the Bangladesh war of 1971", *Journal of the Royal Anthropological Institute* 12 (2): 433–450.

Navarro, Marysa. 1989. "The Personal is Political: Las Madres de Plaza de Mayo". In *Power and Popular Protest. Latin American Social Movements*, edited by Susan Eckstei, 241–258. Berkeley, CA: University of California Press.

Nevins, Joseph. 2003. "Restitution over coffee: truth, reconciliation, and environmental violence in East Timor", *Political Geography* 22 (6): 677–701.

Niezen, Ronald. 2016. "Templates and exclusions: victim centrism in Canada's Truth and Reconciliation Commission on Indian residential schools", *Journal of the Royal Anthropological Institute* 22 (4): 920–938.

Pieces of the Past Project. 2014. *Living Through the Conflict: Belfast Oral Histories*. Belfast: Dúchas Oral History Archive.

Robarchek, Clayton A. 1979. "Conflict, emotion and abreaction: Resolution of conflict among the Semai Senoi", *Ethos* 7 (2): 104–123.

Robins, Simon. 2011. "Towards Victim-Centred Transitional Justice: Understanding the Needs of Families of the Disappeared in Postconflict Nepal", *The International Journal of Transitional Justice* 5 (1): 75–98.

Ross, Fiona C. 2001. "Speech and Silence: Women's Testimony in the First Five Weeks of Public Hearings of the South African Truth and Reconciliation Commission". In *Remaking a World: Violence, Social Suffering, and Recovery*, edited by Veena Das, Arthur Kleinman, Margaret Lock, Mamphela Ramphela and Pamela Reynolds, 250–279. Berkeley, CA: University of California Press.

Ross, Fiona. 2003a. *Bearing Witness: Women and the Truth and Reconciliation Commission in South Africa*. London: Pluto Press.

Ross, Fiona. 2003b. "On Having a Voice and Being Heard", *Anthropological Theory* 3 (3): 325–341.

Shaw, Rosalind. 2007a. "Displacing Violence: Making Pentecostal Memory in Postwar Sierra Leone", *Cultural Anthropology* 22 (1): 66–93.

Shaw, Rosalind. 2007b. "Memory Frictions: Localizing the Truth and Reconciliation Commission in Sierra Leone", *The International Journal of Transitional Justice* 1 (2): 183–207.

Shaw, Rosalind. 2014. "The TRC, the NGO and the child: young people and post-conflict futures in Sierra Leone", *Social Anthropology* 22 (3): 306–325.

Sluka, Jeffrey A. 1990. *Hearts and Minds, Water and Fish: Support for the IRA and INLA in a Northern Irish Ghetto*. Bingley, UK: Emerald Group Publishing.

Theidon, Kimberly. 2007. "Gender in Transition: Common Sense, Women and War", *Journal of Human Rights* 6 (3): 653–678.

Truth and Reconciliation Commission. 1998. *Truth and Reconciliation Commission of South Africa Report*. 5 vols. Vol. 1. Johannesburg: Palgrave Macmillan.

Vella, Louise. 2014. "'What Will You Do with Our Stories?' Truth and Reconciliation in the Solomon Islands", *International Journal of Conflict and Violence* 8 (1): 91–103.

Verdoolaege, Annelies. 2002. The Human Rights Violations Hearings of the South African TRC: A Bridge Between Individual Narratives of Suffering and a Contextualizing Master-Story of Reconciliation. Department of African Languages and Cultures, Ghent University, Belgium.

Verdoolaege, Annelies. 2006. "Managing reconciliation at the human rights violations hearings of the South African TRC", *The Journal of Human Rights* 5 (1): 61–80.

White, Geoffrey M. 1991. "Rhetoric, Reality, and Resolving Conflicts: Disentangling in a Solomon Islands Society". In *Conflict Resolution: Cross-Cultural Perspectives*, edited by Kevin Avruch, Peter W. Black and Joseph A. Scimecca, 187–212. Westport, CT: Greenwood Publishing Group.

Wilson, Richard A. 2000. "Reconciliation and Revenge in Post-Apartheid South Africa: Rethinking Legal Pluralism and Human Rights", *Current Anthropology* 41 (1): 75–98.

Wilson, Richard A. 2001. *The Politics of Truth and Reconciliation in South Africa: Legitimizing the Post-Apartheid State*. Cambridge, UK: Cambridge University Press.

Zunino, Marcos. 2016. "Subversive Justice: The Russell Vietnam War Crimes Tribunal and Transitional Justice", *International Journal of Transitional Justice* 10 (2): 211–229.

5

INTERNATIONAL CRIMINAL JUSTICE

In May 1993, Resolution 827 of the United Nations Security Council created the International Criminal Tribunal for the Former Yugoslavia (ICTY), the resolution stating that prosecuting individuals for "serious violations of international humanitarian law" would ensure "that such violations are halted and effectively redressed" and "would contribute to the restoration and maintenance of peace" (United Nations 1993). The ICTY, which would ultimately indict 161 individuals, was followed by the International Criminal Tribunal for Rwanda (ICTR, established in 1994; with ninety-three individuals indicted); the Special Panels for Serious Crimes in East Timor (SPSC, established in 2000; 400 individuals indicted); the Special Court for Sierra Leone (SCSL, established in 2002; fourteen individuals indicted); and the Extraordinary Chambers in the Courts of Cambodia (ECCC, established in 2003; five individuals indicted). Each of these institutions was created in response to specific events: the 1991–2001 war in the former Yugoslavia (ICTY); the 1994 Rwandan genocide of the Tutsi and crimes against humanity and war crimes against Hutu and Tutsi (ICTR); the 1999 withdrawal of occupying Indonesian forces from East Timor (SPSC); the 1991–2002 civil war in Sierra Leone (SCSL); and the 1975–1979 Khmer Rouge regime of Democratic Kampuchea (ECCC). Three of these courts (SCSL, SPSC, ECCC) are/were "hybrids" which use a combination of domestic and international law and are staffed by a combination of national and international lawyers and judges (see Hinton 2016, 49).

In a parallel development, the International Criminal Court (ICC) was created by the Rome Statute of 1998 and came into operation in 2002. Unlike the restrictive jurisdiction of the context-specific courts, the ICC has jurisdiction over any crime committed since July 2002 if the crime(s) was committed by a national of a state party (states must agree to come under the ICC's jurisdiction); in the territory of a state party; in a state that has accepted the jurisdiction of the court; or if the crime has been referred to the ICC prosecutor by the United Nations

Security Council in order "to maintain or restore international peace and security". All six of these institutions have/had jurisdiction over war crimes (mistreatment of civilians or prisoners of war); crimes against humanity (a widespread or systematic attack on a civilian population, whether or not in a time of war); and genocide (the intent to destroy, in whole or in part, a national, ethnic, racial or religious group). Individuals are held personally accountable for committing these crimes, continuing the precedent established after the Second World War at the International Military Tribunal (Major War Criminals) at Nuremberg (1945–1946) and the International Military Tribunal for the Far East in Tokyo (1946–1948). I shall use the term "international criminal court" in this chapter as a generic term for such institutions.

Reflecting on the ECCC, the anthropologist Alexander Laban Hinton (2018, 5) asks the simple question, "What is the point of holding international tribunals?" Those tasked with speaking on behalf of institutions provide a variety of answers, ranging from discovering and publicising the "truth"; punishing perpetrators; responding to the needs of victims; and promoting the rule of law and reconciliation (see Fletcher & Weinstein 2002, 586–601). I encountered this variety of purported purposes during my own ethnographic fieldwork at the ICTR between 2005 and 2007. On my first day at the ICTR I was handed a twenty-six-minute video produced in 2005 entitled *Towards Reconciliation* and a leaflet entitled "*The ICTR at a Glance*" (ICTR n.d.), which stated that the ICTR was created "to contribute to the process of national reconciliation in Rwanda and to the maintenance of peace in the region, replacing an existing culture of impunity with one of accountability" (see Eltringham 2014, 549–550). Over time, however, I became aware that, rather than discuss whether the ICTR had achieved the objectives of reconciliation and peace, ICTR officials tended to foreground the strictly quantifiable (number of arrests, number of convictions) and tangible contributions of the ICTR to the global project of international criminal justice (jurisprudence). This suggested that while those who spoke on behalf of the ICTR made "grandiose statements about its supposed benefits ('peace,' 'transition,' 'truth,' 'reconciliation')" (Mégret 2016, para 50), evidence to support such claims was, and continues to be, thin on the ground. Given the lack of evidence, anthropologists and other ethnographers have sought to interrogate "grandiose statements" by starting "with the facts and not the ideology" (Branch 2011, 125). This has been done in a number of ways: by challenging the restricted mandate of these institutions; by assessing the degree of success in enabling "peace" and "reconciliation" in affected communities; and by evaluating the way in which trials generate a historical record. I will consider each of these assessments in turn.

The "fiction" of individual criminal responsibility

In Chapter 4 I discussed how the restrictive mandates given to truth commissions can obscure important parts of a violent past. For example, by concentrating on violence to the body, the South African Truth and Reconciliation Commission (SATRC) suppressed testimony regarding collective, socio-economic deprivation that would have revealed the true "depths of apartheid" (Ross 2001, 253 270). The

110 International criminal justice

same argument has been levelled at international trials, that they suppress consideration of important aspects of violent conflict. The anthropologist Kamari Clarke (2009, 13–15) suggests that those who promote international criminal courts justify their existence by employing a "tragic spectacle of suffering – the spectre of a victim representing the condition of oppression in need of salvation", that, without such a "victim", the "moral – and thus institutional – power" of such institutions would be weakened (see Eltringham 2019, 124–127). Similarly, the legal scholar Christine Schwöbel-Patel (2016, 256) argues that international criminal courts employ the already established "fundraising image" used by humanitarian NGOs in ways that simultaneously disempower the "victim" while legitimising powerful, international "saviours" (see Abu-Lughod 2002; Kendall & Nouwen 2014; McEvoy & McConnachie 2013). The result of international criminal courts relying on the image of a victim in need of rescue is a simplistic narrative of the "evil warlord", the "innocent victim" and the "hero lawyer" (Schwöbel-Patel 2016, 268–269). This simplistic narrative has two interrelated consequences: by placing the responsibility for mass atrocity crimes on individual "evil warlords", the causes and dynamics of such crimes are misrepresented; this, in turn, masks the responsibility of international actors (political and commercial). I shall consider these two consequences in turn.

Regarding the first consequence, political scientist Adam Branch (2011, 121–123) rejects the "fiction of individual criminal responsibility for mass violence". Such an understanding, argues Branch, depends on seeing the work of institutions like the ICC through the lens of the "domestic analogy", that the ICC is simply a "scaled-up" version of domestic courts which punish individuals who commit individual crimes. However, such "scaling up" does not work, Branch (2011, 126) argues, as those put on trial in international criminal courts end "up being burdened individually with what is in fact a vast collective and structural responsibility" (see Glasius & Meijers 2012). Such misrepresentation makes international criminal justice ineffective because it:

> reduces mass violence to cynical acts undertaken by self-interested "conflict entrepreneurs" who are thought to lead misguided or coerced followers. It ignores the affirmative character of identity-based violence and the ways in which radicalised identity-based political forces will not be defused through punishing their leaders, but will often be further radicalised as punishment inflames divisions.
>
> *(Branch 2011, 128)*

Branch's assertion is reflected in the response by "ordinary" people to an ICTY "outreach" event (see below) at which the conviction of individuals from their own community did not defuse ethnic animosity but, rather, "contributed to cementing ethno-political fault lines" (Mannergren Selimovic 2010, 51). While representing mass violence as the consequence of the individual actions of "evil warlords" misrepresents its collective nature, it has another, more insidious, consequence. Branch (2011, 126–135) notes that although "mass violence is embedded in international and global structures of domination and injustice", by promoting individual prosecution as a solution, international criminal courts have "placed certain fundamental issues outside the scope of what can be defined as unjust and thus subject to challenge". These fundamental issues include "economic exploitation, Western sponsorship of violent and anti-democratic political forces, internationally enforced disparities in access to medicines, trade regimes that undermine development and food security", all of which need to be addressed if sustainable peace is to be realised (Branch 2011, 135; see Branch 2007). By trying individuals for mass crimes and ignoring global structures, the "ICC is thus uniquely unsuited to address the very acts it was established to prosecute" (Branch 2011, 126).

Branch's list of "fundamental issues" indicates ways in which international political and commercial interests are integral to mass atrocity crimes (war crimes, crimes against humanity and genocide). This is particularly relevant to Sub-Saharan Africa which has, up to now, been a key focus of international criminal justice (at the time of writing, twelve situations were under investigation by the ICC, of which nine are in Sub-Saharan Africa, and all of the thirty-seven individuals who have so far been indicted by the court are from the continent of Africa). Clarke (2011, 34–35) notes how neoliberal capitalism privileges free-market methods which open up foreign markets to "corporate colonisation", resulting in an increase in "paramilitary contests over resources, furthering militarisation and sectarian violence". Clarke (2010, 641) argues that there has been a new scramble for African resources involving "local, national, regional and international interests" which "shapes and fuels" the conflicts so often portrayed outside of Africa as ancient, local "ethnic clashes" (see Eltringham 2013b, 4–11). This includes the on-going war in the Democratic Republic of Congo which, since 1996, has resulted in the deaths of more than six million people, a conflict fuelled, in part, by regional and international exploitation of natural resources that include diamonds, cobalt, coltan and gold (see Prunier 2011; United Nations 2001). Such conflicts must, therefore, be understood as being "part of a larger set of global interconnections in which violence, war, arms and mineral extraction are all part of the same cycle", with the consequence that "the responsibility for such violence goes well beyond that of an individual commander" (Clarke 2010, 641–642). Clarke (2010, 630) summarises the consequences of this:

> where there are mass struggles over the management of resources and competing forces vying for control, reassigning the guilt of thousands of people to a single chief commander and a few of his/her top aides neither ends violence nor captures adequately the complicity of multiple agents involved in the making of war.

The way in which international criminal justice can obscure how "mass violence is embedded in international and global structures of domination and injustice" (Branch 2011, 126) is illustrated by Hinton's (2013) discussion of a cartoon booklet entitled *Uncle San, Aunty Yan and the KRT* (Khmer Rouge Tribunal), produced in 2008 by the Khmer Institute of Democracy as part of an "outreach" programme on behalf of the ECCC, which began in 2005. At the start of the booklet Uncle San "dozes fitfully in a hammock, dreaming about the Khmer Rouge past" (Hinton 2013, 89). Next, Uncle San is shown attending an "outreach" meeting at which he is told about the 2003 agreement between the Cambodian government and the UN to create the ECCC, followed by a visit to the ECCC itself. Uncle San's journey, therefore, illustrates a movement from the past of "regressive savagery, violence, chaos, anarchy" to a "civilised, peaceful, ordered, progressive" future made possible by trials at the ECCC (Hinton 2013, 94). Hinton (2013, 96) suggests that the booklet relies on what he calls "transitional justice time" which erases historical and socio-cultural complexities (see Shaw 2014). Because the ECCC was created to bring to trial the "senior leaders of Democratic Kampuchea" for their actions during Khmer Rouge rule of "17 April 1975 to 6 January 1979" (United Nations/Royal Government of Cambodia 2003), the outreach booklet makes no mention of the origins or immediate aftermath of Khmer Rouge rule, including the Vietnam War (1955–1975), the hundreds of thousands of Cambodians killed by the illegal carpet bombing of Cambodia by the United States of America in 1973, or that the United States rearmed and supported the Khmer Rouge after they were toppled by a Vietnamese invasion in 1979 (see Manning 2011, 167). Hinton (2013, 92) argues that there is an irony that the "critical backdrop and aftermath" of Khmer Rouge rule is erased (including the involvement of foreign states), given that a purported purpose of international criminal trials is to establish "truth" (see Hinton 2016, 35).

FIGURE 5.1 Pronouncement of the judgement in Case 002/02 (Khieu Samphan and Nuon Chea) on 16 November 2018. (Photo courtesy of the Extraordinary Chambers in the Courts of Cambodia)

Clarke (2010, 635) notes that international criminal courts need not exclude consideration of "global structures of domination and injustice" (Branch 2011, 126). The 1991 Draft Code of Crimes Against the Peace and Security of Mankind (prepared by a Preparatory Commission established by the UN General Assembly) included a broader set of crimes than just war crimes, crimes against humanity and genocide, including "colonial domination and other forms of alien domination; apartheid; recruitment use, financing and training of mercenaries; wilful and severe damage to the environment; international terrorism; and illicit traffic in narcotic drugs" (International Law Commission 1991). These crimes, however, were removed by the Special Rapporteur (appointed by the International Law Commission) from the 1995 Draft Code of Crimes Against the Peace and Security of Mankind because the crimes were "too controversial or widespread" (Clarke 2010, 635). In the end, the crimes over which the ICC has jurisdiction (following the examples of the ICTY and ICTR) are "genocide, war crimes, crimes against humanity and the crime of aggression". In contrast, in 2014 member states of the African Union adopted the Malabo Protocol which extends the jurisdiction of the yet to be established African Court of Justice and Human Rights to include not only genocide, crimes against humanity and war crimes but also crimes including "mercenarism", "corruption", "trafficking in hazardous wastes" and "illicit exploitation of natural resources" (see Werle & Vormbaum 2017), reflecting the breadth of the Draft Code of Crimes Against the Peace and Security of Mankind.

The list of crimes contained in the 1991 Draft Code of Crimes Against the Peace and Security of Mankind suggests that there are individuals who should be held to account for mass atrocity crimes but who evade prosecution, such as those who finance and train mercenaries. Furthermore, by concentrating only on the individual responsibility of "evil warlords", international criminal courts could be considered as "dangerous, potentially masking power and diverting attention from geopolitical interest, domestic manipulations, and structural violence" (Hinton 2018, 7). Such a concern corresponds to my discussion in the Introduction regarding "structural violence", and Johan Galtung's (1969, 170) distinction between "personal or direct" violence and "structural or indirect" violence. As Galtung (1969, 172) notes, institutions such as international criminal courts that are "directed against *intended* violence will easily fail to capture structural violence in their nets – and may hence be catching the small fry and letting the big fish loose". Rectifying this failure is one of the objectives of the Permanent Peoples' Tribunal I discussed in Chapter 4, which – in addition to being concerned with war crimes, crimes against humanity and genocide – is also concerned with "ecological crimes", "economic crimes" and "system crimes", defined as crimes "not imputable to specific persons, but of which it is possible to identify the causes as being not natural, but political or economic, in the functioning of legal and social systems" (Permanent Peoples' Tribunal 2018, Art. 7). Such an approach provides an alternative vision for international criminal courts, but one that is unlikely to be supported by nation states.

114 International criminal justice

Local responses to international criminal justice

The purpose of international criminal courts has been justified in relation to facilitating "reconciliation" and "peace" among affected communities: for example, that the ICTY "would contribute to the restoration and maintenance of peace" (United Nations 1993); the SCSL "would contribute to the process of national reconciliation and to the restoration and maintenance of peace" (United Nations 2000); and that the ECCC is part of the "pursuit of justice and national reconciliation, stability, peace and security" by the government and people of Cambodia (United Nations/Royal Government of Cambodia 2003). This "purported link between trials and reconciliation has solidified into articles of faith" (Fletcher & Weinstein 2002, 600). One way in which to assess that link is through the "outreach" programmes established by international criminal courts to disseminate information about their activities to affected communities. Here I shall consider three "outreach" programmes – in Bosnia-Herzegovina (Mannergren Selimovic 2010; 2015), Cambodia (Lesley-Rozen 2014; Manning 2011) and Sierra Leone (Anders 2012).

Peace studies scholar Johanna Mannergren Selimovic (2010, 50) gives an account of two, one-day conferences organised by the "Outreach Program of the ICTY" in 2004–2005 in Srebrenica (concerned with crimes committed against Bosniak civilians) and Konjic (concerned with crimes committed against Serb civilians). In July 1995 the UN-protected enclave of Srebrenica in north-eastern Bosnia was overrun by the Army of Republika Srpska (VRS), resulting in the murder of an estimated 8,000 Bosnian men and boys. At the time of Mannergren Selimovic's fieldwork, Radislav Krstic (deputy commander and later Chief of Staff of the VRS) had been found guilty (in 2004) by the ICTY of "aiding and abetting genocide" (following an appeal). Subsequently, Radovan Karadžić (President of Republika Srpska during the war) was convicted by the ICTY of genocide at Srebrenica in 2016 and, in 2017, Ratko Mladić (who led the VRS) was also convicted of the Srebrenica genocide by the ICTY. As regards Konjic, the ICTY convicted three Bosniak soldiers of the rape, torture and murder of eight civilians in a detention camp established outside the town (Mannergren Selimovic 2010, 53).

At the outreach events, organised as part of a "belated effort to connect with local communities" (Mannergren Selimovic 2010, 50), representatives of the ICTY prosecutor's office explained the trials, showed videos of the trials and answered a few pre-selected questions from local power holders and ordinary citizens who made up the audience. The central message from the ICTY prosecutors was that "singling out individual perpetrators puts an end to the demonizing of entire groups, deflates ideas of collective guilt, and paves the way for reconciliation in divided societies" (Mannergren Selimovic 2010, 51). And yet none of Mannergren Selimovic's respondents in either Srebrenica or Konjic believed that the presentations would affect the positions taken by the other side regarding collective victimhood. Participants described perpetrators on their own side as "'not really' perpetrators" and, while they acknowledged that people on the other side had suffered, they insisted that those on the other side were "'not really' victims" because they had not suffered to the same extent (Mannergren Selimovic 2010, 54). Furthermore, both groups:

> tended to interpret every ICTY sentence against an individual perpetrator as an action directed against the entire group. The assumption was that every person belonging to the other group was (more or less) guilty, apart from a few innocent ones—an innocence that was determined individually instead of in court. The opposite logic applied to perpetrators within one's own group—they were defined as "crazy" and responsibility was isolated.
>
> *(Mannergren Selimovic 2010, 58)*

Mannergren Selimovic (2010, 51 58) concludes that the outcome of the ICTY outreach events was "utterly contrary" to their intention (to establish the principle of individual rather than collective guilt) and, instead, "contributed to cementing ethno-political fault lines". As anthropologist Tim Allen (2010, 259) observes, it is "not certain, even in Europe, that the ritual humiliation of a small group of individuals, who are held to be most responsible for terrible acts, contributes to social healing. Perhaps the proceedings of courts and tribunals just remind people why they hate each other so much" (see Pavlakovic 2010).

Mannergren Selimovic's (2015, 236) further research in the town of Foča (in Republika Srpska, eastern Bosnia-Herzegovina) strengthens what she had observed at the earlier outreach events. Ten Bosnian Serbs were indicted by the ICTY for crimes against humanity and war crimes committed in Foča. These indictments (leading to eight convictions) were seen as a challenge to the ethno-nationalist narrative that Bosnian Serbs had been defending their "homeland". As a consequence, every conviction of a Bosnian Serb was interpreted as "a collective punishment based on ethnic belonging" (Mannergren Selimovic 2015, 236). The Bosniak collective narrative followed the same logic: any acts by Bosniaks defined as a crime by the ICTY were excused as "acts of self-defence against Serb aggression" (Mannergren Selimovic 2015, 236). Despite this, and unlike the "outreach" events in Srebrenica and Konjic, Mannergren Selimovic (2015, 239) found in Foča "less aligned" individuals who had never embraced exclusionist, ethno-nationalist narratives and who had opposed the war (see Kulle 2003). These people accepted the verdicts of the ICTY as factual accounts of the war and more readily accepted the ICTY's narrative of individual guilt, because "they categorized people not according to ethnic collectives but according to whether they were 'good people' or 'bad people'" (Mannergren Selimovic 2015, 239). While these "non-aligned" people were evidence that the ICTY trials did deflate ideas of collective guilt, the overwhelming sense was that the trials "contributed to cementing ethno-political fault lines" (Mannergren Selimovic 2010, 58 51; see Clark 2009; 2012).

In the context of the ECCC, anthropologist Elena Lesley-Rozen (2014, 131) describes how, since 2004, civil society organisations, supported by the ECCC, have organised "study tours" that bring groups of Cambodians to the ECCC courtroom, the former torture centre at Tuol Sleng and to Choeung Ek (the

116 International criminal justice

nearby "killing fields", where many of those tortured at "S-21" were killed; see Chapter 6). The "study tours" are designed to support the historical narrative promoted by the ECCC and Cambodian government that "a few top leaders" were responsible for the crimes committed during the Democratic Kampuchea period (1974–1979; brought to an end by a Vietnamese invasion), despite responsibility for crimes being much more widespread. This narrative grants *de facto* amnesty to lower-level Khmer Rouge perpetrators, thereby shielding from prosecution former Khmer Rouge in the current government, including Hun Sen, prime minister since 1985 (Lesley-Rozen 2014, 133). Unsurprisingly, Lesley-Rozen (2014, 141–142) found that "study tour" participants who had lived in areas controlled by the Khmer Rouge after 1979 challenged the ECCC, some rejecting the court outright and others acknowledging that killing had taken place but casting doubt on whether the leaders of Democratic Kampuchea had been responsible. In contrast, those who had lived in areas not controlled by the Khmer Rouge after 1979 were "mostly supportive of prosecutions underway at the ECCC". In conversations with Lesley-Rozen, however, they "tended to focus on seemingly fragmented personal experiences without connecting them to a larger political or historical narrative" (Lesley-Rozen 2014, 141). This may be because of the contradictory manner in which Democratic Kampuchea has been treated since 1979. Initially "Hate Day" (20 May) was established to "sustain an implacable hatred of the [Khmer Rouge]" (Williams 2004, 249). When the Vietnamese withdrew from Cambodia in September 1989, followed by United Nations intervention, remnants of the Khmer Rouge were invited to join the government and "Cambodians were asked to forgive Pol Pot and other leaders" (Williams 2004, 249). This changed again when the surviving leadership was put on trial at the ECCC. Given this shifting attitude, Lesley-Rozen (2014, 142) suggests that Cambodians who participated in these "study tours" concentrated on personal experiences because they were unsure of whether any "historical/political narrative" they proposed would be "accurate or endorsed by current and future authorities". This raises the question of whether the ECCC's preferred historical narrative (the culpability of "a few top leaders") that was promoted in the "study tours" would gain support if those who had experienced Democratic Kampuchea shied away from such historical-political narratives.

The sociologist Peter Manning (2011) also participated in an ECCC outreach activity, a "public forum" on "Justice and Reconciliation" organised in 2008 by a Cambodian NGO in Pailin region in western Cambodia, a region that had remained a Khmer Rouge stronghold long after the fall of the regime in 1979. Prior to the forum, sixty residents of the region had been taken to Phnom Penh to visit the ECCC courtroom, the former torture centre at Tuol Sleng and the Choeung Ek "killing fields". During the visit and the forum, Manning (2011, 171) witnessed a desire among former Khmer Rouge to "address a broader historical and contextual truth about the [Khmer Rouge] period". The jurisdiction of the ECCC, however, is restricted to the actions of "senior leaders" between 1975 and 1979. Manning (2011, 174) found that while former Khmer Rouge soldiers who participated in the "public forum" did not necessarily deny the ECCC's claims regarding 1975–1979, they argued that what had happened before 1975 and after 1979 was also important. The outreach event, therefore, drew attention to "alternative accounts of political violence that are silenced by ECCC proceedings, particularly those memories of suffering that occurred before and after the ECCC's temporal jurisdiction" (Manning 2011, 179). While Lesley-Rozen (2014) found participants in ECCC outreach events to be unwilling to engage in the historical narrative of the Khmer Rouge regime promoted by the ECCC, Manning (2011) found that Khmer Rouge participants were frustrated by the restricted focus of the ECCC (see Hinton 2013, 92). Neither finding suggested that the ECCC was perceived by outreach participants as a straightforward means to achieve "national reconciliation, stability, peace and security" (United Nations/Royal Government of Cambodia 2003).

Anthropologist Gerhard Anders (2012, 94) provides an account of Sierra Leonean "outreach officers" working for the SCSL who were tasked with informing the population about the court through "outreach events" of one to two hours' duration in villages, town halls, schools, police stations and army barracks. At these events footage of the trials would be screened, followed by an explanation of the relevant law and the opportunity for the audience to ask questions. Anders accompanied "outreach officers" to a number of events, including one in Mukump Gbana, near Makeni in northern Sierra Leone. Once the formal presentation had

FIGURE 5.2 Residents of the former Khmer Rouge stronghold of Pailin visit Tuol Sleng Genocide Museum as part of an ECCC outreach visit in November 2010. (Photo courtesy of the Extraordinary Chambers in the Courts of Cambodia)

118 International criminal justice

been completed the town chief criticised the court for putting Issa Sesay on trial, arguing that Sesay was a responsible commander who had ordered the RUF to disarm (Sesay was the interim leader of the rebel Revolutionary United Front [RUF], 2000–2002; Anders 2012, 106). Behind this criticism voiced in northern Sierra Leone was the fact that the 2002 elections had been won by the Sierra Leone People's Party (SLPP), which had its main power base in the east of the country and among the Mende ethnic group in the south. For those living in Mukump Gbana in the north, the arrest and trial of Sesay (a member of the Temne ethnic group from the north) by the SCSL was seen as an attempt by the SLPP government to further consolidate power in a context in which the north had been politically and economically marginalised since independence (Anders 2012, 108). Anders (2012, 109–110) found that criticism of the SCSL was reversed at an out-reach event in Tissor, in the eastern part of the country dominated by the Mende. Here the town chief criticised the SCSL for arresting Sam Hinga Norman (a Mende traditional ruler) who had formed the civil defence forces that had fought the RUF. In other words, within the context of long-standing regional power struggles, the SCSL's even-handed indictment of individuals from different sides was dismissed as being politically motivated and as targeting groups collectively.

The SCSL outreach events demonstrated, as in the case of Mannergren Seli-movic's (2010, 51) ICTY events, that the prosecution of individuals did little to break down "ethno-political fault lines". Furthermore, Anders (2012, 108) found that Sierra Leoneans that spoke at the outreach events were in agreement that the $150 million that had been spent on the SCSL would have been better spent on development projects and compensation for victims. In Mukump Gbana, for example, one younger chief asked why those detained by the SCSL were "'growing fat' on three meals a day ... while the villagers in Mukump Gbana were hungry" (Anders 2012, 108). In response, the "outreach officers" stuck to an "official script", stating that the court's limited jurisdiction did not include devel-opment or social justice (Anders 2012, 113). This corresponds with the rejection of the SLTRC by Sierra Leoneans that I discussed in Chapter 4, that those who tes-tified and demanded material assistance were told this was not part of the SLTRC's mandate (Shaw 2007, 201–202; see Millar 2011, 524). The fact that this criticism was raised at both outreach events indicates that, for Sierra Leoneans, "justice" was not about "fuzzy concepts such as national reconciliation or the symbolic punish-ment of a few individuals", but about "concrete development in their commu-nities, including roads, schools, hospitals, clean water, electricity and, above all, employment" (Anders 2012, 107 114; see Meith 2013).

Research by Mannergren Selimovic (2010; 2015), Lesley-Rozen (2014), Manning (2011) and Anders (2012) appears to confirm Branch's (2011, 128) warning that "radicalised identity-based political forces will not be defused through punishing their leaders, but will often be further radicalised as punishment inflames divisions". Whereas ICTY prosecutors suggested that "singling out individual perpetrators puts an end to the demonizing of entire groups, deflates ideas of collective guilt, and paves the way for reconciliation in divided societies" (Mannergren Selimovic 2010,

51), international trials in both Sierra Leone and the former Yugoslavia appeared to strengthen (or do little to dissipate) the sense of collective victimhood of one's own group and collective guilt of one's opponents. Furthermore, in the case of the SCSL, Sierra Leoneans demonstrated a concern for a "present- and future-oriented justice, one that focuses on survival and moving forward, instead of investigating the past" (Millar 2011, 524). In Cambodia, the historical narrative promoted by the ECCC, one that was politically expedient for the government, was either rejected in favour of recounting individual experiences or as being too restrictive as it excluded consideration of events prior to and after the Khmer Rouge regime. Although research at "outreach" events provides only a limited snapshot, these findings cast doubt on the claim that trials in international criminal courts "contribute to the restoration and maintenance of peace" (United Nations 1993).

The historical record

The critique of international criminal courts that I have considered so far has not been particularly complimentary. The focus on individual responsibility for mass crimes, it has been argued, masks power by "diverting attention from geopolitical interest, domestic manipulations, and structural violence" (Hinton 2018, 7). Meanwhile, the claim that prosecution of individuals "deflates ideas of collective guilt, and paves the way for reconciliation in divided societies" (Mannergren Selimovic 2010, 51), is not supported by the examples of the ICTY, ECCC or SCSL "outreach" events.

A third area in which anthropologists and other ethnographers have assessed international criminal courts is through the claim that trials produce a valuable "historical record". This was a view I encountered in my fieldwork at the ICTR (see Eltringham 2019, 157–162; Moghalu 2005, 204). In 2008, for example, the ICTR President (the chief judge) addressed the UN General Assembly, stating that the ICTR had:

> established an important, judicially verified factual record of those atrocities. The importance and value of that record and the archival collections of the Tribunal to national, regional and international history should not be underestimated. They have contributed and will continue to contribute to the peace and reconciliation process in Rwanda and in the Great Lakes region.
>
> *(United Nations 2008, 2)*

The claim that a "historical record" is an important purpose of international criminal trials can be traced back to the predecessors of the more recent institutions. Judges and lawyers who participated in the International Military Tribunal (Major War Criminals) at Nuremberg (1945–1946), which after the Second World War tried twenty-four high-ranking Nazis for war crimes, crimes against humanity and wars of aggression, also considered the "historical record" as an important contribution of trials. Sir Hartley Shawcross, (British Attorney General and chief

120 International criminal justice

prosecutor for the United Kingdom), for example, stated that the trial would provide "an authoritative and impartial record to which future historians may turn for truth and future politicians for warning" (International Military Tribunal 1947, 594). Addressing the American Bar Association less than a month after the execution of ten of the Nuremberg defendants, Norman Birkett (British alternate judge of the IMT) stated that "the fate of the individual defendants was perhaps the least important result of the Nuremberg trial"; more important was the record of "the dreadful consequences which come to a great nation when the rights of the individual are disregarded", a record that was "now available, not merely for the present generation, but for all generations to come" (Hyde 1964, 529).

In contrast to the perspective of lawyers and judges at Nuremberg, having witnessed the trial of Adolf Eichmann (German Nazi SS-Obersturmbannführer and a key organiser of the Holocaust) in Jerusalem in 1962 (see Chapter 3), Hannah Arendt (1994 [1963], 253) argued that:

> the purpose of the trial is to render justice, and nothing else: even the noblest of ulterior purposes — "the making of a record of the Hitler regime which would withstand the test of history" ... can only detract from the law's main business: to weigh the charges brought against the accused, to render judgement, and to mete out due punishment.

Anthropologist Richard Ashby Wilson (2011, 1) notes that it is because of this tension between the individual and broader frameworks in which alleged perpetrators operate (see above) that it is often argued "the justice system should not attempt to write history at all, lest it sacrifice high standards of judicial procedure", and that a consensus has emerged in the literature on legal responses to mass atrocity crimes that "courts of law produce mediocre historical accounts of the origins and causes of mass crimes". Based on his research at the ICTY, ICTR and ICC, Wilson (2011, 220) argues, however, that the "legal testing" that takes place in the course of a trial means that "historical points of view are all aired openly and are all challenged robustly, thus illustrating their strengths and weaknesses and leading the court to search for new material to make sense of the past" (see Douglas 2001, 265n264). For those reasons, Wilson (2011, 19) argues that "there is a compelling case for rethinking the long-standing view that the pursuit of justice and the writing of history are inherently irreconcilable". The legal scholar Kirsten Campbell (2013, 255) agrees, suggesting that the "law 'acts as a historian' in its legal function of establishing and recording an objective history of the conflict" (see Turner 2008).

The claim that law "acts as a historian" is also supported by the way in which historians actively collaborate in the creation of the archives of international criminal courts when they are called as expert witnesses or when extracts from their publications are submitted as evidence (see Anders 2014; Buss 2014; Wilson 2011, 49–68). As I found at the ICTR, historians themselves changed their positions in response to information emerging from the trials (Eltringham 2013a). For example, when a historian, called by the defence at the ICTR as an expert witness in 2006, was challenged by a prosecution lawyer on why he had changed his opinion since publishing a book ten years earlier, the historian responded: "When I wrote my book of 1996, proceedings at the ICTR were still in their infancy. Today, ninety per cent of the documents on the basis of which we can have a contemporaneous vision of the situation, are based on documents produced by the ICTR." On the one hand, this statement indicates the value placed on the archive by the historian, but it also indicates that trials and the production of works by historians are intertwined, rather than simply being a matter of historians consulting an archive after the fact.

While acknowledging that historians and their writings are often embedded in international criminal trials, it remains the case that such trials "produce a body of evidence that is invaluable for historians" so that the impact of trials "as producers of history lasts long after the trials are completed" (Wilson 2011, 18). An ICTR prosecution lawyer described this record to me:

> The historical record is every record, every piece of oral evidence before a Chamber [composed of three judges]. There are also documents released from US State Department, Human Rights groups, Radio broadcasts etc., all sources recording the events, all are part of the historical record. Like Nuremberg, we preserve everything because scholars have different interests. Therefore, this is the record.

FIGURE 5.3 The ICTR courtroom from the prosecution end. (Photo courtesy of the International Residual Mechanism for Criminal Tribunals)

122 International criminal justice

Among ICTR lawyers and judges with whom I spoke the key concern was whether the accumulation of a historical record should be viewed as an intentional objective of the trials or merely an incidental by-product (see Eltringham 2019, 157–162). On the one hand, a judge was adamant that a "'historical record' is not a purpose of the Tribunal, even if it is an inevitable result"; on the other hand, another judge argued that the ICTR was not a normal situation, that "the ICTR performs more functions than a normal court" and that it would "establish an historical record and individual guilt and innocence of an individual, the general and the specific". The prevalent position among lawyers and judges at the ICTR with whom I spoke was that a "historical record is an inevitable result" although not an intentional objective, as summarised by a prosecution lawyer:

> I see concentric circles. The outer circle: while acting as a court, it's also preserving evidence, cutting a path through a thicket. So, if the circle of law establishes truth, then it preserves history. ... So, the core is legal, but at the periphery there are other things. History is not the primary role, but the trials do it. No matter how you cut and dice it, the primary responsibility of the Tribunal is justice, but there are other secondary things including a factual, historical record.

Whereas Arendt's (1994 [1963], 253) position implies an either/or (granting primacy to either a historical record or individual prosecution), the lawyers and judges with whom I spoke at the ICTR implied that both could be pursued simultaneously. While the position adopted by Arendt offers a stark choice, many legal practitioners at the ICTR suggested a "middle ground" was possible, in which a historical record as an inevitable (valued) by-product could exist alongside the "core" objective of prosecution. A prosecution lawyers summed up the position, that the "historical record" should be valued for, after all, "You're going to have a version of history anyway, so better to have an accurate legal version rather than a watered down version."

My own research and that of Wilson (2011) suggest that international criminal courts do indeed "produce a body of evidence that is invaluable for historians" (Wilson 2011, 18). As already indicated, such a perspective finds support among many lawyers and judges at international criminal courts (see Turner 2008). For example, the ICTR prosecutor's former spokesperson stated that:

> The judicial records and ICTR Archives are perhaps the best historical narrative of the genocide and hold a great potential for re-imaging Rwanda based on the truth about the past. The Archives present a rich source for re-education in the recent history of the country and for reconciliation.
>
> (Gallimore 2008, 255 258)

While laudable, such aspirations do not acknowledge the possibility that the archive may be employed to write histories that are at odds with legal judgements.

The assumption, evident in the statement by the prosecutor's spokesperson above, is that the ICTR archive (and by extension the archives of other international criminal courts) will only be used in ways that correspond with legal judgements. The assumption was also evident in a response from an assistant legal officer (ALO; a judge's assistant) at the ICTR when I asked whether he considered the archive or the judgements to be the "historical record", to which he responded that "only by looking at the judgement can one ascertain whether [an item in the archive] is trustworthy or not. Future researchers should always read the judgements before they use any document."

There are a number of problems, however, in assuming that consulting the ICTR archives (and those of other international criminal courts) would be this straightforward. Different trials at the same international criminal court may have come to different conclusions about the same events. As the legal scholar Lawrence Douglas (2016, 46) notes, as "prosecutors, judges, and other legal actors master the learning curve of complex crimes – atrocity trials typically come to frame a richer, more nuanced treatment of the larger historical complex". Barrie Sander (2018, 554–568), also a legal scholar, notes that while in the judgement of Jean-Paul Akayesu (1998) and Clément Kayishema and Obed Ruzindana (1999) the ICTR judges concluded in unambiguous terms that the 1994 genocide of the Tutsi had been planned in advance, by the time of the judgement of Théoneste Bagosora et al. (2008) the judges concluded that the prosecution had failed to prove beyond reasonable doubt that the four accused had conspired to commit the genocide before its commencement. This raises the question of which judgement should be consulted as guidance in interpreting the archive.

Furthermore, assessing the credibility of an exhibit in the archive would not be straightforward as the archives contain multiple copies of the same exhibit that served different, possibly contradictory, purposes in different trials (and their concluding judgements) As Tom Adami (2007, 216), former chief archivist and head of the Judicial Records and Archives Unit at the ICTR, notes:

> A transcript of the Rwandan [Radio Télévision Libre des Mille Collines] ethnic hatred radio broadcasts may be submitted as exculpatory material [clears someone of guilt] by one of the parties and then it may again appear as an exhibit for the opposite side. Also, the same transcripts may again appear in another case defending or refuting a different set of actions attributed to a different defendant. Records are used, re-used, interpreted, and reinterpreted according to a complex set of requirements of the prosecution and/or defence teams.

Not only may trials within the same institution relate to the archive in different ways, but future trials in different courts may challenge ICTR judgements and how, therefore, the contents of the archive should be interpreted. Douglas (2001, 4) notes, for example, how the trial of Klaus Barbie (in 1987, for crimes committed while he directed the Nazi Gestapo in Lyon 1942–1944) revisited and revised the Nuremberg judgement (see Rousso 2001, 67). While Douglas (2001, 4) observes

124 International criminal justice

that "Individual trials must be staged to reach closure ... the discourse of legal judgement and the historical understanding it contains remain fluid and can be completely revised." Part of the reason for this is because subsequent trials "revisit and revise their judicial precursors" (Douglas 2006b, 191). ICTR judges themselves acknowledge this possibility. Sander (2018, 557) notes, for example, that while the officials in the ICTR judgement of Théoneste Bagosora et al. (ICTR 2008, para. 2112) concluded that the prosecution had not proven the genocide had been planned in advance, it remained conceivable that "newly discovered information, subsequent trials or history" would support that conclusion. This raises further problems for using judgements as a guide to interpreting the archives of international criminal courts.

A final issue is that those consulting the archives of international criminal courts may not be as compliant as the ALO quoted above assumes. This is illustrated by Danny Hoffman (2007), an anthropologist who published a version of the expert report he prepared for the defence in the trial of leaders of civil defence forces militia (CDF) at the SCSL. Hoffman (2007, 640) argues that:

> I believe the Special Court transcripts and archive will be the primary historical record of the war. ... Though there are a number of excellent books, articles, reports, and websites dedicated to analysing or documenting the CDF, no other body collected the sheer volume of data that the Special Court did. A great deal of this material is freely available online. In my view, much of the Prosecution's interpretation of that material was inaccurate. My report and the current article are therefore meant as a dissenting voice in the CDF archive.

In this statement Hoffman indicates that he values the SCSL archive and believes the SCSL has produced an invaluable body of evidence (see Wilson 2011, 18), but his interpretation of it is contrary to that promoted by the prosecution at the SCSL. Hoffman's approach illustrates that "future researchers" will not be bound by the judgements in their interpretation of the archives of international criminal courts, as the ALO quoted above assumed.

While Hoffman belongs to the anticipated category of "researchers and historians" envisaged by the prosecutor's spokesperson (Gallimore 2008, 255), his "dissenting voice" raises the spectre of more extreme dissent, as hinted at by ICTR defence lawyers who claimed that the archives could support an "untold story of the Rwanda War" (Erlinder 2009, 20) that had not been told by the judgements. This suggests that while international trials should be valued "as producers of history", whose impact lasts long after the trials have been completed (Wilson 2011, 18), judgements will not control the way in which the archives are used and that the archives may "face a long-term state of contestation" (Kaye 2014, 392; see Campbell 2013, 258). This corresponds with the view of Eric Ketelaar (2012, 210), a former national archivist of the Netherlands and a member of the Advisory Committee on the Archives of the ICTY and ICTR (2007–2008). He argues, in the context of the ICTY, that archives never speak for themselves; rather, it is users who determine what information they will get out of an archive. As a consequence, "archives are never closed and never complete: every individual and every generation are allowed their own interpretation of the archive, to reinvent and reconstruct its view on and narrative of the past" (Ketelaar 2012, 210).

And what of the assumption that it will be "researchers and historians" (Gallimore 2008, 255–258) who will be the principal consumers of the archive? These consumers will be multiple and unpredictable and, as anthropologist Michel-Rolph Trouillot (1995, 25–26) suggests in another context, not restricted to "researchers and historians":

> theories of history … grossly underestimate the size, the relevance, and the complexity of the overlapping sites where history is produced, notably outside of academia … Next to professional historians we discover artisans of different kinds, unpaid or unrecognised field labourers who augment, deflect or reorganise the work of the professionals as politicians, students, fiction writers, filmmakers and participating members of the public.

Such "artisans" will "subject the [archives] to different and unpredictable readings [and put them] to different and unpredictable" uses (Schaffer & Smith 2004, 32). This raises the question of whether such contestation is something that can or should be avoided. Speaking of the ICTY archives, Ketelaar (2012, 217) welcomes the fact that it will be a "living archive" that will "continue to be challenged, contested, and expanded". Like memory, "an archive is not just an agency of storage, but a process", and is, therefore, "a space to escape from a monolithic truth, history and memory, by allowing the questioning of myth and rationality".

My own research (Eltringham 2019) and that of Wilson (2011, 18) suggest that trials contribute to history immediately (through "legal testing") and in the longer term by preserving an archive ("a body of evidence that is invaluable for historians"). An archive will not only be used by historians but by "artisans of different kinds" (Trouillot 1995, 26). This includes future generations. As a resident of Foča told Mannergren Selimovic (2015, 240), "I think the archives of the ICTY will be there for the future. The youth of today will be able to go through them and find the truth." Likewise, a defence lawyer at the ICTR reported to me that his client told him to "Put everything on the record and then later our children will decide on the truth. People will be able to read and make their own decisions in the future. We have all the records. The judgement is not made now; the judgement will be made in the future." This suggests the archives of international criminal courts will face a "long-term state of contestation" (Kaye 2014, 392). While, on one hand, this would make archives "a potential, future antidote to permanent amnesia" (Mannergren Selimovic 2015, 240), archives may also be employed to write histories that are at odds with judgements and which may fuel division rather than achieve "the restoration and maintenance of peace" (United Nations 1993).

126 International criminal justice

Conclusion

I began the chapter by suggesting that although claims are made for the value of putting individuals on trial for mass atrocity crimes (war crimes, crimes against humanity and genocide) – including discovering and publicising the "truth"; responding to the needs of victims; and promoting the rule of law and reconciliation (see Fletcher & Weinstein 2002, 586–601) – there is a need to start with the "facts and not the ideology" (Branch 2011, 25) of their impact. That impact, it has been argued, is artificially restrained by the focus on the actions of "evil warlords", which misrepresents the collective nature of violent conflict and the complicity of international actors. As Douglas (2006a, 100–101) observes regarding all criminal trials:

> trials exaggerate the roles of individuals ... the law overlooks and mischaracterizes larger forces – political, ideological, military, bureaucracy ... thus [creating] an odd disconnect between the magnitude of the crimes adjudicated and the solitary individual in the dock ... creating a false sense of legal closure as other perpetrators go unpunished and history remains unexamined, undigested.

In the case of international criminal courts, the "history that remains unexamined" includes the "corporate colonisation" which results in an increase in "paramilitary contests over resources" (Clarke 2011, 34–35), during which mass atrocity crimes are committed. Rather than publicising and discovering the "truth", it can be argued that indicting individuals at international criminal courts is a way of "diverting attention from geopolitical interest, domestic manipulations, and structural violence" (Hinton 2018, 7).

The artificial focus on the culpability of individuals could be considered a price worth paying if international criminal courts achieved the objectives of ending the demonisation of entire groups and deflating ideas of collective guilt (Mannergren Selimovic 2010, 51). And yet the response of the local population to ICTY "outreach" events in Srebrenica and Konjic (in the former Yugoslavia) and SCSL "outreach" events in Mukump Gbana and Tissor (in Sierra Leone) suggested that international criminal trials had strengthened (or done little to dissipate) a sense of collective victimhood of one's own group and the collective guilt of one's own opponents (see Anders 2012; Mannergren Selimovic 2010). Meanwhile, in Cambodia, participants in ECCC outreach events were either unwilling to engage in the historical narrative promoted by the ECCC or were frustrated by its restricted focus (see Lesley-Rozen 2014; Manning 2011).

Finally I considered the long-standing debate regarding the "main business" (Arendt 1994 [1963], 253) of trials for mass atrocity crimes. Given their concern with the guilt or innocence of individuals, can/should criminal trials provide "an authoritative and impartial record to which future historians may turn" (International Military Tribunal 1947, 594)? Recent research has suggested that international criminal courts can "produce a body of evidence that is invaluable for historians" (Wilson 2011, 18; see Eltringham 2019, 152–180). And yet how those archives may be used is unpredictable. While there is no doubt that the archives of international criminal courts will "face a long-term state of contestation" (Kaye 2014, 392), this may allow them to be "a potential, future antidote to permanent amnesia" (Mannergren Selimovic 2015, 240). But they also may be drawn upon to write histories that are at odds with judgements and which fuel division rather than achieve "the restoration and maintenance of peace" (United Nations 1993).

Bibliography

Abu-Lughod, Lila. 2002. "Do Muslim Women Really Need Saving? Anthropological Reflections on Cultural Relativism and Its Others", *American Anthropologist* 104 (3): 783–790.

Adami, Tom. 2007. "'Who will be left to tell the tale?' Recordkeeping and international criminal jurisprudence", *Archival Science* 7 (3): 213–221.

Allen, Tim. 2010. "Bitter Roots: the 'invention' of Acholi traditional justice". In *The Lord's Resistance Army: Myth and Reality*, edited by Tim Allen and Koen Vlassenroot, 242–261. London: Zed Books.

Anders, Gerhard. 2012. "Juridification, Transitional Justice and Reaching out to the Public in Sierra Leone". In *Law against the State: Ethnographic Forays into Law's Transformations*, edited by Julia Eckert, Brian Donahoe, Christian Strümpell and Zerrin Özlem Biner, 94–117. Cambridge, UK: Cambridge University Press.

Anders, Gerhard. 2014. "Contesting Expertise: Anthropologists at the Special Court for Sierra Leone", *Journal of the Royal Anthropological Institute* 20 (3): 426–444.

Arendt, Hannah. 1994 [1963]. *Eichmann in Jerusalem: A Report on the Banality of Evil.* Harmondsworth, UK: Penguin.

Branch, Adam. 2007. "Uganda's Civil War and the Politics of ICC Intervention", *Ethics & International Affairs* 21 (2): 179–198.

Branch, Adam. 2011. "Neither Liberal nor Peaceful? Practices of 'Global Justice' by the ICC". In *A Liberal Peace? The Problems and Practices of Peacebuilding*, edited by Susanna Campbell, David Chandler and Meera Sabaratnam, 121–137. London: Zed Books.

Buss, Doris. 2014. "Expert Witnesses and International War Crimes Trials: Making Sense of Large-Scale Violence in Rwanda". In *Narratives of Justice in and out of the Courtroom: Former Yugoslavia and Beyond*, edited by Dubravka Zarkov and Marlies Glasius, 23–44. New York: Springer.

Campbell, Kirsten. 2013. "The Laws of Memory: The ICTY, the Archive, and Transitional Justice", *Social and Legal Studies*: 22 (2): 247–269.

Clark, Janine Natalya. 2009. "The limits of retributive justice: findings of an empirical study in Bosnia and Hercegovina", *Journal of International Criminal Justice* 7 (3): 463–487.

Clark, Janine Natalya. 2012. "The ICTY and Reconciliation in Croatia: A Case Study of Vukovar", *Journal of International Criminal Justice* 10 (2): 397–422.

Clarke, Kamari Maxine. 2009. *Fictions of Justice: The International Criminal Court and the Challenge of Legal Pluralism in Sub-Saharan Africa.* Cambridge, UK: Cambridge University Press.

Clarke, Kamari Maxine. 2010. "Rethinking Africa Through Its Exclusions: The Politics of Naming Criminal Responsibility", *Anthropological Quarterly* 83 (3): 625–651.

Clarke, Kamari Maxine. 2011. "The Rule of Law Through Its Economies of Appearances: The Making of the African Warlord", *Indiana Journal of Global Legal Studies* 18 (1): 7–40.

Douglas, Lawrence. 2001. *The Memory of Judgment: Making Law and History in the Trials of the Holocaust.* New Haven, CT: Yale University Press.

128 International criminal justice

Douglas, Lawrence. 2006a. "History and Memory in the Courtroom: Reflections on Perpetrator Trials". In *The Nuremberg Trials: International Criminal Law Since 1945*, edited by Herbert R. Reginbogin and Christoph Safferling, 95–105. Munich: Saur.

Douglas, Lawrence. 2006b. "Perpetrator Proceedings and Didactic Trials". In *The Trial on Trial: Volume 2: Judgment and Calling to Account*, edited by Antony Duff, Lindsay Farmer, Sandra Marshall and Victor Tadros, 191–206. London: Bloomsbury.

Douglas, Lawrence. 2016. "Truth and Justice in Atrocity Trials", *The Cambridge Companion to International Criminal Law*, edited by William A. Schabas, 34–51. Cambridge, UK: Cambridge University Press.

Eltringham, Nigel. 2013a. "'Illuminating the Broader Context': Anthropological and Historical Knowledge at the International Criminal Tribunal for Rwanda", *Journal of the Royal Anthropological Institute*. 19 (2): 338–355.

Eltringham, Nigel (ed.). 2013b. "Introduction: Cinema or Chimera?: The Re-presencing of Africa in 21st Century Film". In *Framing Africa: portrayals of a continent in contemporary mainstream cinema*, 1–20. Oxford: Berghahn Books.

Eltringham, Nigel. 2014. "'When we walk out; what was it all about?': Views on 'new beginnings' from within the International Criminal Tribunal for Rwanda", *Development and Change* 45 (3): 543–564.

Eltringham, Nigel. 2019. *Genocide Never Sleeps: Living Law at the International Criminal Tribunal for Rwanda*. Cambridge, UK: Cambridge University Press.

Erlinder, Peter. 2009. *Preventing the Falsification of History: An Unintended Consequence of ICTR Disclosure Rules?* In International Criminal Tribunal for Rwanda: An Independent Conference on its Legacy from the Defence Perspective. The Hague.

Fletcher, Laurel E. and Harvey M. Weinstein. 2002. "Violence and Social Repair: Rethinking the Contribution of Justice to Reconciliation", *Human Rights Quarterly* 24 (3): 573–639.

Gallimore, Timothy. 2008. "The Legacy of the International Criminal Tribunal for Rwanda (ICTR) and its Contributions to Reconciliation in Rwanda", *New England Journal of International and Comparative Law* 14 (2): 239–263.

Galtung, Johan. 1969. "Violence, Peace and Peace Research", *Journal of Peace Research* 6 (3): 167–190.

Glasius, Marlies and Tim Meijers. 2012. "Constructions of Legitimacy: The Charles Taylor Trial", *International Journal of Transitional Justice* 6 (2): 229–252.

Hinton, Alexander Laban. 2013. "Transitional Justice Time: Uncle San, Aunty Yan, and Outreach at the Khmer Rouge Tribunal". In *Genocide and Mass Atrocities in Asia: Legacies and Prevention*, edited by Deborah Mayersen and Annie Pohlman, 86–98. New York: Routledge.

Hinton, Alexander Laban. 2016. *Man or Monster? The Trial of a Khmer Rouge Torturer*. London: Duke University Press.

Hinton, Alexander Laban. 2018. *The Justice Facade: Trials of Transition in Cambodia*. Oxford: Oxford University Press.

Hoffman, Danny. 2007. "The meaning of a militia: Understanding the civil defence forces of Sierra Leone", *African Affairs* 106 (425): 639–662.

Hyde, Harford Montgomery. 1964. *Norman Birkett: The Life of Lord Birkett of Ulverston*. London: H. Hamilton.

ICTR. (n.d.). *The ICTR at a Glance*. Arusha: ICTR.

ICTR. 2008. Prosecutor v. Théoneste Bagosora et al. No. ICTR-98–41-T. Judgement and Sentence. 18 December.

International Law Commission. 1991. *Draft Code of Crimes against the Peace and Security of Mankind*. Geneva: International Law Commission.

International Military Tribunal. 1947. *Trial of the Major War Criminals Before the International Military Tribunal.* Vol. I. Nuremberg: International Military Tribunal.

Kaye, David. 2014. "Archiving justice: conceptualizing the archives of the United Nations International Criminal Tribunal for the Former Yugoslavia", *Archival Science* 14 (3): 381–396.

Kendall, Sara and Sarah M.H.Nouwen. 2014. "Representational Practices at the International Criminal Court: The Gap between Juridified and Abstract Victimhood", *Law & Contemporary Problems* 76 (3&4): 235–262.

Ketelaar, Eric. 2012. "Truths, Memories and Histories in the Archives of the International Criminal Tribunal for the Former Yugoslavia". In *The Genocide Convention: The Legacy of 60 Years*, edited by Harmen van der Wilt, Jeroen Vervliet, Göran Sluiter and Johannes Houwink ten Cate, 199–221. Leiden: Brill.

Kulle, Dorte. 2003. "Where's the middle? The less-aligned in a context of absolutes – An anthropological perspective on identities in pre-post conflict Northern Ireland", *Nordic Irish Studies* 2 (1): 95–120.

Lesley-Rozen, Elena. 2014. "Memory at the Site: Witnessing, Education and the Repurposing of the Tuol Seng and Choeung Ek in Cambodia". In *Remembering Genocide*, edited by Nigel Eltringham and Pam Maclean, 131–151. London: Routledge.

Mannergren Selimovic, Johanna. 2010. "Perpetrators and victims: Local responses to the International Criminal Tribunal for the Former Yugoslavia", *Focaal* 57: 50–61.

Mannergren Selimovic, Johanna. 2015. "Challenges of Postconflict Coexistence: Narrating Truth and Justice in a Bosnian Town", *Political Psychology* 36 (2): 231–242.

Manning, Peter. 2011. "Governing memory: Justice, reconciliation and outreach at the Extraordinary Chambers in the Courts of Cambodia", *Memory Studies* 5 (2): 165–181.

McEvoy, Kieran and Kirsten McConnachie. 2013. "Victims and Transitional Justice: Voice, Agency and Blame", *Social and Legal Studies* 22 (4): 489–513.

Mégret, Frédéric. 2016. "International Criminal Justice as a Juridical Field", *Champ Pénal/ Penal Field* 13.

Meith, Friederike. 2013. "Bringing Justice and Enforcing Peace? An Ethnographic Perspective on the Impact of the Special Court for Sierra Leone", *International Journal on Conflict and Violence* 7 (1): 1–15.

Millar, Gearoid. 2011. "Local Evaluations of Justice through Truth Telling in Sierra Leone: Postwar Needs and Transitional Justice", *Human Rights Review* 12 (4): 515–535.

Moghalu, Kingsley Chiedu. 2005. *Rwanda's Genocide: The Politics of Global Justice.* New York: Palgrave Macmillan.

Pavlakovic, Vjeran. 2010. "Croatia, the International Criminal Tribunal for the Former Yugoslavia, and General Gotovina as a Political Symbol", *Europe-Asia Studies* 62 (12): 1707–1740.

Permanent Peoples' Tribunal. 2018. New Statute of the Permanent Peoples' Tribunal. 27 December. Permanent Peoples' Tribunal.

Prunier, Gerard. 2011. *Africa's World War: Congo, the Rwandan Genocide, and the Making of a Continental Catastrophe.* Oxford: Oxford University Press.

Ross, Fiona C. 2001. "Speech and Silence: Women's Testimony in the First Five Weeks of Public Hearings of the South African Truth and Reconciliation Commission". In *Remaking a World: Violence, Social Suffering, and Recovery*, edited by Veena Das, Arthur Kleinman, Margaret Lock, Mamphela Ramphela and Pamela Reynolds, 250–279. Berkeley, CA: University of California Press.

Rousso, Henry. 2001. *The Haunting Past: History, Memory, and Justice in Contemporary France.* Philadelphia, PA: University of Pennsylvania Press.

Sander, Barrie. 2018. "History on Trial: Historical Narrative Pluralism Within and Beyond International Criminal Courts", *International & Comparative Law Quarterly* 67 (3): 547–576.

Schaffer, Kay and Sidonie Smith. 2004. *Human Rights and Narrated Lives: The Ethics of Recognition*. Basingstoke, UK: Palgrave Macmillan.

Schwöbel-Patel, Christine. 2016. "Spectacle in international criminal law: the fundraising image of victimhood", *London Review of International Law* 4 (2): 247–274.

Shaw, Rosalind. 2007. "Memory Frictions: Localizing the Truth and Reconciliation Commission in Sierra Leone", *The International Journal of Transitional Justice* 1 (2): 183–207.

Shaw, Rosalind. 2014. "The TRC, the NGO and the child: young people and post-conflict futures in Sierra Leone", *Social Anthropology* 22 (3): 306–325.

Trouillot, Michel-Rolph. 1995. *Silencing the Past: Power and the Production of History*. Boston, MA: Beacon.

Turner, Jenia Iontcheva. 2008. "Defense Perspectives on Law and Politics in International Criminal Trials", *Virginia Journal of International Law* 48 (3): 529–594.

United Nations. 1993. *Resolution 827 (1993). Adopted by the Security Council at its 3217th meeting*. S/RES/827. 25 May. New York: United Nations.

United Nations. 2000. *Security Council resolution 1315 (2000)*. S/RES/1315. 14 August. New York: United Nations.

United Nations. 2001. Letter from the Secretary General to the Council President transmitting the Report of the Panel of Experts on the Illegal Exploitation of Natural Resources and Other Forms of Wealth of the Democratic Republic of the Congo. A/2001/357. 12 April.

United Nations. 2008. *Address to the United Nations General Assembly by the President of the ICTR. 13th Annual Report of the ICTR*. A/63/209. 13 October. New York: United Nations General Assembly.

United Nations/Royal Government of Cambodia. 2003. Agreement between the United Nations and the Royal Government of Cambodia concerning the prosecution under Cambodian law of crimes committed during the period of Democratic Kampuchea. 6 June. Phnom Penh.

Werle, Gerhard and Moritz Vormbaum (eds.). 2017. *The African Criminal Court: A Commentary on the Malabo Protocol*. New York: Springer.

Williams, Paul. 2004. "Witnessing Genocide: Vigilance and Remembrance at Tuol Sleng and Choeung Ek", *Holocaust and Genocide Studies* 18 (2): 234–254.

Wilson, Richard Ashby. 2011. *Writing History in International Criminal Trials*. Cambridge, UK: Cambridge University Press.

6

MEMORIAL SITES

Across the globe, memorial or "trauma sites" (Violi 2012, 39) where violent events occurred are preserved and made accessible to the general public, including Nazi extermination camps (Auschwitz-Birkenau in Poland), Khmer Rouge torture centres (Tuol Sleng in Cambodia) and genocide massacre sites (Murambi in Rwanda). Having visited more than one hundred "trauma memorials" in seventeen countries, Laurie Beth Clark (2011) suggests three interrelated purposes such sites serve: to enable therapeutic "closure" (for survivors and their descendants); to facilitate educational and preventative "disclosure" (for future generations); and to reinforce political "foreclosure" (supporting a selective narrative of past events for political purposes). Given that therapeutic "closure" tends to be a private practice that does not lend itself to ethnographic investigation, I will concentrate in this chapter on "disclosure" and "foreclosure". While the educative and preventative objectives associated with "disclosure" are easy to grasp, that "lessons can be drawn and applied to contemporary problems" (Hamber 2012, 271), how this is to be achieved is less straightforward, given that generalising past events in order to draw contemporary lessons may distort the understanding of the original events. While there is no doubt that memorial sites contribute to "foreclosure" as political authorities choose what "to explicitly "remember" or deliberately silence" (Viejo-Rose 2011, 469) in the aftermath of violent conflict, such manipulation is not static but changes as political authorities respond to new challenges to their legitimacy.

I will assess the two issues of "disclosure" and "foreclosure" through two "trauma sites" that have been extensively researched by anthropologists and other ethnographers: the Tuol Sleng Museum of Genocide Crimes in Phnom Penh, Cambodia, which was the site of a torture centre (known as "S-21") during the Khmer Rouge regime of Democratic Kampuchea (1975–1979), and the Murambi Genocide Memorial Centre in Rwanda, which was the site of a massacre of an estimated 50,000 Tutsi men, women and children between 20–21 April 1994

132 Memorial sites

during the genocide of the Tutsi. Before discussing the two case studies in detail I will reflect further on the ambiguous quality of "disclosure" at memorial sites.

"Disclosure" at memorial sites

As noted above, Clark (2011) suggests that a supposed purpose of "disclosure" at memorial sites is to educate the uninformed about past events and prevent the recurrence of violence in the future. The nature of what is being disclosed may, however, be misunderstood. In his study of Holocaust memorials, James Young (1993, 121) notes there is a danger that visitors to memorial sites may mistake the "debris of history for history itself" and assume that Nazi extermination and concentration camps are "unreconstructed realities" in which visitors can experience "unmediated history". In reality, memorial sites tend to be "heavily mediated" by "[r]oped sections, glassed walls, guides and ... restricted areas" (Williams 2004, 242). Just as individual survivors do not simply "speak for themselves", but give testimonies that pass through a "collage of intervening presences – witness, editor, transcriber, translator, reader" (Douglass 2003, 68; see Chapter 3), so memorial sites do not speak for themselves but are an intentional, "monumentalized vision" (Young 1998, 174).

It is not only the case that memorial sites, while appearing "unreconstructed", are, in reality, presented in a particular way, but that the form the presentation takes tends to be reproduced around the globe. The social geographer Rachel Hughes (2003b, 180), writing in the context of the Tuol Sleng Genocide Museum in Cambodia (see below), notes how, following the overthrow of the Khmer Rouge regime (1975–1979) by the Vietnamese, consistent efforts were made to align Cambodia's genocide with the Holocaust, the "emblematic horror against which all other horrors are measured" (Novick 2001, 255; see Eltringham 2004, 51–68). In designing the Tuol Sleng exhibition, Vietnamese General Mai Lam (who had organised the Museum of American War Crimes Exhibition in Ho Chi Minh City, Vietnam) travelled to Poland to study the Auschwitz-Birkenau Museum (Williams 2004, 248; see Ledgerwood 1997, 89; Young 1993, 49). The piles of prisoners' clothes at Tuol Sleng Genocide Museum reflect the piles of clothes and belongings at Auschwitz-Birkenau, for example. Other museums reflect this cross-referencing. The Srebrenica-Potočari Memorial Center and Cemetery in Bosnia-Herzegovina, created in 2000 to commemorate the 8,000 Bosnian men and boys murdered by the Army of Republika Srpska (VRS) in 1995, was initially the idea of the British politician Lord Ashdown (the fourth High Representative in Bosnia-Herzegovina, a position created under the General Framework Agreement for Peace in Bosnia and Herzegovina of 1995). This followed his visit to the Holocaust Exhibition at the Imperial War Museum in London (Bardgett 2007) which was, in turn, inspired by the United States Holocaust Memorial Museum (Bardgett 1998, 32). Similar cross-referencing can be seen in the way in which the Beth Shalom Holocaust Centre in Nottingham (established in 1995 and run by the Aegis Trust) was created after a visit by its founders to Jerusalem's Yad Vashem, Israel's official memorial to the victims of the Holocaust (see Smith 1999). In turn, having visited the Beth Shalom Holocaust Centre in 2003, the Rwandan Minister for Youth, Sports and Culture and the Mayor of Kigali requested that the Aegis Trust take over responsibility for the creation of the Kigali Genocide Memorial and the Murambi Memorial Centre (see Sodaro 2011).

The anthropologist Nayanika Mookherjee (2011, 80), in her study of the Bangladesh Liberation War Museum (BLWM), provides a detailed illustration of such "cross-referencing". As discussed in Chapter 4, West Pakistan's administrative and economic domination of East Pakistan, combined with a strategy of forced cultural assimilation, led to a nine-month "war of liberation" in 1971 that resulted in the creation of Bangladesh (Mookherjee 2006, 435). In 1996 the BLWM was created in Dhaka, the capital of Bangladesh, to house 21,000 artefacts and documents associated with the "war of liberation" (Mookherjee 2011, S74). Mookherjee (2011, S74) notes that the museum was built primarily as a "citizen's effort" in order to provide an account of the civilian contribution to "liberation", which had been overshadowed until 1990 by military governments that emphasised military victory. Mookherjee (2011, S80) considers the museum to be an example of "genocidal cosmopolitanism" reflecting a "transnational cross-referencing of historical atrocities". Mookherjee (2011, S83) provides the example of images of skulls and bones at the BWLM that re-create the display of such remains in Cambodia and Rwanda (see below), while at the front of the BWLM is the "recognizably global icon of the eternal flame" (also present at the USHMM and Yad Vashem). This cross-referencing is not accidental as the BLWM was built on the template of the USHMM and is a founder member of the International Coalition of Sites of Conscience, a global network of historic sites, museums and memorials that is dedicated to promoting and protecting human rights across the world (other members include the Kigali Genocide Memorial, the Tuol Sleng Genocide Museum and the Srebrenica-Potočari Memorial Center and Cemetery) (Mookherjee 2011, S74; see Ševčenko 2010). Furthermore, the trustees of the BLWM use the "globally recognizable injunction against genocide 'never again'", or *aar kohkhono nay* in Bengali (Mookherjee 2011, S73–S79; see Hamber 2012). While on one hand the BLWM was an "attempt to bring into being the Bangladeshi nation ... based on common suffering" (Mookherjee 2011, S72 S78), the way in which the museum positions itself as teaching a "global moral-historical lesson" in collaboration with other "sites of conscience" means there is a danger that "specificity is decontextualised" (Mookherjee 2011, S88).

Peace studies scholar Johanna Mannergren Selimovic (2016) illustrates the dangers of such decontextualisation in relation to the Kigali Memorial Centre (Gisozi), the main national memorial museum in Rwanda at which the remains of more than 250,000 victims of the 1994 Rwandan genocide of the Tutsi are interred. As noted above, it is not surprising that the museum employs a common, global format for representing genocide and mass atrocity, given that it was designed by the Aegis Trust, whose Beth Shalom Holocaust Centre in Nottingham in the United Kingdom was inspired by Yad Vashem in Jerusalem (see Smith 1999). Like the BLWM, the Kigali museum is designed to teach a "global moral-historical

134 Memorial sites

lesson" (Mookherjee 2011, S88), with the museum's director describing it as "a place of warning for humankind" (Mannergren Selimovic 2016, 55). This aspiration for global relevance is reflected in the way in which the exhibition makes reference to the Nazi Holocaust (1941–1945), the genocide of 1.5 million Armenians by the Ottoman Empire (1914–1923) and the Srebrenica genocide (1995). Mannergren Selimovic (2016, 56) argues that this "seamless insertion of the Rwandan genocide into cosmopolitan memory-making" serves to silence discussion of crimes against humanity committed by the ruling Rwandan Patriotic Army/Front (RPA/F) against Hutu (see Eltringham 2004, 100–146; 2019, 38–41). By generalising the Rwandan genocide of the Tutsi for "global consumption", the RPA/F government legitimises a selective genocide narrative, leaving experiences inconvenient to the current political authorities unacknowledged (Mannergren Selimovic 2016, 58).

So far in this section I have reflected on the way in which memorial sites in the process of disclosing the past cross-reference one another to make themselves globally relevant as places of education and prevention. The question remains, however, whether the educational and preventative objectives of "disclosure" are achieved. In response to a lack of research into this question, Brandon Hamber, Liz Ševčenko and Ereshnee Naidu (2010) oversaw an evaluation of the youth education programmes of three "trauma museums": the BLWM (see above); the Monte Sole Peace School in Italy (commemorating the massacre of up to 770 people, mostly women and children by Nazi troops and Italian Fascist forces in 1944); and the Villa Grimaldi Peace Park in Chile (the site of a torture centre (1974–1978) during the Pinochet regime). Hamber, Ševčenko and Naidu (2010, 415–416) found that "experiential learning" at the three sites did have a "strong emotional impact" on young people, who "spoke about how it changed their views about [contemporary] issues and certain groups". While acknowledging this short-term impact, Hamber, Ševčenko and Naidu (2010, 419) warn that it remains to be seen whether sites can achieve the kinds of long-term, society-wide changes associated with the prevention of violence in the future.

While Hamber, Ševčenko and Naidu (2010) are cautiously positive about the impact on young people of structured, educational visits to "trauma sites", the assessment of unstructured visits to memorial sites by broader categories of visitors has been far less positive. It has been argued that "trauma sites" serve "dark tourism", defined by J. John Lennon and Malcolm Foley (1996, 198) as "the presentation and consumption (by visitors) of real and commodified death and disaster sites" (alternative terms include "death tourism", "thanatourism", "grief tourism" and "tragic tourism", (Clark 2011, 68)). Lennon and Foley (2000, 58) argue that "horror and death have become established commodities, on sale to tourists who have an enduring appetite for the darkest elements of human history". Given this "appetite", there is a "fundamental difficulty of delineating education and entertainment/spectacle" (Lennon & Foley 2000, 284). As a consequence, the intended educational and preventative impact of visits to "trauma sites" may be overwhelmed by "entertainment/spectacle". Olivera Simić (2009, 286) illustrates this with an account of visiting an exhumation of a mass grave in

Bosnia-Herzegovina with a group of law and history scholars. She notes that some took their cameras into the open grave and took photographs. Simić (2009, 286) found it difficult to imagine what people intended to do with the images: "Were they going to look at them over and over again at home?" Experiences such as this led Simić (2009, 273 279) to conclude that there is a "blurring between voyeurism and educational enlightenment" as memorial sites "become a mixture of politics, education, entertainment and financial gain".

In this section I have considered that although "trauma sites" appear to be "unreconstructed" sites of "gruelling historical spectacle" (Williams 2004, 243), they are, in fact, an intentional, "monumentalized vision" (Young 1998, 174). Furthermore, the form that these sites take tends to be reproduced around the globe, as memorial sites cross-reference one another (the Auschwitz-Birkenau Museum influenced the Tuol Sleng Museum of Genocide Crimes; the USHMM in Washington DC influenced the BLWM in Dhaka and the Holocaust Exhibition at the Imperial War Museum in London; which, in turn, influenced the Srebrenica-Potočari Memorial Center and Cemetery in Bosnia-Herzegovina). While cross-referencing enables "memorial sites" to teach a "global moral-historical lesson" (Mookherjee 2011, S88), the process of generalisation can be used as an opportunity to silence experiences inconvenient to political authorities, as is the case at the Kigali Memorial Centre (Gisozi) (see King 2010). Finally, memorial sites may, by appealing to a global audience, become places of "entertainment/spectacle" rather than education and prevention (Lennon & Foley 2000, 284). I shall now explore these issues in further detail with two case studies: the Tuol Sleng Museum of Genocide Crimes in Cambodia and the Murambi Genocide Memorial Centre in Rwanda.

Tuol Sleng Museum of Genocide Crimes, Cambodia

Between 1975 and 1979 the Communist Party of Kampuchea (CPK), led by Pol Pot and known as the Khmer Rouge (KR), ruled Cambodia, which was renamed Democratic Kampuchea (DK) (see Kiernan 2008). During this period between 1.5 and two million people died through execution, starvation or preventable diseases, nearly a quarter of Cambodia's 1975 population of approximately 7.8 million (see Hinton 2005; Kiernan 2003). "S-21", named after the *Santebal* ("keeper of the peace", the internal security service of the KR), was the largest interrogation centre in DK, housed in a high school in Phnom Penh, Cambodia's capital city. Between 14,000 and 16,000 people (most of whom were DK administrative insiders accused of betraying the revolution) were interrogated and tortured at "S-21" before being executed (see Chandler 1999; Ledgerwood 1997, 84). Following the overthrow of the DK by a Vietnamese invasion in January 1979 and the creation of the People's Republic of Kampuchea (PRK), "S-21" became the Tuol Sleng Museum of Genocide Crimes (the high school had been called Tuol Svay Prey; Tuol Sleng – the "hillock of the poisonous Sleng Tree" – had been the name of a nearby primary school (Ledgerwood 1997, 83)). The Tuol Sleng Museum of Genocide Crimes illustrates three issues related to "disclosure" and "foreclosure" that are

136 Memorial sites

applicable to many memorial sites: their (evolving) role in legitimating ruling political authorities; the inadvertent perpetuation of the perpetrators' logic; and insufficient explanatory information. I will consider each of these in turn.

The Tuol Sleng Museum of Genocide Crimes illustrates how, in the aftermath of violent conflict, attempts are made to "mould memories in order to give legitimacy to the post-war administration" (Viejo-Rose 2011, 469). In advance of their invasion, the Vietnamese created the Kampuchean United Front for National Salvation, composed of pro-Vietnamese Cambodian communists and KR defectors, including Hun Sen, who has been Prime Minister of Cambodia since 1985 (Hinton 2016, 23). Despite the involvement of Cambodian leaders in the invasion, Cambodians tended to view the new PRK regime with suspicion, given that it was socialist like the KR and had been installed by Vietnam, the historical enemy (Hinton 2016, 24). In addition, the United States of America, China and the United Nations condemned the Vietnamese invasion and continued to recognise the DK/KR government. The principal purpose of the new museum, therefore, was to justify the Vietnamese invasion as a "humanitarian intervention" saving Cambodians from Pol Pot (Hughes 2003b, 178; Ledgerwood 1997, 85).

Hughes (2003b, 176) notes how, despite "the country-wide demand for emergency welfare, administration and infrastructure" following the fall of the DK regime, the new authorities prioritised opening Tuol Sleng in July 1980 to inform international delegations (predominantly from other communist countries) and foreign journalists about the violence of the KR regime, with the museum becoming the "archetype of prison and killing sites reported throughout the country" (Hughes 2003b, 178). The term "Genocide Crimes" in the title of the museum was chosen in order to distinguish the "legitimate communism" of Vietnam, the Soviet Union and China (all of which eliminated political opponents) from the "'fascist,' DK communism" which committed "genocide" against its own people (even though the majority of killing under the KR did not correspond to the definition of genocide contained in the United Nations Convention for the Prevention and Punishment of Genocide of 1948, in which targets are defined as "national, ethnical, racial or religious groups" Williams 2004, 248).

Hughes (2003b, 178) suggests that while the initial purpose of the museum was to legitimise the PRK regime by communicating the "true horror of Democratic Kampuchea", including a "wall arrangement of skulls in the shape of the Cambodian territory" (removed in 2002), the political utility of the site changed when the Vietnamese withdrew in 1989 and, in 1991, remnants of the KR were invited to join the government and Cambodians asked to forgive Pol Pot and other KR leaders (Williams 2004, 249).With the creation of the Extraordinary Chambers in the Courts of Cambodia (ECCC) in 2003 to put on trial those accused of mass atrocity crimes (war crimes, crimes against humanity and genocide) during DK (see Chapter 5), including "Duch" (Kaing Guek Eav), the director of "S-21" between 1975 and 1979, Tuol Sleng was "repurposed" to support the narrative promoted by the court and the Cambodian government that only "a few top leaders" were responsible for the crimes committed (Lesley-Rozen 2014, 133; see Dunlop 2009; Hinton 2016).

FIGURE 6.1 The entrance to Tuol Sleng Museum. (Photo courtesy of Alexander Laban Hinton)

The anthropologist Elena Lesley-Rozen (2014, 131) describes how, since 2004, civil society organisations have organised "study tours" bringing groups of Cambodians to Tuol Sleng, Choeung Ek (the nearby "killing fields", where many of those tortured at "S-21" were killed) and the ECCC courtroom. The ECCC and the associated "study tours" observed by Lesley-Rozen promoted a historical narrative of the DK period that suited the purposes of the Cambodian government in that it emphasised the culpability of "a few top leaders" who were to be tried at the ECCC (even though responsibility for crimes committed during the DK era was much more widespread), thereby granting a *de facto* amnesty to lower-level perpetrators and shielding from prosecution former KR in the current government, including Hun Sen (Lesley-Rozen 2014, 133). The Tuol Sleng Museum of Genocide Crimes, therefore, evolved from justifying the 1979 Vietnamese invasion to, following a period of abeyance, promoting the ECCC's and Cambodian government's historical narrative. This evolution illustrates that while no memorial site is "ever-lasting", its meaning is "contingent on evolving political realities" (Young 1993, 154).

In addition to illustrating the (evolving) role memorial sites play in legitimating ruling political authorities, Tuol Sleng also demonstrates a dilemma faced by those who administer memorial sites; whether to anonymise victims or restore their identity. At the Srebrenica-Potočari Memorial Center, for example, twenty of the 8,000 victims are individually identified with a photo, a short biography and one of their belongings recovered from a mass grave (Simič 2009, 278). In contrast, at Murambi Genocide Memorial more than 800 unidentified dead bodies are displayed (see below). Sara Guyer (2009, 163 174) argues that refusing to "return names, identities, or individualities to the dead" perpetuates "genocide's logic … the logic of impersonality whereby persons are recognized only as members of a population". This places the observer in the position of the perpetrator, "leading us to see the dead as the perpetrators of the genocide saw the living", as an anonymised mass.

The same accusation can be levelled at Tuol Sleng, where retaining the anonymity of victims was an intentional choice. On display in "Building C" at Tuol Sleng are thousands of portraits taken of individuals when they arrived at "S-21", each with a number pinned to their shirt (see Hughes 2003a; Sion 2011). Lacking any information, "the photographs are left to speak for themselves" (Hinton 2016, 20). Hughes (2003b, 183) notes how, in the first two years of the museum's operation, relatives and friends who recognised a person in a photograph would write the person's name on the displayed photograph as "an act of personal and public remembrance". Hughes (2003b, 183) suggests that the subsequent prohibition of this practice by museum authorities was because it threatened the museum's narrative of "collective suffering engendering popular resolve and resistance". In intentionally maintaining the anonymity of those in the portraits, the museum perpetuated the logic and "mechanisms of the perpetrators" who replaced individual identity with a lethal number (Williams 2004, 247).

FIGURE 6.2 The portrait room at Tuol Sleng. (Photo courtesy of Elena Lesley)

Not only are "the photographs ... left to speak for themselves" (Hinton 2016, 20) at Tuol Sleng; the whole site contains very little explanatory information, suggesting it is a museum "to be felt rather than to be known or understood" (Violi 2012, 48). For example, in the middle of rooms in "Building A" are rusted metal beds, underneath which are shackles, spikes and ammunition boxes with a photograph on the wall of the mutilated corpse found on the bed when the centre was discovered by the Vietnamese army on 14 January 1979 (Hinton 2016, 14). The lack of "explanatory signage" is because the exhibition was "initially created to be interpreted by those who had experienced its horrors", including Ung Pech, a survivor of "S-21" who was also the first director of the museum (Lesley-Rozen 2014, 136; see Hughes 2008, 325–326; Ledgerwood 1997, 83). Today, however, guided tours are rare for those arriving independently of organised groups, so the "authoritative narration given by survivors ... so much a part of early visitors' experiences, is no longer heard" (Hughes 2008, 326). As a consequence, foreign tourists leave with the feeling that their knowledge of the site is "incomplete" (Hughes 2008, 325–328), while Cambodians who have participated in "study tours" since 2004 also left with many unanswered questions and no greater understanding of "the functioning of [DK], how the regime had come to power and why its reign had been so deadly" (Lesley-Rozen 2014, 145).

Having evolved from justifying the 1979 Vietnamese invasion to then promoting the ECCC's historical narrative (which also suited the Cambodian government), the Tuol Sleng Museum of Genocide Crimes demonstrates the way in which memorial sites are appropriated to serve the evolving needs of political authorities. In the context of mass atrocity crimes (war crimes, crimes against humanity and genocide), those who administer memorial sites face a dilemma between communicating the enormity of the crime by using a mass of anonymous victims or restoring to victims their individual identities, denied by perpetrators who defined them solely as members of a generic category destined for torture and extermination. It can be argued that deliberately retaining the anonymity of victims at Tuol Sleng perpetuates the perpetrators' logic, as the visitor sees the dead as the perpetrators saw them (Guyer 2009, 174). Finally, while the lack of information provided at Tuol Sleng can be explained by an initial design that relied on tour guides, the lack of guides in the present day means that both foreign tourists and Cambodians leave with unanswered questions, thereby putting in doubt the educational and preventative purpose of "disclosure" of the past.

Murambi Genocide Memorial Centre, Rwanda

Between 20–21 April 1994 an estimated 50,000 Tutsi men, women and children were murdered at Murambi Technical School in south-western Rwanda by the *interahamwe* militia of the ruling party (Mouvement Républicain National pour la Démocratie et le Développement) and *gendarmes* (part of the military) (ICTR 2005, para 88). In February 2003 the Aegis Trust, a UK-based genocide prevention charity, was invited by the Rwandan government to take over responsibility for

140 Memorial sites

the creation of the Kigali Genocide Memorial, the Murambi Memorial Centre and preservation work at an additional five major sites around the country. Like Tuol Sleng, the Murambi Memorial Centre illustrates three issues related to "disclosure" and "foreclosure" that are applicable to many memorial sites: their (evolving) role in legitimating ruling authorities; insufficient explanatory information; and the danger of inadvertently perpetuating the perpetrators' logic. I will consider each of these in turn.

Rwanda, in the aftermath of the 1994 genocide of the Tutsi, provides a good illustration of how memorial sites are "a means for national elites to cultivate a shared understanding of the past and to construct political legitimacy" (Ibreck 2010, 330) by selectively highlighting some memories of violence and repressing others (see King 2010, 293), even if this government strategy is not wholly successful (see Longman & Rutagengwa 2006, 243; Thomson 2011b). The 1994 genocide was more complex than simply Hutu killing Tutsi, given that "some Tutsi killed Hutu, some Hutu protected Tutsi [and] others stood by" (Thomson 2011a, 379). Despite this, the current RPA/F government has employed simplistic categories in which Tutsi are survivors and Hutu are perpetrators (see Eltringham 2004, 97). The way in which these simplistic categories silence other experiences before, during and after the 1994 genocide is apparent at the Kigali Memorial Centre (Gisozi) which, like the Murambi Genocide Memorial Centre, is under the care of the Aegis Trust. Drawing on interviews, the political scientist Elisabeth King (2010, 296–303) identifies "five main genres of civilian memories" in post-genocide Rwanda: "Recognised Tutsi Memories" (narratives of Tutsi targeted in the 1994 genocide); "Somewhat Recognised Hutu Memories" (narratives of Hutu who helped Tutsi during the 1994 genocide); "unrecognised Hutu memories" (narratives of Hutu who suffered at the hands of the RPA/F before, during and after the 1994 genocide); "unrecognised Tutsi memories" (narratives of Tutsi who feared the RPA/F before and during the 1994 genocide); and "unrecognised memories of ethnically mixed Rwandans" (narratives of those whose experience does not correspond with the simplistic categories; see Conway 2011; McLean Hilker 2012). King (2010) notes that when she visited the Kigali Memorial Centre it was only "Recognised Tutsi Memories" and "Somewhat Recognised Hutu Memories" that were represented on exhibition panels, with a passing reference to the experience of ethnically mixed Rwandans. King (2010, 303–304) concludes that by only fully acknowledging two categories of memories, the Kigali Memorial Centre legitimates RPA/F rule and, by leaving experiences unacknowledged, "could lay the foundations for future intergroup conflict".

The evolution of the Murambi Genocide Memorial Centre also reflects the exclusion of certain experiences in order to legitimate RPA/F rule. When I visited the memorial centre in 2007 the Rwandan government website described the museum's exhibition as:

> a simple narrative outlining the development of the genocidal ideology from pre-colonial and colonial times through to the post-colonial policies of division between ethnic groups. It describes the role of propaganda and the systematic organization of the killing during the genocide.

Memorial sites **141**

This description reflects a standardised history of Rwanda promoted by the ruling RPA/F which maintains that ethnicity was created, or substantially distorted, by colonial authorities, thereby disrupting a pre-colonial unity, and that the genocide had begun in 1959 with the overthrow of the Tutsi monarchy (see Buckley-Zistel 2009, 34–41; Eltringham 2004, 163–177; 2011; Sodaro 2011, 80–81; Zorbas 2009). Although the government website described the exhibition in these terms, the exhibition was not, in fact, open to the public at the time of my visit. Although the Murambi memorial was supposed to be completed by 2004, the tenth anniversary of the genocide, the exhibition was criticised by a government "ad hoc commission" for having "photographs that do not make any sense" and that did "not reflect the truth about history, politics or Rwandese Culture" (Laville 2006). Aimé Kayinamura, who coordinated the project, responded:

> the contested photos had to do with the story of a young Tutsi boy who lost his parents, survived his machete wounds, and was taken in by a Hutu family. After the genocide, the family fled to the former Zaire [now Democratic Republic of the Congo], taking the boy with them. The depiction of the family's journey included scenes of large-scale suffering of Hutu refugees in the former Zaire.
>
> *(International Justice Tribune 2008, 2)*

According to Kayinamura, the "ad hoc commission" had "felt that these photos could suggest a double genocide and we had to remove them". Accusations of "double genocide" refer to evidence that the RPA/F was responsible for massacres of Hutu refugees in the Democratic Republic of Congo between 1996 and 1998 in the aftermath of the 1994 genocide of the Tutsi (see Eltringham 2004, 118–142; Office of the United Nations High Commissioner for Human Rights 2010). In other words, the photos were unacceptable to the government as they indicated "unrecognised Hutu memories" (narratives of Hutu who suffered at the hands of the RPA/F) that challenged the government's selective genocide narrative (King 2010, 293; see Conway 2011; Mannergren Selimovic 2016, 58).

The manner in which the Murambi Memorial Centre has been used to legitimate RPA/F rule is also demonstrated by the minimal explanatory information at the site when I visited in 2007. The only information provided was on three, apparently recently installed, maroon-painted shields which read, in English, French and Kinyarwanda: "FRENCH SOLDIERS WERE PLAYING VOLLEY HERE"; "MASS GRAVE OF VICTIMS"; and "PLACE OF FRENCH FLAG DURING OPERATION TURQUOISE". The signs refer to the fact that the Murambi school site was used by French paratroopers who, with UN Security Council approval, entered Rwanda on 23 June 1994 under "Operation Turquoise". While described as a humanitarian mission, because the French government had given extensive assistance to the pre-genocide government "Operation Turquoise" was controversial (see African Rights 2007, 142–150; Kroslak 2007). One explanation for the erection of this minimal information in 2007 relates to the

FIGURE 6.3 The half-completed Murambi Technical School in southern Rwanda. (Photo: Nigel Eltringham)

event that marked the start of the 1994 genocide of the Tutsi, the shooting down on 6 April 1994 of the plane carrying Rwandan President Juvénal Habyarimana and President Cyprien Ntaryamira of Burundi who were returning to Kigali from a summit in Dar es Salaam, where Habyarimana had apparently consented to a power-sharing government with the RPA/F, which had invaded Rwanda in 1990. The aircraft was brought down at around 8:23 p.m., having been hit by surface-to-air missiles launched from a location near Kigali airport. All on board died. The killing of Hutu politicians committed to a peace process commenced immediately, followed soon after by the widespread killing of Tutsi. In November 2006, in relation to the plane attack, the French anti-terrorist judge Jean-Louis Bruguière issued international arrest warrants against nine close associates of Paul Kagame, Rwandan President and leader of the RPA/F. The judge added that he thought Kagame should also stand trial but that, as serving head of state, he was immune. Although experts commissioned by a French judge concluded in 2012 that the missile was fired from a position held by the Presidential Guard and not the RPA/F (Oosterlinck et al. 2013), Murambi was to play an important role in the Rwandan government's response to Judge Bruguière's 2006 arrest warrants.

In April 2007 the national commemoration of the genocide was held at Murambi, during which President Kagame stated that "part of the international community has participated in the Rwandan genocide" and had "[played] on the

Memorial sites 143

FIGURE 6.4 Sign in English, French and Kinyarwanda at Murambi. (Photo: Nigel Eltringham)

graves of those who were killed during the genocide ... play[ed] volleyball on their graves ... they proclaimed they had come to save people, on the contrary it was to kill them" (see Eltringham 2014, 212). It appears that, to ensure the allegation of French complicity in the 1994 genocide was beyond doubt, the three signs had been erected, with their lack of contextual information explained by the fact that they were not intended to be read by casual visitors but by the foreign dignitaries and press who had attended the 2007 commemoration ceremony and heard President Kagame's speech. While the removal of the exhibition at Murambi because of the photos of Hutu refugees in the Democratic Republic of the Congo is an example of deliberate silencing in the service of political authorities, the erection of the signs in 2007 is an example of explicit remembering (Viejo-Rose 2011, 469).

At the Murambi Genocide Memorial Centre, as at Tuol Sleng, the decision was taken to communicate the enormity of the crime committed on the site by retaining the anonymity of victims. Whereas at Tuol Sleng the "vast dead" (Major 2015, 171) is communicated through anonymous portraits, when I visited Murambi Genocide Memorial in 2007 there were twenty-four classrooms housing around 800 corpses of the victims of the massacre preserved in lime. Immediately after the massacre, the Gikongoro Préfectural office provided two bulldozers to use to bury victims in order to prevent disease (African Rights 2007, 116). During exhumations in 1995 one mass grave was found in which the bodies had barely

144 Memorial sites

begun to decompose (Scully 2012, 15). The survivors of the massacre, along with the government of Rwanda and the National Museum of Rwanda, stopped the decomposition by covering the bodies in lime and putting them on display. Not only did this display transgress "in an unheard of way traditional relationships with the dead" (Vidal 2004, 578), but, as Guyer (2009, 163 174) argues, by refusing to "return names, identities, or individualities to the dead" such displays perpetuate "genocide's logic … the logic of impersonality whereby persons are recognized only as members of a population". Such displays place the observer in the position of the perpetrator, "leading us to see the dead as the perpetrators of the genocide saw the living", as an anonymised mass.

Given the danger of perpetuating the logic and "mechanisms of the perpetrators" (Williams 2004, 247), what were the reasons for the display of these remains? Strengthening the legitimacy of the RPA/F appears to have played a part. The sociologist Claudine Vidal (2004, 580–582) argues that the decision to put the remains at Murambi on display in 1995/1996 must be understood within a confrontation between the post-genocide government and the Roman Catholic Church, which has been accused of complicity with the government that oversaw the 1994 genocide of the Tutsi (see Eltringham 2000). In 1995, elements of the Roman Catholic Church had denounced the opening and reinternment of mass graves, often involving the forced labour of the local population, as unnecessarily traumatic, disrespectful to the dead and lacking a sacred element. Vidal (2004, 585), therefore, sees the display of bodies, including those at Murambi, as the RPA/F government asserting its power against the Roman Catholic Church.

The decision to display the bodies also coincided with emerging criticism of the post-genocide government. On 29 August 1995 several prominent Hutu politicians resigned from the coalition "Government of National Unity" in protest at extra-judicial killings and human rights violation by the RPA/F. The political scientist Jens Meierhenrich (2011, 288–289) suggests that the decision by the government to display "macabre" remains was, and continues to be, a means to "disable comprehension"; that, "by appealing to emotions rather than reason", such displays disable reflection on the post-genocide regime and "facilitate a forgetting of the present" (see Guyer 2009, 170).

These two explanations for the display of the remains relate to the way in which memorial sites are used to strengthen the legitimacy of political authorities. It is also important, however, to consider the role played by genocide survivors. The forensic anthropologist Shannon Scully (2012) defends the display of the remains as the "right of an affected group" because a majority of the ten survivors of the Murambi massacre support the bodies remaining on display. One survivor, Emmanuel Nshimyimana, stated, "Originally we didn't like having our people on display. But we know it is for the future and therefore it is important that they are preserved for future generations" (Scully 2012, 17). Describing the attitude of survivors, Freddy Mutanguha, Country Director for the Aegis Trust in Rwanda, has stated, "There are those who feel that only reburial can offer dignity for the dead, but [they] fear that unless the ultimate evidence of genocide is there to see, it could be denied and perhaps one day happen again" (Aegis Trust 2011).

While research by anthropologist Laura Major (2015) concerns the reinternment of remains, rather than their display, her findings give further insight into the relationship between the wishes of genocide survivors and the display of remains at Murambi. Major (2015, 165) describes a government-led programme of exhumation of Tutsi victims of the genocide buried in mass and individual graves, with the bodies then reinterred in purpose-built memorials. Teams, largely composed of genocide survivors, separated remains into clothing, personal possessions and bones. These were then disarticulated, washed and divided into "rough anatomical type", ready for reinternment (Major 2015, 169–170). Having worked as part of a team, Major (2015, 170–171) reports not only the discovery of identifying possessions among the remains (including identity cards and clothing) but that exhumers even identified the remains of their relatives. Despite this opportunity to identify specific remains, there was a "determined discarding of remnants of individuated identities from bodily remains" (Major 2015, 166). This is in stark contrast to other post-violent conflict contexts where the identification of individual remains is considered a priority (see Renshaw 2010; Robben 2016; Wagner 2010). Major (2015, 167) suggests that the reason for this rejection of the opportunity to identify remains is because the RPA/F uses the "genocide corpse" as a "political tool" and that many of the genocide-survivor exhumers rely on the RPA/F for social and economic security. The refusal to identify individual remains even when that was possible is, therefore, an "acceptable compromise" for genocide survivors (Major 2015, 167). What emerges from this process of exhumation is "a mass of bones that imply a vast dead", an "undifferentiated collective of genocide victims … which is intended to productively consolidate a dominant narrative of the past that is closely tied to the RPF [RPA/F] politics and legitimacy" (Major 2015, 171 176). While an "undifferentiated collective" of victims may be politically expedient for the RPA/F, it raises the problem of perpetuating genocide's logic, in which anonymised members of a generic category are destined for torture and extermination (Guyer 2009, 163 174). Major's (2015) research indicates that survivors are not necessarily in favour of creating an "undifferentiated collective" of victims, as is the case at Murambi, but that this is a pragmatic response in a context of survivors' economic and physical insecurity.

The way in which genocide survivors can acquiesce with government policy towards human remains while pursuing other objectives is illustrated by Julia Viebach's (2020, 25) research in Rwanda among "care-takers", genocide survivors who clean newly discovered remains and preserve the remains of genocide victims (bones and dead bodies) at genocide memorials, including Murambi. Viebach (2020, 3 25) argues that, for these survivors, memorials are a "social home" in which they can "project the personhood of their loved ones" onto the human remains they care for, thereby transforming "the anonymity of the remains into individual human beings". Through this process the survivors reimagine the anonymous remains as "'real persons' and thereby give them back an identity in

146 Memorial sites

the face of a collective mass of bones and remains" (Viebach 2020, 25). This suggests that while sites such as Murambi and the "undifferentiated collective of genocide victims" (Major 2015, 176) they contain are appropriated for political purposes, the imaginative return of identity to anonymous bones by survivors demonstrates that memorial sites serve "political, collective and individual purposes" and that the actions of survivors may be "distinct and sometimes at odds with the state's attempts to employ memorials and human remains to consolidate its power" (Viebach 2020, 3 5). The research by Major (2015) and Viebach (2020) suggests a degree of caution is required when assessing why anonymised remains were displayed at Murambi. While the display of human remains is a means by which the RPA/F can "facilitate a forgetting of the present" (Meierhenrich 2011, 288–289), there are parallel "informal and personal" practices (Viebach 2020, 3) that serve the interests of survivors rather than those of the government, including reimagining the anonymous remains as real persons in a way contrary to the government's intention.

The evolution of the Murambi Genocide Memorial Centre illustrates how memorial sites are "a means for national elites to cultivate a shared understanding of the past and to construct political legitimacy" (Ibreck 2010, 330) by selectively highlighting some memories of violence and repressing others (see King 2010, 293). While the removal of the exhibition at Murambi because of the photos of Hutu refugees in the Democratic Republic of the Congo is an example of deliberate silencing in the service of political authorities, the erection of the signs in 2007 is an example of explicit remembering (Viejo-Rose 2011, 469). Likewise, the display of remains appears to be part of a more general government policy to reject the identification of individual remains in favour of presenting an "undifferentiated collective of genocide victims ... which is intended to productively consolidate a dominant narrative of the past that is closely tied to the RPF [RPA/F] politics and legitimacy" (Major 2015, 171 176). While genocide survivors participate in this process by cleaning remains and as "care-takers", it appears to be a pragmatic involvement behind which is a rejection by survivors of anonymising victims and, instead, transforming "the anonymity of the remains into individual human beings" (Viebach 2020, 25).

Conclusion

In this chapter I have considered the way in which memorial sites seek to facilitate educational and preventative "disclosure" (for future generations), but also reinforce political "foreclosure" (supporting a selective narrative of past events for political purposes) (Clark 2011). While the first of these objectives would appear worthy, there are a number of obstacles: that visitors may fail to recognise that what appears "unreconstructed" is, in reality, an intentional presentation; that the way in which memorial sites cross-reference one another may lead to a loss of specificity and be used as an opportunity to silence experiences inconvenient to political authorities; and, finally, by appealing to a global audience memorial sites

Memorial sites 147

may become places of "entertainment/spectacle" rather than of education and prevention.

Both the Tuol Sleng Museum of Genocide Crimes and Murambi Genocide Memorial Centre illustrate three issues related to "disclosure" and "foreclosure" that are applicable to many memorial sites: their (evolving) role in legitimating ruling political authorities; the danger of inadvertently perpetuating the perpetrators' logic; and insufficient explanatory information. In the service of the needs of political authorities, Tuol Sleng evolved from justifying the 1979 Vietnamese invasion to supporting the politically expedient message of the ECCC. Likewise, Murambi has served the RPA/F in its power struggles with the Roman Catholic Church, human rights organisations and the French judiciary. Such evolution means that memorials must be understood as "processes rather than objects"; that while the meaning the sites communicate may appear to be relatively fixed, "these sites prove to be far more malleable, the meanings associated with them changing with use and over time" (Viejo-Rose 2011, 469 471).

Perhaps the most important dilemma facing those who administer memorial sites is whether to communicate the enormity of the crime by retaining the anonymity of victims or by restoring to victims their individual identities denied by perpetrators. At both Tuol Sleng and Murambi it was the first option that prevailed, in line with the priorities of political authorities. Such an approach may perpetuate the perpetrators' logic, so that visitors see the dead as perpetrators saw them, as anonymised members of a generic category destined for torture and extermination (Guyer 2009, 163 174). And yet, as the example of Rwanda demonstrates, there are hidden "informal and personal" practices (Viebach 2020, 3) whereby victims who, while seemingly acquiescing to the political desire for an "undifferentiated collective" of victims (Major 2015, 171 176), privately restore identity by projecting the personhood of their loved ones onto otherwise anonymous remains (Viebach 2020, 3).

Bibliography

Aegis Trust. 2011. *Genocide Memorial Opens at Murambi*, Rwanda. 25 May. Nottingham, UK: The Aegis Trust.

African Rights. 2007. *"Go. If you die, perhaps I will live": A Collective Account of Genocide and Survival in Murambi, Gikongoro, April–July 1994*. Kigali: African Rights.

Bardgett, Suzanne. 1998. "The Genesis and Development of the Imperial War Museum's Holocaust Exhibition Project", *The Journal of Holocaust Education* 7 (3): 28–37.

Bardgett, Suzanne. 2007. "Remembering Srebrenica", *History Today* 57 (11).

Buckley-Zistel, Susanne. 2009. "Nation, narration, unification? The politics of history teaching after the Rwandan genocide", *Journal of Genocide Research* 11 (1): 31–53.

Chandler, David P. 1999. *Voices from S-21: Terror and History in Pol Pot's Secret Prison*. Berkeley, CA: University of California Press.

Clark, Laurie Beth. 2011. "Never again and its discontents." *Performance Research* 16 (1): 68–79.

Conway, Paul. 2011. "Righteous Hutus: Can stories of courageous rescuers help in Rwanda's reconciliation process", *International Journal of Sociology and Anthropology* 3 (7): 217–223.

148 Memorial sites

Douglass, Ana. 2003. "The Menchu Effect: Strategies, Lies and Approximate Truths in Texts of Witness". In *Witness and Memory: The Discourse of Trauma*, edited by Ana Douglass and Thomas A. Vogler, 55–88. New York: Routledge.

Dunlop, Nic. 2009. *The Lost Executioner: The Story of Comrade Duch and the Khmer Rouge*. London: Bloomsbury.

Eltringham, Nigel. 2000. "The Institutional Aspect of the Rwandan Church". In *Conflict and Ethnicity in Central Africa*, edited by Didier Goyvaerts, 225–250. Tokyo: Tokyo University of Foreign Studies.

Eltringham, Nigel. 2004. *Accounting for Horror: Post-Genocide Debates in Rwanda*. London: Pluto.

Eltringham, Nigel. 2014. "Bodies of evidence: Remembering the Rwandan Genocide at Murambi". In *Remembering Genocide*, edited by Nigel Eltringham and Pam Maclean, 200–219. London: Routledge.

Guyer, Sara. 2009. "Rwanda's Bones", *boundary* 2 36 (2): 155–175.

Hamber, Brandon. 2012. "Conflict Museums, Nostalgia, and Dreaming of Never Again", *Peace and Conflict: Journal of Peace Psychology* 18 (3): 268–281.

Hamber, Brandon, Liz Ševčenko and Ereshnee Naidu. 2010. "Utopian Dreams or Practical Possibilities? The Challenges of Evaluating the Impact of Memorialization in Societies in Transition", *International Journal of Transitional Justice* 4 (3): 397–420.

Hinton, Alexander Laban. 2005. *Why Did They Kill?: Cambodia in the Shadow of Genocide*. Berkeley, CA: University of California Press.

Hinton, Alexander Laban. 2016. *Man or Monster? The Trial of a Khmer Rouge Torturer*. London: Duke University Press.

Hughes, Rachel. 2003a. "The abject artefacts of memory: photographs from Cambodia's genocide", *Media, Culture and Society* 25 (1): 23–44.

Hughes, Rachel. 2003b. "Nationalism and Memory at the Tuol Sleng Museum of Genocide Crimes, Phnom Penh, Cambodia". In *Memory, History, Nation*, edited by Susannah Radstone, 175–192. London: Routledge.

Hughes, Rachel. 2008. "Dutiful Tourism: Encountering the Cambodian Genocide", *Asia Pacific Viewpoint* 49 (3): 318–330.

Ibreck, Rachel. 2010. "The politics of mourning: Survivor contributions to memorials in post-genocide Rwanda", *Memory Studies* 3 (4): 330–343.

ICTR. 2005. Prosecutor v. Aloys Simba Case No. ICTR-01–76-T. Judgement and Sentence. 13 December.

International Justice Tribune. 2008. Shaming the world at Murambi. Radio Netherlands Worldwide. 1 December.

Kiernan, Ben. 2003. "The Demography of Genocide in Southeast Asia: The Death Tolls in Cambodia, 1975–1979, and East Timor, 1975–1980", *Critical Asian Studies* 35 (4): 585–597.

Kiernan, Ben. 2008. *The Pol Pot Regime: Race, Power, and Genocide in Cambodia Under the Khmer Rouge, 1975–79*. New Haven, CT: Yale University Press.

King, Elisabeth. 2010. "Memory Controversies in Post-Genocide Rwanda: Implications for Peacebuilding", *Genocide Studies and Prevention* 5 (3): 293–309.

Kroslak, Daniela. 2007. *The Role of France in the Rwandan Genocide*. London: Hurst & Co.

Laville, Sandra. 2006. Two years late and mired in controversy: the British memorial to Rwanda's past. *The Guardian*, 13 November.

Ledgerwood, Judy. 1997. "The Cambodian Tuol Sleng Museum of Genocidal Crimes: National Narrative", *Museum Anthropology* 21 (1): 82–98.

Lennon, J. John and Malcolm Foley. 1996. "JFK and dark tourism: A fascination with assassination", *International Journal of Heritage Studies* 2 (4): 198–211.

Lennon, J. John and Malcolm Foley. 2000. *Dark Tourism*. London: Continuum.

Lesley-Rozen, Elena. 2014. "Memory at the Site: Witnessing, Education and the Repurposing of the Tuol Sleng and Choeung Ek in Cambodia". In *Remembering Genocide*, edited by Nigel Eltringham and Pam Maclean, 131–151. London: Routledge.

Longman, Timothy and Theoneste Rutagengwa. 2006. "Memory and Violence in Post-Genocide Rwanda". In *States of Violence: Politics, Youth, and Memory in Contemporary Africa*, edited by Edna G. Bay and Donald L. Donham, 236–260. Charlottesville, VA: University of Virginia Press.

Major, Laura. 2015. "Unearthing, Untangling and Re-articulating Genocide Corpses in Rwanda", *Critical African Studies* 7 (2): 164–181.

Mannergren Selimovic, Johanna. 2016. "Frictional Commemoration: Local Agency and Cosmopolitan Politics at Memorial Sites in Bosnia-Herzegovina and Rwanda". In *Peacebuilding and Friction: Global and Local Encounters in Post-Conflict Societies*, edited by Annika Björkdahl, Kristine Höglund, Gearoid Millar, Jair van der Lijn and Willemijn Verkoren, 48–63. London: Routledge.

McLean Hilker, Lyndsay. 2012. "Rwanda's 'Hutsi': Intersections of Ethnicity and Violence in the Lives of Youth of 'Mixed' Heritage", *Identities* 19 (2): 229–247.

Meierhenrich, Jens. 2011. "Topographies of Remembering and Forgetting: The Transformation of *Lieux de Mémoire* in Rwanda". In *Remaking Rwanda: State Building and Human Rights after Mass Violence*, edited by Scott Straus and Lars Waldorf, 283–296. Madison, WI: University of Wisconsin Press.

Mookherjee, Nayanika. 2006. "'Remembering to forget': public secrecy and memory of sexual violence in the Bangladesh war of 1971", *Journal of the Royal Anthropological Institute* 12 (2): 433–450.

Mookherjee, Nayanika. 2011. "'Never again': aesthetics of 'genocidal' cosmopolitanism and the Bangladesh Liberation War Museum", *Journal of the Royal Anthropological Institute* 17 (1): S71–S91.

Novick, Peter. 2001. *The Holocaust and Collective Memory*. London: Bloomsbury.

Office of the United Nations High Commissioner for Human Rights. 2010. *Report of the Mapping Exercise documenting the most serious violations of human rights and international humanitarian law committed within the territory of the Democratic Republic of the Congo between March 1993 and June 2003*. Geneva: Office of the United Nations High Commissioner for Human Rights.

Oosterlinck, Claudine, Daniel Van Schendel, Jean Huon, Jean Sompayrac, Olivier Chavanis and Jean-Pascal Serre. 2013. *Rapport D'expertise: Destruction En Vol Du Falcon 50 Kigali (Rwanda)*. Paris: Cour d'appel de Paris Tribunal de Grande Instance de Paris.

Renshaw, Layla. 2010. "The Scientific and Affective Identification of Republican Victims from the Spanish Civil War", *Journal of Material Culture* 15 (4): 449–463.

Robben, Antonius C.G.M. 2016. "Disappearance and Liminality: Argentina's Mourning of State Terror". In *Ultimate Ambiguities: Investigating Death and Liminality*, edited by Peter Berger and Justin Kroesen, 99–125. New York: Berghahn.

Scully, Shannon. 2012. "*The Politics of the Display of Human Remains: Murambi Genocide Memorial, Rwanda*". Presented at the International Network of Genocide Scholars' Biennial Conference. Genocide: Knowing the Past, Safeguarding the Future.

Ševčenko, Liz. 2010. "Sites of Conscience: New Approaches to Conflicted Memory", *Museum International* 62 (1–2):20–25.

Simič, Olivera. 2009. "Remembering, Visiting and Placing the Dead: Law, Authority and Genocide in Srebrenica", *Law Text Culture* 13 (1): 273–310.

Sion, Brigitte. 2011. "Conflicting sites of memory in post-genocide Cambodia", *Humanity: An International Journal of Human Rights, Humanitarianism, and Development* 2 (1): 1–21.

Smith, Stephen D. 1999. *Making Memory: Creating Britain's First Holocaust Centre*. Newark, UK: Quill.

Sodaro, Amy. 2011. "Politics of the Past: Remembering the Rwandan Genocide at the Kigali Memorial Centre". In *Curating Difficult Knowledge: Violent Pasts in Public Places*, edited by Erica T. Lehrer, Cynthia E. Milton and Monica Patterson, 72–88. Basingstoke, UK: Palgrave Macmillan.

Thomson, Susan. 2011a. "The Darker Side of Transitional Justice: The Power Dynamics Behind Rwanda's Gacaca Courts", *Africa* 81 (3): 373–390.

Thomson, Susan. 2011b. "Whispering truth to power: The everyday resistance of Rwandan peasants to post-genocide reconciliation", *African Affairs* 110 (440): 439–456.

Vidal, Claudine. 2004. "Les commémorations du génocide au Rwanda", *Cahiers d'Etudes Africaines* XLIV (3): 575–592.

Viebach, Julia. 2020. "Mediating 'absence-presence' at Rwanda's genocide memorials: of care-taking, memory and proximity to the dead", *Critical African Studies* 12 (2): 237–269.

Viejo-Rose, Dacia. 2011. "Memorial functions: Intent, impact and the right to remember", *Memory Studies* 4 (4): 465–480.

Violi, Patrizia. 2012. "Trauma Site Museums and Politics of Memory: Tuol Sleng, Villa Grimaldi and the Bologna Ustica Museum", *Theory, Culture & Society* 29 (1): 36–75.

Wagner, Sarah. 2010. "Tabulating loss, entombing memory: The Srebrenica-Potočari Memorial Centre". In *Memory, Mourning, Landscape*, edited by Elizabeth Anderson, Avril Maddrell and Kate McLoughlin, 61–78. Amsterdam: Rodopi.

Williams, Paul. 2004. "Witnessing Genocide: Vigilance and Remembrance at Tuol Sleng and Choeung Ek", *Holocaust and Genocide Studies* 18 (2): 234–254.

Young, James E. 1993. *The Texture of Memory: Holocaust Memorials and Meaning*. New Haven, CT: Yale University Press.

Young, James E. 1998. *Writing and Rewriting the Holocaust: Narrative and the Consequences of Interpretation*. Bloomington, IN: Indiana University Press.

Zorbas, Eugenia. 2009. "What does reconciliation after genocide mean? Public transcripts and hidden transcripts in post-genocide Rwanda", *Journal of Genocide Research* 11 (1): 127–147.

CONCLUSION

In the Introduction to this book I suggested that in the aftermath of violent conflict the strength of anthropology lies in the ethnographic method characterised by a commitment to an "insider" point of view (see Avruch 2009, 11). Understanding "processes, events, ideas and practices in an informant's own terms rather than ours" (Shaw 2007, 188) forces us to revise or even abandon our preconceived assumptions and received wisdom. Challenging assumptions in this way is, undoubtedly, a hallmark of anthropology, as summarised by Clifford Geertz (1984, 275): "We have, with no little success, sought to keep the world off balance; pulling out rugs, upsetting tea tables, setting off firecrackers." Keeping the world off balance does not mean anthropologists are inveterate naysayers. Rather, an unswerving commitment to recording the "insider's" point of view often generates this kind of disruption. The value of such an approach is, I hope, borne out by this book, in which I have avoided "vats of theory" (Geertz 1984, 275) in favour of rich, ethnographic examples.

In the Introduction I reflected on the two terms that appear in the book's title: "peace" and "reconciliation". I suggested that while we may define "peace" as constructive, in opposition to destructive conflict, such an approach is inadequate once we recognise that conflict is also constructive, acting as a binding element between groups that are in conflict, potentially revitalising the norms by which group members are supposed to live (Coser 1956, 121–128). This can be interpreted as implying that there is no "peace" without conflict, as intermittent conflict is needed to re-educate members of a group on how they should live "in peace" with one another. Similarly counter-intuitive is the suggestion that it is multiple, cross-cutting allegiances, rather than unity, that maintain "peace". Conflict is defused and "peace" maintained in situations where "people who are friends on one basis are enemies on another" (Gluckman 1963, 4). I also discussed how "harmony", which we would assume to be a virtuous objective, may in reality be a coercive ideology

152 Conclusion

that was not only used to strengthen colonial rule but continues to suppress legit-imate grievances caused by social and economic inequality, by portraying grievance as being solely a matter of interpersonal conflict (Nader 1997, 713–714). My fourth counter-intuitive proposition was that "peace" is not simply the absence of violence if we conceive of violence as not just being "personal or direct" but also "structural or indirect", as reflected in widespread poverty and discrimination (see Galtung 1969). This has consequences for how we might envisage "peace", whether as "negative peace" (the absence of "direct, personal violence") or "positive peace" (the absence of "indirect, structural violence") (Galtung 1969, 183). I illustrated my dis-cussion of these four counter-intuitive assertions (conflict can be constructive; "peace" relies on division; seeking "harmony" can be coercive; and peace is not the absence of violence) with ethnographic examples from Malawi, Mexico, Rwanda, South Sudan, South Africa, Sierra Leone and Zambia.

Regarding "reconciliation", received wisdom might suggest parties must "freely discuss the past conflict and take responsibility for past injustice and wrongdoing" (Bar-Tal & Cehajic-Clancy 2013, 131). And yet the ethnographic examples I considered from Bosnia-Herzegovina, Cambodia, East Timor, Indonesia, Mozam-bique, Sierra Leone and Rwanda suggest that survivors of violent conflict tend to avoid direct discussion of the past and, instead, foreground "relational and embo-died forms of communication, rather than public, verbal disclosure" (Kent 2016, 42). Such communication draws upon the "seemingly mundane" (Ketterer 2014, 5) performance of everyday life as survivors seek to (re)construct "normal life" (Jansen 2013, 234). Such reconstruction requires acts of imagination (Nordstrom 1998) that may draw on a fabricated, nostalgic image of past relations prior to violent conflict (Zorbas 2009b). These examples suggest that it is through everyday, mundane interactions that viable relationships are (re)established, rather than through formal processes that are explicitly proclaimed as enabling "reconciliation". Such mundane interactions, including eating and drinking, may, however, be ignored because re-establishing "everyday life" is not amenable to the same kinds of instrumental formalisation, replication, monitoring and evaluation sought by national governments and international agencies as they seek to foster "reconcilia-tion" (Martin 2016). Furthermore, formal interventions and their emphasis on speaking about the violent past may, in fact, undermine the (re)construction of mundane relations (Kent 2016, 37), although they may also, paradoxically, draw those from opposing sides closer together in their mutual distrust of political authorities.

In Chapter 1 I reflected on anthropology's long-standing concern with how societies maintain "social cohesion" by managing conflict (Avruch 2007). Drawing on ethnographic examples from Hawaii, Indonesia, Liberia, Malaysia, Nigeria and Papua New Guinea, I tentatively suggested five common features of these conflict management mechanisms (restoring the "harmony" of the group; reintegrating the "wrongdoer"; sharing food and drink; the active participation of the community; the airing of comprehensive information). I also acknowledged the dilemma of comparison and that the drive to identify "recurring cultural patterns" should not

Conclusion **153**

be at the expense of appreciating the context specificity of each mechanism (Fry & Bjorkqvist 1996, 5). Furthermore, given that different readers of the same ethnographies or different ethnographies would generate alternative common features, the five common features I identified must be considered as provisional.

One of the purposes of Chapter 1 was to lay the foundations for the discussion of the "re-traditionalisation" movement in Chapter 2. In recent years a new "received wisdom" has emerged as "traditional" conflict management mechanisms have been "lauded for their authenticity and presumed efficiency" (Horne 2014, 18; see United Nations 2004, paras 17 36). Anthropologists have, however, been less enthusiastic. Some of the reasons for this I discussed in Chapter 1, principally the dangers of essentialising "culture" by misrepresenting a "culture" as if it is "free of dissensions, of internal contradictions or paradoxes" (Avruch 2000, 341). Furthermore, describing conflict management mechanisms as "traditional" may lend them an aura of prestige when, in reality, they are a "product of the colonial encounter" (Falk Moore 1989, 289) and continue to change over time. Finally, an essentialised, "authentic" conflict management mechanism may be used to enforce a "coercive harmony" that subordinates certain members of a community (Nader 1997, 715).

In Chapter 2 I discussed a number of other concerns regarding "re-traditionalisation": that international and national authorities may choose a caricature of "tradition" to serve their own interests; that while the "local" is presented as being intrinsically good, what is "local" is a matter of perspective; that flexible mechanisms may lose their efficacy if they are codified; and that prompting "tradition" may reinforce the exploitative authority of leaders. While acknowledging these critiques, I considered whether there are degrees of "re-traditionalisation" and whether there are ways in which "local" responses can still be promoted whilst avoiding the pitfalls identified by anthropologists. To answer this question I considered ethnographic accounts from Rwanda, Uganda and Mozambique. The case of *Inkiko-Gacaca*, which was created following the 1994 genocide of the Tutsi in Rwanda, substantiated the critique to a large degree, given that the government-backed institution bore little resemblance to "traditional" *gacaca* and, according to the research I considered, failed to achieve its stated objectives because of "cultural" norms that gave rise to a "pragmatic" rather than an "objective" truth; people using the opportunity for revenge and material gain; the exclusion of crimes committed against Hutu by the current ruling party; and the lack of comfort the process brought to Tutsi survivors. *Inkiko-Gacaca* appears, therefore, to be an example of how governments can appropriate "local tradition" but fail to achieve the intended results (Merry 1988, 882). *Mato oput* in Uganda and *gamba* spirits in Mozambique, however, presented a more complicated picture. While in Uganda there were moves akin to those in Rwanda to formalise and promote *mato oput*, which would have potentially robbed the process of its essential flexibility, when left to operate "out of sight" (Finnström 2010, 146) spirit divination and *mato oput* were used in a creative way to reintegrate Lord's Resistance Army abductees into their communities. Likewise in Mozambique, ways of working with the spirit world were modified to restore peace and stability to communities following the

154 Conclusion

civil war, further demonstrating that "tradition" is effective because it is "flexible, fluid and enduring" (Nordstrom 1998, 114). As such, the ethnographic research considered in Chapter 2 does not reject outright the assumption that "traditional" conflict management practices can be effective responses to violent conflict. Rather, by emphasising that it is the flexibility of such practices that allows their creative adaptation, research raises questions about the codification of such practices by national governments and international aid agencies.

In Chapter 3 I considered more "received wisdom", that in this "age of testimony" (Felman & Laub 1992, 201) the "telling of truth" enables "healing" and future peace. Anthropologists, however, have voiced concern that such benefits have been elevated to a global paradigm of "redemptive remembering through truth-telling" (Shaw 2007, 189), despite a lack of evidence for such benefits (Summerfield 1999, 1456); that the manner in which testimony is taken and disseminated may be detrimental to the person giving testimony (Brounéus 2008); and that the paradigm claims as universal assumptions that originated in Europe and North America. While there is evidence that survivors of violent conflict can benefit from giving testimony, in that they "make sense of the experiences" and can reclaim "status and self-worth" (Baines & Stewart 2011, 16), such testimony should be considered a "personal narrative" rather than a "forensic" truth (Truth and Reconciliation Commission 1998, 1:112); meaning that it is a "truth" that changes over time as the testifier incorporates "foreign material" (Levi 1986, 130) and adapts testimony for different audiences (French 2009) and to the changing needs of the present (see Eastmond & Mannergren Selimovic 2012). Furthermore, testimony is rarely simply survivors speaking for themselves. Rather, testimony is generated in collaboration with an elicitor who co-authors the testimony and may steer it in ways contrary to the intention of the person giving the testimony. In addition, there is a process of "entextualisation" (French 2009, 97) in which oral testimony is translated from one language to another, is transcribed and extracts used in reports or books which may, in turn, be selectively quoted in other reports or books (Williamson 2016). There is, therefore, a "collage of intervening presences" (Douglass 2003, 68) between initial testimony and dissemination, which may lead those who give testimony to experience a "loss of voice, of agency, and of self" (Ross 2003, 335). I supported my discussion of these key features of testimony (the manner in which testimony is taken and disseminated; the changing nature of testimony; and the co-production of testimony) with ethnographic examples from Argentina, Australia, Bosnia-Herzegovina, Guatemala, Rwanda, Uganda, the United States of America and South Africa.

In Chapter 4 I considered truth commissions which, in the aftermath of violent conflict, "have become fetish objects to which almost mystical powers of future making are attributed" (Shaw 2014, 315). While there is no doubt that truth commissions "narrow the range of permissible lies" (Hamber & Wilson 2002, 36–37; see Ignatieff 1996, 113), anthropologists and other ethnographers have been sceptical regarding the two objectives that truth commissions claim to serve: transforming "common knowledge – into official acknowledgement" (Bickford 2007,

Conclusion **155**

996) and providing an opportunity for victims to give an account of the violations and abuses they suffered. Drawing on ethnographic research conducted in Bangladesh, Canada, East Timor, Peru, Sierra Leone, the Solomon Islands and South Africa, I considered how the restricted nature of truth commission mandates has resulted in obscuring important parts of the past. Likewise, the manner in which witness statements are taken prior to hearings and how they are controlled during hearings suggest that truth commissions are not necessarily contexts in which survivors can "ventilate [their] truth" (Verdoolaege 2006, 67). I contrasted these critiques of formal truth commissions with community-based "unofficial truth projects" in Northern Ireland, which overcome some of the problems associated with truth commissions as they give survivors the opportunity to edit their testimony so that they become active participants in truth-telling, rather than just being involved in "passive telling to third-party authors" (Laplante 2007, 435; see Lundy & McGovern 2006, 84). In addition I suggested that assessing truth commissions on whether they successfully "draw a line" under the past may obscure a more profound benefit that they have as an impetus for "victim-survivors to continue to tell their story" as part of a continuing struggle over representing the past (Laplante 2007, 434–435).

In Chapter 5 I considered how trials at international criminal courts for mass atrocity crimes (war crimes, crimes against humanity and genocide) are promoted as a means to discover and disseminate the "truth"; for victims to be heard; and for the rule of law and reconciliation to be promoted (see Fletcher & Weinstein 2002, 586–601). Anthropologists and other ethnographers have, however, suggested that putting individuals on trial for mass atrocity crimes can obscure the way in which "mass violence is embedded in international and global structures of domination and injustice" (Branch 2011, 126), meaning that "other perpetrators go unpunished and history remains unexamined" (Douglas 2006, 100–101). Regarding the contribution of trials to "reconciliation", I considered ethnographic research from Bosnia–Herzegovina and Sierra Leone that suggests trials appeared to strengthen (or do little to dissipate) the sense of collective victimhood of one's own group and collective guilt of one's opponents, while research from Cambodia suggests that the temporal jurisdiction of the court was too restrictive, silencing experiences prior to and in the aftermath of the Khmer Rouge regime (1975–1979). Finally, drawing on my own research at the International Criminal Tribunal for Rwanda, I considered the claim that international criminal trials provide an important "historical record". On one hand, recent research has suggested that international criminal courts can "produce a body of evidence that is invaluable for historians" (Wilson 2011, 18; see Eltringham 2019, 152–180). And yet how those archives may be used is unpredictable. While there is no doubt that the archives of international criminal courts will "face a long-term state of contestation" (Kaye 2014, 392) and may act as "a potential, future antidote to permanent amnesia" (Mannergren Selimovic 2015, 240), they may also be drawn upon to write histories that are at odds with judgements and which fuel division rather than achieve "the restoration and maintenance of peace" (United Nations 1993).

156 Conclusion

In Chapter 6 I considered memorial or "trauma sites" (Violi 2012, 39) where violent events occurred and which are preserved and made accessible to the general public. On one hand, these sites are considered to be a valuable place of "disclosure", educating the uninformed about past events and preventing the recurrence of violence in the future (Clark 2011). Drawing on ethnographic research from Bangladesh, Bosnia-Herzegovina and Rwanda I suggested that "disclosure" is not without its problems, given that the way in which memorial sites cross-reference one another may lead to a loss of specificity and be used as an opportunity to silence experiences inconvenient to current political authorities. Meanwhile, by appealing to a global audience, memorial sites may become places of "entertainment/spectacle" rather than of education and prevention. A detailed consideration of two memorial sites, the Tuol Sleng Museum of Genocide Crimes in Cambodia and the Murambi Genocide Memorial Centre in Rwanda, illustrated how such sites are also utilised for "foreclosure" (supporting a selective narrative of past events for political purposes) (Clark 2011). Tuol Sleng evolved from justifying the 1979 Vietnamese invasion to supporting the politically expedient message of trials at the Extraordinary Chambers in the Courts of Cambodia; Murambi has served the Rwandan government in its power struggles with the Roman Catholic Church, human rights organisations and the French judiciary. I also considered the dilemma facing those who administer such sites of whether to communicate the enormity of the crime by retaining the anonymity of victims or restoring to victims their individual identities, denied them by perpetrators. At both Tuol Sleng and Murambi it was the first option that prevailed, in line with the priorities of political authorities. Such an approach may perpetuate the perpetrators' logic, so that visitors see the dead as perpetrators saw them, as anonymised members of a generic category destined for torture and extermination (Guyer 2009, 163 174). However, ethnographic research in Rwanda also suggests that "informal and personal" memorial practices privately restore identity, as those who care for anonymous human remains project the personhood of their loved ones onto the remains (Viebach 2020, 3).

What emerges from this overview of ethnographic research is not that "received wisdom" is necessarily incorrect, but that it is partial or overly simplistic. For example, it is not the case that "traditional" conflict management practices in Uganda and Mozambique cannot be effective responses, but that the limitations of codifying what is flexible must be taken into account (see Chapter 2). Likewise, while for some in Bosnia-Herzegovina the trials at the International Criminal Tribunal for the Former Yugoslavia do not put an end to the demonising of other groups, there are "less aligned" people who more readily accepted the ICTY's narrative of individual guilt, (Mannergren Selimovic 2015, 239). Similarly, and contrary to claims, truth commissions may not allow survivors to "ventilate" their truth, but they can instil an "insatiable desire among victim-survivors to continue to tell their story" (Laplante 2007, 434–435). The ethnographic record considered in this book is full of examples demonstrating that the value of ethnography lies not in countering simplistic "received wisdom" with an equally simplistic rejection but in adding texture through "thick" accounts; accounts which are never intended to be the last word but, rather, the means to continue to keep "the world off balance" (Geertz 1984, 275).

Bibliography

Avruch, Kevin. 2000. "Culture and negotiation pedagogy", *Negotiation Journal* 16 (4): 339–346.

Avruch, Kevin. 2007. "A Historical Overview of Anthropology and Conflict Resolution", *Anthropology News*: 48 (6): 13–14.

Avruch, Kevin. 2009. "Transforming conflict resolution education: applying anthropology alongside your students", *Learning and Teaching* 2 (2): 8–22.

Baines, Erin and Beth Stewart. 2011. "'I cannot accept what I have not done': Storytelling, Gender and Transitional Justice", *Journal of Human Rights Practice* 3 (3): 245–263.

Bar-Tal, Daniel and Sabina Cehajic-Clancy. 2013. "From Collective Victimhood to Social Reconciliation: Outlining a Conceptual Framework". In *War, Community, and Social Change: Collective Experiences in the Former Yugoslavia*, edited by Dario Spini, Guy Elcheroth and Dinka Corkalo Birusk, 125–136. New York: Springer.

Bickford, Louis. 2007. "Unofficial Truth Projects", *Human Rights Quarterly* 29 (4): 994–1035.

Branch, Adam. 2011. "Neither Liberal nor Peaceful? Practices of 'Global Justice' by the ICC". In *A Liberal Peace? The Problems and Practices of Peacebuilding*, edited by Susanna Campbell, David Chandler and Meera Sabaratnam, 121–137. London: Zed Books.

Brounéus, Karen. 2008. "Truth Telling as Talking Cure? Insecurity and Retraumatization in the Rwandan Gacaca Courts", *Security Dialogue* 39 (1): 55–76.

Clark, Laurie Beth. 2011. "Never again and its discontents", *Performance Research* 16 (1): 68–79.

Coser, Lewis A. 1956. *The Functions of Social Conflict*. London: Routledge and Kegan Paul.

Douglas, Lawrence. 2006. "History and Memory in the Courtroom: Reflections on Perpetrator Trials". In *The Nuremberg Trials: International Criminal Law Since 1945*, edited by Herbert R. Reginbogin and Christoph Safferling, 95–105. Munich: Saur.

Douglass, Ana. 2003. "The Menchu Effect: Strategies, Lies and Approximate Truths in Texts of Witness". In *Witness and Memory: The Discourse of Trauma*, edited by Ana Douglass and Thomas A. Vogler, 55–88. New York: Routledge.

Eastmond, Marita and Johanna Mannergren Selimovic. 2012. "Silence as Possibility in Postwar Everyday Life", *The International Journal of Transitional Justice* 6 (3): 502–524.

Eltringham, Nigel. 2019. *Genocide Never Sleeps: Living Law at the International Criminal Tribunal for Rwanda*. Cambridge, UK: Cambridge University Press.

Falk Moore, Sally. 1989. "History and the Redefinition of Custom in Kilimanjaro". In *History and Power in the Study of Law: New Directions in Legal Anthropology*, edited by J. Starr and J.F. Collier, 277–301. Ithaca, NY: Cornell University Press.

Felman, Shoshana and Dori Laub. 1992. *Testimony: Crises of Witnessing in Literature, Psychoanalysis, and History*. London: Routledge.

Finnström, Sverker. 2010. "Reconciliation Grown Bitter?: War, Retribution, and Ritual Action in Northern Uganda". In *Localizing Transitional Justice: Interventions and Priorities after Mass Violence*, edited by Rosalind Shaw, Lars Waldorf and Pierre Hazan, 135–156. Stanford, CA: Stanford University Press.

Fletcher, Laurel E. and Harvey M. Weinstein. 2002. "Violence and Social Repair: Rethinking the Contribution of Justice to Reconciliation", *Human Rights Quarterly* 24 (3): 573–639.

French, Brigittine M. 2009. "Technologies of Telling: Discourse, Transparency, and Erasure in Guatemalan Truth Commission Testimony", *Journal of Human Rights* 8 (1): 92–109.

Fry, Douglas P. and Kaj Bjorkqvist (eds.). 1996. "Introduction: Conflict Resolution Themes". In *Cultural Variation in Conflict Resolution: Alternatives to Violence* 3–8. London: Routledge.

Galtung, Johan. 1969. "Violence, Peace and Peace Research", *Journal of Peace Research* 6 (3): 167–190.

158 Conclusion

Geertz, Clifford. 1984. "Distinguished Lecture: Anti Anti-Relativism", *American Anthropologist* 86 (2): 263–278.

Gluckman, Max. 1963. *Custom and Conflict in Africa*. Oxford: Basil Blackwell.

Guyer, Sara. 2009. "Rwanda's Bones", *boundary 2* 36 (2): 155–175.

Hamber, Brandon and Richard A. Wilson. 2002. "Symbolic Closure Through Memory, Reparation and Revenge in Post-Conflict Societies", *Journal of Human Rights* 1 (1): 35–53.

Horne, Cynthia M. 2014. "Reconstructing 'Traditional' Justice from the Outside In: Transitional Justice in Aceh and East Timor", *Journal of Peacebuilding & Development* 9 (2): 17–32.

Ignatieff, Michael. 1996. "Articles of faith", *Index on Censorship* 25 (5): 110–122.

Jansen, Stef. 2013. "If reconciliation is the answer, are we asking the right questions", *Studies in Social Justice* 7 (2): 229–243.

Kaye, David. 2014. "Archiving justice: conceptualizing the archives of the United Nations International Criminal Tribunal for the Former Yugoslavia", *Archival Science* 14 (3): 381–396.

Kent, Lia. 2016. "Sounds of Silence: Everyday Strategies of Social Repair in Timor-Leste", *Australian Feminist Journal* 42 (1): 31–50.

Ketterer, Stephanie Hobbis. 2014. "'Love Goes through the Stomach': A Japanese–Korean Recipe for Post-conflict Reconciliation", *Anthropology in Action* 21 (2): 2–13.

Laplante, Lisa J. 2007. "The Peruvian Truth Commission's Historical Memory Project: Empowering Truth-Tellers to Confront Truth Deniers", *Journal of Human Rights* 6 (4): 433–452.

Levi, Primo. 1986. "The Memory of Offense". In *Bitburg in Moral and Political Perspective*, edited by Geoffrey Hartman, 131–137. Bloomington, IN: Indiana University Press.

Lundy, Patricia and Mark McGovern. 2006. "Participation, Truth and Partiality: Participatory Action Research, Community-based Truth-telling and Post-conflict Transition in Northern Ireland", *Sociology* 40 (1): 71–88.

Mannergren Selimovic, Johanna. 2015. "Challenges of Postconflict Coexistence: Narrating Truth and Justice in a Bosnian Town", *Political Psychology* 36 (2): 231–242.

Martin, Laura S. 2016. "Practicing Normality: An Examination of Unrecognizable Transitional Justice Mechanisms in Post-Conflict Sierra Leone", *Journal of Intervention and Statebuilding* 10 (3): 400–418.

Merry, Sally Engle. 1988. "Legal Pluralism", *Law and Society Review* 22 (5): 869–896.

Mertus, Julie. 2000. "Truth in a Box: The Limits of Justice through Judicial Mechanisms". In *The Politics of Memory: Truth, Healing and Social Justice*, edited by Ifi Amadiume and Abdullahi An-Na'im, 142–161. London: Zed Books.

Nader, Laura. 1997. "Controlling Processes: Tracing the Dynamic Components of Power", *Current Anthropology* 38 (5): 711–737.

Nordstrom, Carolyn. 1998. "Terror Warfare and the Medicine of Peace", *Medical Anthropology Quarterly* 12 (1): 103–121.

Ross, Fiona. 2003. "On Having a Voice and Being Heard", *Anthropological Theory* 3 (3): 325–341.

Shaw, Rosalind. 2007. "Memory Frictions: Localizing the Truth and Reconciliation Commission in Sierra Leone", *The International Journal of Transitional Justice* 1 (2): 183–207.

Shaw, Rosalind. 2014. "The TRC, the NGO and the child: young people and post-conflict futures in Sierra Leone", *Social Anthropology* 22 (3): 306–325.

Summerfield, Derek. 1999. "A critique of seven assumptions behind psychological trauma programmes in war-affected areas", *Social Science & Medicine* 48 (10): 1449–1462.

Truth and Reconciliation Commission. 1998. *Truth and Reconciliation Commission of South Africa Report*. 5 vols. Vol. 1. Johannesburg: Palgrave Macmillan.

United Nations. 1993. *Resolution 827 (1993) Adopted by the Security Council at its 3217th meeting*. S/RES/827. 25 May. New York: United Nations.

United Nations. 2004. *The rule of Law and Transitional Justice in Conflict and Post-Conflict Societies*. New York: United Nations.

Verdoolaege, Annelies. 2006. "Managing reconciliation at the human rights violations hearings of the South African TRC", *The Journal of Human Rights* 5 (1): 61–80.

Viebach, Julia. 2020. "Mediating absence-presence' at Rwanda's genocide memorials: of care-taking, memory and proximity to the dead", *Critical African Studies* 12 (2): 237–269.

Violi, Patrizia. 2012. "Trauma Site Museums and Politics of Memory: Tuol Sleng, Villa Grimaldi and the Bologna Ustica Museum", *Theory, Culture & Society* 29 (1): 36–75.

Williamson, Caroline. 2016. "Post-traumatic growth at the international level: The obstructive role played by translators and editors of Rwandan Genocide testimonies", *Translation Studies* 9 (1): 33–50.

Wilson, Richard A. 2011. *Writing History in International Criminal Trials*. Cambridge, UK: Cambridge University Press.

Zorbas, Eugenia. 2009. "What does reconciliation after genocide mean? Public transcripts and hidden transcripts in post-genocide Rwanda", *Journal of Genocide Research* 11 (1): 127–147.

INDEX

Note: Illustrations are indicated by page numbers in *italics*

AAR *see* Agreement on Accountability and Reconciliation (AAR)
Aceh 48
Acholi people 8, 49, 55–56
Acholi Religious Leaders Peace Initiative 56
ACP *see* Ardoyne Commemoration Project (ACP)
Adami, Tom 123
ADR *see* Alternative Dispute Resolution (ADR)
Africa 111; *see also specific countries*
African Union 113
Agreement on Accountability and Reconciliation (AAR) 57
Akayesu, Jean-Paul 123
Allen, Tim 47–48, 50, 58, 115
Alternative Dispute Resolution (ADR) 5
Anders, Gerhard 117–118
Ardoyne Commemoration Project (ACP) 92, 101–103
Arendt, Hannah 79, 120, 122
Argentina 76, 91–92
Army of Republika Srpska (VRS) 18, 114, 132
Asad, Talal 73
Auschwitz-Birkenau Museum 78, 132, 135
Australia 80–81
Avruch, Kevin 26, 36

Bagosora, Théoneste 124
Baines, Erin 57, 59–60, 76

Bangladesh 98, 133, 155–156
Bangladesh Liberation War Museum (BLWM) 133
Barbie, Klaus 123–124
bcaraa' 36, 38, 40
Beverley, John 77
Bickford, Louis 96, 100
Birkett, Norman 120
Black, Peter W. 26
Blommaert, Jan 80
BLWM *see* Bangladesh Liberation War Museum (BLWM)
Bock, Mary 80
Borneman, John 8–9, 17, 70
Bosnia-Herzegovina 12–13, 16–18, 37, 74–76, 115, 132, 134–135, 155; *see also* International Criminal Tribunal for the Former Yugoslavia (ICTY)
Branch, Adam 49–50, 110–111
Brounéus, Karen 74, 97
Burnet, Jennie 75

Cambodia 12, 108, 112, *112,* 114–117, *117,* 119, 131–132, 135–139, 155–156
Campbell, Kirsten 120
Canada 94–96, *95,* 103
CAVR *see* Commission for Reception, Truth and Reconciliation (CAVR) (East Timor)
Chagga people 27–28
charismatic victim 69–70

Index **161**

Chile 91, 134
Clark, Laurie Beth 131
Clarke, Kamari 110, *112,* 113
Clifford, James 26x
coerciveness: of harmony 2, 4–6, 8, 19, 35, 40, 151–153; law and 25
cohesion, social 4, 16, 25, 152
Cole, Catherine 96
colonialism 27–28, 58, 71
Colvin, Christopher 71
Commission for Reception, Truth and Reconciliation (CAVR) (East Timor) 13–14, 48, 93, 96–97, 103
community participation 38–39
comparison 28–30
conflict: as constructive 2–4; defined 3; memory and testimony in aftermath of 68–83, 77; as opposite of peace 2; peace and 151; truth in aftermath of 90–104, *95*; violence and 3
conflict management: and airing of comprehensive information 39–40; case studies 30–40; and community participation 38–39; harmony and 35–36; in Hawaii 32; in Indonesia 30–31, 33; law as 25; in Liberia 30; in Malaysia 32–33; in Nigeria 33–34; in Papua New Guinea 34; and reintegration of "wrongdoer" 36–37; re-traditionalising 45–63, *52, 57, 62*; and sharing of food and drink 37–38; "traditional" 25–41, *31*
constructiveness: of conflict 2–4
co-production of testimony 79–82
corporate colonisation 126
Coser, Lewis A. 2–3, 36
criminal justice, international 155; historical record and 119–125, *121*; local responses to 114–119, *117*
criminal responsibility, individual 109–113
Croatia 18
culture: essentialisation of 26–27, 153; as homogeneous 26; local 46–47; of secrecy 102; therapy 29, 73; as verb 26
"customary law" 6, 26–28, 48
CVR *see* Truth and Reconciliation Commission (CVR) (Peru)

"dark tourism" 134
Das, Veena 70
Davis, Madeleine 68
"death tourism" 134
Democratic Republic of Congo 111, 141
Dickson-Gomez, Julia 69
"Dirty War" 76

disclosure 131–132
division: and maintenance of peace 4
Donnan, Hastings 68
Dou Donggo 30–31, *31,* 35, 38–39
Douglas, Lawrence 123
Douglass, Ana 78
Draft Code of Crimes Against the Peace and Security of Mankind 113
drink, sharing of 37–38
Duncan, Christopher 12, 47

Eades, Diana 78
Eastmond, Marita 13
East Timor 13–14, 38, 48, 93, 96–97, 103, 108
ECCC *see* Extraordinary Chambers in the Courts of Cambodia (ECCC)
Eichmann, Adolf 69, 78–79, 120
Eliot, T. S. 4
El Salvador 69
Epstein, Arnold 34, 36, 39
esop isöñ 33–34, 37
essentialisation of culture 26–27, 153
Etcheson, Craig 12
ethnography 1–2, 6, 27–28
Evans-Pritchard, E. E. 4
Extraordinary Chambers in the Courts of Cambodia (ECCC) 108, *112, 112,* 114–117, *117,* 119, 147, 156

Falk Moore, Sally 27–28
Falls Community Council 102–103
Farabundo Martí National Liberation Front 69
female genital circumcision (FGC) 46
FGC *see* female genital circumcision (FGC)
Finnström, Sverker 56, 58–59
Foley, Malcolm 134
food, sharing of 37–38
foreclosure 131–132
"foreign material" 78–79
forensic truth 75–79, 77
FRELIMO (Front for the Liberation of Mozambique/Frente de Libertação de Moçambique) 10, 15, 60
Fry, Douglas 29, 35

Galtung, Johan 113
gamba spirits 60–63, *62*
Geertz, Clifford 151
Gibbs, James 29–30
Gono Adalat 98
Good Friday Agreement 101
"grief tourism" 134

162 Index

Guatemala 78, 101, 154
Guthrey, Holly 14, 97–98

Habyarimana, Juvénal 142
Halmahera 47
Hamber, Brandon 134
harmony 151–152; as coercive 2, 4–6, 8, 19, 35, 40, 151–153; in conflict management 35–36
Hausner, Gideon 69–70
Hawaii 32, 38
Hinton, Alexander Laban 109, 111
Hoebel, E. Adamson 2
Hoffman, Danny 124
Holocaust 69–70, 78–80, 132–134
Holy Spirit Army (HSA) 55
homogeneity: of culture 26
Honwana, Alcinda Manuel 61, 74
Ho'oponopono 32, 36, 38–39
Horne, Cynthia 48–49
HRVC *see* Human Rights Violations Committee (HRVC) (South Africa)
HSA *see* Holy Spirit Army (HSA)
Human Rights Industry 70–71
Human Rights Violations Committee (HRVC) (South Africa) 5, 7, 70, 80, 92, 99
Hungary 80–81
Hun Sen 116

Ibibio people 33–34, 37
ICC *see* International Criminal Court (ICC)
ICTR *see* International Criminal Tribunal for Rwanda (ICTR)
ICTY *see* International Criminal Tribunal for the Former Yugoslavia (ICTY)
Igreja, Victor 61–62
Indian Residential School Settlement Agreement (Canada) 95
individual criminal responsibility 109–113
Indonesia 28, 30–31, *31,* 33, 35, 47–49, 93
information, comprehensive: and conflict management 39–40
Ingelaere, Bert 12, 37–38, 53
Inkiko-Gacaca 51–55, *52,* 74–75, 153
International Criminal Court (ICC) 108–110
International Criminal Tribunal for Rwanda (ICTR) 51, 79, 82, 109, 113, 119–121, *121,* 121–124
International Criminal Tribunal for the Former Yugoslavia (ICTY) 108, 110, 113–115, 118–119, 124–126, 156
Ireland 68, 101–103

Israel 69, 132–133
Italy 134
Ito, Karen 32

Jackson, Michael 70
Jansen, Stef 16
Japan 16–17, 38
Jewish Holocaust Museum and Research Centre (JHMRC) 80–81
Just, Peter 30–31, 38–39

Kagak, Alan *95*
Kagak, Rosie *95*
Kagame, Paul 51, 142–143
Kakwena, Alice 55
Kampuchea 108, 112, 116, 135–139; *see also* Cambodia
Karadžić, Radovan 114
Kayinamura, Aimé 141
Kayishema, Clément 123
Kent, Lia 13, 38
Kenya 46
Ketelaar, Eric 76
Ketterer, Stephanie Hobbis 16, 38
Khmer Rouge 12, 108, 111–112, 116–117, *117,* 131–132, 135–139
Khulumani Support Group 71
Khutwane, Yvonne 72, 99
Kigali Genocide Memorial 133–134, 140
Kleinman, Arthur 70
Kony, Joseph 55
Korea 16–17
Kpelle moot 29–30, 37–40

Langfield, Michele 80
Laplante, Lisa 91
law: coercion and 25; conflict management as 25; customary 6, 26–28, 48; as historian 120; international 108; rule of 109, 126, 155
Lebanon 37
Lennon, J. John 134
Lesley-Rozen, Elena 115–116
Levi, Primo 78
Leydesdorff, Selma 18
Liberia 28–30, 152
Llewellyn, Karl 2
Lord's Resistance Army (LRA) 8, 49, 55–57, 59, 63, 76–77, 96
LRA *see* Lord's Resistance Army (LRA)
Lundy, Patricia 102

Macdonald, Anna 47–48, 50
Mac Ginty, Roger 48, 58

Maclean, Pam 80
Madlingozi, Tshepo 71
Madres de Plaza de Mayo 91
Major, Laura 145–146
Malabo Protocol 113
Malawi 5, 152
Malaysia 32–33, 96, 152
Mamdani, Mahmood 92
Mannergren Selimovic, Johanna 13, 19, 75, 114–115, 118, 125, 133
Manning, Peter 116
Martin, Laura 16–17
mato oput 55–60, *57*, 153
McCormick, Kay 80
McGovern, Mark 102
McKinley, Michelle 71–72
McWilliam, Andrew 33, 47, 50, 63
memorial sites *see* trauma sites
memory: in aftermath of violent conflict 68–83, 77; collective 68; historical 68; implicit transmission of 68–69; inter-generational transmission of 69; personal 68; as revisionist 76; social 68
Menchú, Rigoberta 78, 80
Merry, Sally 27, 52
Meto people 33, 37, 47
Mexico 2, 5, 152
Millar, Gearoid 94
Mladić, Ratko 114
Mookherjee, Nayanika 98, 133
Mozambique 10–11, 17–18, 60–63, *62*, 74, 153–154
Murambi Genocide Memorial Centre 131, 133, 135, 138–146, *142–143*
Museveni, Yoweri 55

Nader, Laura 4–5
Naidu, Ereshnee 134
Namotemo, Hein 49
narrative truth 75–79, 77
National Commission on the Disappeared (Argentina) 92
National Commission on Truth and Reconciliation (Chile) 91
National Resistance Army (NRA) 55
Nazi Germany 69, 78–79, 123–124, 126–127, 131–134; *see also* Holocaust
negative peace 7–8, 93, 152
Nevins, Joseph 93
Nigeria 28, 33–35, 40, 152
Nordstrom, Carolyn 14, 17, 60
"normal life" 15–18
Norman, Sam Hinga 118
Northern Ireland 68, 101–103

nostalgia 17–18
NRA *see* National Resistance Army (NRA)
Ntaryamira, Cyprien 142
Nuer 4
Nuremberg Trials 69–70, 109, 119–120, 126–127

O'Barr, William 81
Obote, Milton 55
Offiong, Daniel 33–34, 37–38, 40
Okello, Tito 55

Pain, Dennis 57
Pakistan 98, 133
Papua New Guinea 34, 36, 39
participation, community 38–39
Participatory Action Research (PAR) 102
past: idealised 17–18; silence about 9–15
peace: conflict and 151; division as maintaining 4; negative 7–8, 93, 152; as not absence of violence 6–8; as opposite of conflict 2; positive 7, 93, 152
Peru 75, 91, 93–94, 96, 100–101, 103
Pinochet, Augusto 91
Poland 80, 131–132
Portugal 10, 93
positive peace 7, 93, 152
post-conflict societies 45
post-traumatic stress disorder (PTSD) 73–74
Proyecto de Recuperación de la Memoria Histórica (REMHI) (Guatemala) 101
psychoanalysis 29
PTSD *see* post-traumatic stress disorder (PTSD)

reconciliation 152; defining 8–18; "normal life" and 15–16; in Rwanda 54
REDINFA *see* Red para el Desarrollo Integral del Niño y la Familia (REDINFA)
Red para el Desarrollo Integral del Niño y la Familia (REDINFA) 101
reintegration, of "wrongdoer" 36–37
REMHI *see* Proyecto de Recuperación de la Memoria Histórica (REMHI) (Guatemala)
RENAMO (Mozambican National Resistance) 60–62
re-traditionalisation: of conflict management 45–63, *52, 57, 62*; dangers of 46–50
Rettig, Raúl 91
Rettig Report 91
Revolutionary United Front (RUF) 94, 118
Robarchek, Clayton 32, 38, 40

164 Index

Ross, Fiona 72, 90–91
RUF *see* Revolutionary United Front (RUF)
Ruzindana, Obed 123
Rwanda 3, 9, 12–14, 16, 37–38, 51–55, *52*, 59, 72–75, 79, 82, 95, 109, 113, 119–124, *121*, 131–135, 138–146, *142–143*, 153

Sampson, Steven 9, 17
Sander, Barrie 123–124
SATRC *see* South African Truth and Reconciliation Commission (SATRC)
Schwöbel-Patel, Christine 110
SCSL *see* Special Court for Sierra Leone (SCSL)
Scully, Shannon 144
Semai Sanoi 32–33
Sesay, Issa 118
Ševčenko, Liz 134
sharing, of food and drink 37–38
Shaw, Rosalind 29, 69–70, 73, 90, 94
Shawcross, Hartley 119
Sierra Leone 11, 15, 50, 70, 94–97, 100, 103, 108, 117–118, 124, 155
Sierra Leone People's Party (SLPP) 118
Sierra Leone Truth and Reconciliation Commission (SLTRC) 90, 94, 96–97
silence: about past 9–15
Simić, Olivera 134–135
Simmel, Georg 2
Simpson, Kirk 68
Skaar, Elin 61–62
SLPP *see* Sierra Leone People's Party (SLPP)
SLTRC *see* Sierra Leone Truth and Reconciliation Commission (SLTRC)
social cohesion 4, 16, 25, 152
South African Truth and Reconciliation Commission (SATRC) 5–8, 70, 72, 76, 81, 90–93, 96, 99, 109–110
South Korea 16–17
South Sudan 4, 55
Special Court for Sierra Leone (SCSL) 108, 118, 124
Special Panels for Serious Crimes (SPSC) 108, 117–118
SPSC *see* Special Panels for Serious Crimes (SPSC)
Stefansson, Anders 74–75
Stewart, Beth 76
Stoll, David 78
storytelling 71, 76, 81, 96, 101–103
Stovel, Laura 50

Strejilevich, Nora 76
Strupinskiené, Lina 12, 16
subjectivity 83
Summerfield, Derek 29, 73–74
Sutton, David 17, 38

Taylor, Christopher 3
testimonío 77–78
testimony: in aftermath of violent conflict 68–83, 77; age of 69–75; co-production of 79–82; editing-in of 71–72; editing-out of 72; in truth commissions 96–100
Thailand 46
"thanatourism" 134
Theidon, Kimberly 46, 75, 94
therapy culture 29, 73
third party listening 8
Thomson, Susan 14
Tokyo Trials 109
Tolai people 34, 37
tourism, dark 134
"traditional" conflict management 25–41, *31*
"tragic tourism" 134
trauma sites 156; as dark tourism 134; disclosure and 131–132; examples of 131; foreclosure and 131–132; truth telling and 91; as "unreconstructed" 132
TRCC *see* Truth and Reconciliation Commission of Canada (TRCC)
"Troubles, The" 68, 101–103
Trouillot, Michel-Rolph 125
truth: in aftermath of violent conflict 90–104, *95*; factual 78; forensic *vs.* narrative 75–79, 77; objective 83
Truth and Reconciliation Commission (CVR) (Peru) 75, 91, 93–94, 103
Truth and Reconciliation Commission of Canada (TRCC) 94–96, *95*
truth commissions 154–155; elites and 91; restricted mandates of 92–96; testimony in 96–100; *see also* unofficial truth projects (UTPs); *specific commissions*
truth telling 8, 10, 70–71, 74, 154
Tuol Sleng Museum of Genocide Crimes 115–116, *117*, 132–133, 135–139, *137*
Tyali, Nomonde 80

Uganda 8, 55–60, *57*, 63, 76–77, 77
United States Holocaust Memorial Museum (USHMM) 133
unofficial truth projects (UTPs) 98, 100–103

UTPs *see* unofficial truth projects (UTPs)

Verdoolaege, Annelies 99–100
victim, charismatic 69–70
Vidal, Claudine 144
Viebach, Julia 145–146
Vietnam 98, 132
Vojska Republike Speke (VRS) 18
VRS *see* Army of Republika Srpska (VRS); Vojska Republike Speke (VRS)

Waldorf, Lars 27, 51
West Timor 13–14, 33, 47, 93
Whitehead, Neil 3
Williamson, Caroline 72

Wilson, Richard Ashby 5, 120
World War II 69, 109, 119–120, 123–124, 126–127, 132–134
wrongdoer, reintegration of 36–37

Yad Vashem 132–133
Yugoslavia 108, 110, 113–115, 118–119, 124–126; *see also* International Criminal Tribunal for the Former Yugoslavia (ICTY)

Zambia 2, 5, 152
Zapotec 5
Zechenter, Elizabeth 27, 36
Zimbabwe 71–72
Zorbas, Eugenia 16–17

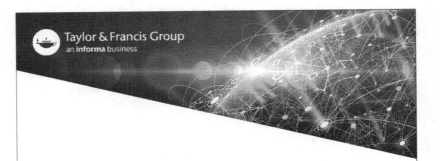

Printed in the United States
by Baker & Taylor Publisher Services